# JANE AUSTEN

# JANE AUSTEN

Tony Tanner

Harvard University Press
Cambridge, Massachusetts
1986

AAU 8481

**Library of Congress Cataloging-in-Publication Data**
Tanner, Tony.
Jane Austen.
Includes index
1. Austen, Jane, 1775–1817—Criticism and interpretation.
I. Title.
PR4037.T36      1986        823'.7        86–4818
ISBN 0–674–47173–3
ISBN 0–674–47174–1 (pbk.)

*For G. H. W. Rylands*

# Contents

*Acknowledgements*                                                    ix

1   Introduction                                                       1
    Jane Austen and the Novel                      1
    Jane Austen and Society                       12
    Jane Austen and Education                     24
    Jane Austen and Language                      35

2   Anger in the Abbey: *Northanger Abbey*                            43

3   Secrecy and Sickness: *Sense and Sensibility*                     75

4   Knowledge and Opinion: *Pride and Prejudice*                     103

5   The Quiet Thing: *Mansfield Park*                                142

6   The Match-Maker: *Emma*                                          176

7   In Between: *Persuasion*                                         208

8   The Disease of Activity: *Sanditon*                              250

*Bibliography*                                                      286

*Index*                                                             289

# Acknowledgements

This book is offered as a reading of Jane Austen's novels, not as a contribution to Jane Austen scholarship. In particular, it attempts to see the novels in their relation to problems concerned with society, education and language. Hence the introductory chapter, which offers a brief discussion of the relevance of these topics before the consideration of the individual novels. The earliest chapter in the book was, substantially, written in 1966, while the most recent chapters were written this year, so the book in effect represents my thoughts about Jane Austen's work ranging, intermittently, over some twenty years. I wish to express my gratitude to Penguin Books for granting me permission to reprint – in somewhat altered form – my introductions to *Sense and Sensibility*, *Pride and Prejudice* and *Mansfield Park*. A much earlier – and very different – version of the chapter on *Persuasion* was given as a talk to the Jane Austen Society. I am much indebted to my editor, Beverley Tarquini, for her patience, help and encouragement. The dedication is a small acknowledgement of the inestimable debt I owe to a man who has been an exemplary and incomparable friend – and 'educator' – for over twenty-five years to me and to countless others.

*King's College,*                                              TONY TANNER
*Cambridge*
*September 1985*

# 1
# Introduction

'You know how interesting the purchase of a sponge cake is to me' – thus Jane Austen in a letter to Cassandra of 1808. Allowing for her habitual cool irony (aimed as much at herself as at others) it is hard to imagine such a sentence being written by any other major English novelist. The received image – or stereotype – of Jane Austen is that of a quiet, though brilliant, spinster living in the sheltered margin of her period. The image or stereotype has some truth – as stereotypes often do. But as many writers about Jane Austen have realised it is an image that has to be re-examined in light of her work. Austen-Leigh in his indispensable *Memoir* probably served to give authoritative status to the stereotype: 'Of events her life was singularly barren: few changes and no great crisis ever broke the smooth current of its course.' And he later lists some of the areas of human activity about which she never attempted to write: 'She never touched upon politics, law, or medicine', and so on. 'Science and philosophy of which I know nothing' – a quotation from a Jane Austen letter of 1815 cited by Austen-Leigh – simply serves to add to that list of what Jane Austen did *not* write about without bringing us much closer to what she did write about. He quotes from letters from Jane Austen which have since become famous, if not mindlessly overused: 'the little bit (two inches wide) of ivory on which I work with so fine a brush, as produces little effect after much labour'. Yes, we know about 'those two inches of ivory', but, since there seem to be people who can inscribe most of the New Testament on a pin's head, and since there have certainly been artists who worked yards of ivory with no residue of interest to engage us, we may say that the question is not one of dimensions but, rather, what did she inscribe on those (metaphorical) two inches of ivory?

Jane Austen – unwittingly surely, since her letters do not read

1

as if they were indirectly addressed to posterity – seems to collude or agree about the necessarily restricted range of her work: 'Three or four families in a country village is the very thing to work on. . . .' This would seem to embrace a 'minimalist' if not marginal conception of her art – almost defensively so. It is rather in line with the conclusion of one of her letters of 1815 where she writes, 'I think I may boast myself to be, with all possible vanity, the most unlearned and uninformed female who ever dared to be an authoress.' We can accept the 'boast', for the ironic hyperbole thinly disguises a gay self-confidence masquerading as modest ignorance. Jane Austen was quite tolerably learned and certainly well informed. If she chose to present herself as a provincial spinster enjoying (or suffering) a very limited horizon of contemporary experience and, more generally, contemporary academic, philosophic and literary work, then that must have been because she realised (or decided) that she was not in any way going to compete with, say, Richardson and Scott – to mention no more. How it was that her own 'modest' works came to be held in more esteem and regard even than the work of those great authors can perhaps only be ascribed to the magic, or what James would call 'the madness', of art.

It seems that we should look in vain for evidence in her work of many of the main historical and political events which occurred during her lifetime. She saw – or lived through – the French Revolution, the rise (and fall) of Napoleon Bonaparte; the American War of Independence (and the war with England of 1812). She died (1817) midway between Waterloo (1815) and Peterloo (1819) and she lived through much of the turmoil which accompanied what E. P. Thompson has described as 'The Making of the English Working Class' (1780–1832 in Thompson's version). She must also have been aware of the Jacobin and anti-Jacobin struggle which went on in England as a result of the French Revolution, a struggle most easily (though not adequately) described as the opposition of the views expressed in Edmund Burke's *Reflections on the French Revolution* (1790) and in Thomas Paine's *Rights of Man* (1791). These tumultuous revolutions, changes and arguments seem to have left very little mark on her fiction, and yet of course she knew what was going on. What effect, if any, all these events had in her writing we shall have to consider in due course.

It is easy enough to draw up a list of what Jane Austen seems to have 'left out' or *not* written about, though as we can see from a brief glance at the biographical details of her and her family's lives she was certainly aware – or made cognisant of – more than appears in her fiction. There she restricted herself to the point where we should do well perhaps to think again about what she did in fact put *in*. We should not expect to find, for instance, anything in Jane Austen's work like the following passage from Charlotte Brontë's *Shirley* (1849):

Time wore on and spring matured. The surface of England began to look pleasant: her fields grew green, her hills fresh, her gardens blooming; but at heart she was no better: still her poor were wretched, still their employers were harassed: commerce, in some of its branches, seemed threatened with paralysis, for the war continued; England's blood was shed and her wealth lavished: all, it seemed, to attain most inadequate ends. Some tidings there were indeed occasionally of successes in the Peninsula, but these came in slowly; long intervals occurred between, in which no quote was heard but the insolent self-felicitations of Bonaparte on his continued triumphs. Those who suffered from the results of the war felt this tedious and – as they thought – hopeless struggle against what their fears or their interests taught them to regard as an invincible power, most insufferable: they demanded peace on any terms: men like Yorke and Moore – and there were thousands whom the war placed where it placed them, shuddering on the verge of bankruptcy – insisted on peace with the energy of desperation.

They held meetings; they made speeches; they got up petitions to extort this boom: on what terms it was made they cared not.

All men taken singly, are more or less selfish; and taken in bodies they are intensely so. The British merchant is no exception to this rule: the mercantile classes illustrate it strikingly. These classes certainly think too exclusively of making money: they are too oblivious of every national consideration but that of extending England's (*i.e.* their own) commerce. Chivalrous feeling, disinterestedness, pride in honour, is too dead in their hearts. A land ruled by them alone

would too often make ignominious submissions – not at all
from the motives Christ teaches, but rather from those
Mammon instils.                                        (Ch. 10)

Since the Peninsular War began in 1809 and the war(s) with
Bonaparte dominated English national concerns for the first
quarter of the nineteenth century – until the decisive battle of
Waterloo (18 June 1815, two years before Jane Austen's death);
and since – looking at home affairs, although the exigencies of the
war had their effect here of course – the Combination Acts of 1799
and 1800 were clearly aimed at suppressing the trade unions
forming among the textile workers of Yorkshire and Lancashire,
there were Scarcity riots in and around 1800, there were the
Luddite riots in 1811, in which frames were broken in
Nottingham, Derbyshire and Leicestershire, and there was a
great deal of disturbance and discontent among the artisans in
the West Riding from 1811 to 1815 – just noting these facts we can
see that Charlotte Brontë's novel was set in the period which fell
within the second half of Jane Austen's life and her most prolific
creative years. We can also see that we should have little notion of
these momentous internal and external events simply by reading
her novels. To quote only one writer, who has made a point made
by many others in various ways, reading Jane Austen's novels 'it
would take an abnormally acute reader to realise that there had
been a war on at all' (Esmé Wingfield-Stratford, *The Squire and his
Relations*). As we shall see, it certainly would not have taken an
'abnormally acute' reader to gather from Jane Austen's novels
that there had been a war on: indeed, it would have taken an
abnormally obtuse one *not* to gather just that, particularly a
reader of *Persuasion* but also a reader of *Pride and Prejudice*. More
generally, it has become clear that Jane Austen was much more
aware of contemporary events, debates and issues, of the wars
and domestic unrest, of the incipiently visible results of the
Industrial Revolution, and of a radical change taking place in the
constitution of English society, than the conventional view
allows, or perhaps wants to allow.

A related objection, and potentially a more serious one, is that
Jane Austen not only did not know what was going on
historically but also remained blithely and comfortably unaware
of the prevailing Tory ideology which informed her work, writing

uncritically from its assumptions and classifications and within the boundaries of its rigid and foreclosing prejudices. Here is one of the more intelligent, if more extreme, versions of this criticism:

> Many critics continue to venerate Jane Austen as a great artist who is also and inseparably a great 'moralist', while doggedly refusing to discuss the way her work mediates contemporary ideological, moral and social conflicts, unwilling or unable to discuss the way it is informed by a peculiarly Tory ideology and its incoherence. The consequence of this ideology is that instead of her art opening out gentry/middle-class reality and assumptions to a genuinely exploratory fiction which takes alternative forms of life and aspiration seriously, Jane Austen systematically closes up her imagination against critical alternatives. In doing so, her art, her religion, her morality and her version of the individual and community quite fail to transcend the narrow limitations of her historical class, albeit a class whose dominant role in English society is still very evident.
>
> (David Aers, 'Community and Morality: Towards Reading Jane Austen', in *Romanticism and Ideology: Studies in English Writing 1765–1830*)

That Jane Austen held many Tory sympathies need hardly be questioned; but it does not follow that her work is uncritical of her society in many profound ways. It surely is. And there is another way of looking at this problem of the writer's relationship to the prevailing ideology of his or her time. Thus, according to Althusser, the works of a writer such as Balzac make us see the ideology from which they are born *because* they remain within that ideology, not because they transcend it. In fact Jane Austen partly remains within the ideology of her class and partly (and increasingly) transcends it. I would argue that almost everything David Aers says about Jane Austen is misleading or wrong, and testifies to another kind of misreading. Even his assertion that Jane Austen 'systematically closes up her imagination against critical alternatives' is an error, as the most superficial reading of *Persuasion* immediately demonstrates. As I hope will be apparent by the end of this book, to my mind it is clear that Jane Austen does both expose and criticise the

ideological assumptions which ground her society and which
may seem to constrain her fiction. If in *some* ways Jane Austen's
vision is complicit with the dominant ideology of her class, in
other ways it very clearly transcends it – for by how few of her
characters taken from that class is she or her writing deceived, or
'taken in'!

What really matters in the work of any writer is not the degree
or kind of referentiality or content. Rather it is the writer's moral
relation to language. The overriding concern of Jane Austen's
novels – and of many of her heroines – is the nature of true
utterance. Language, to state the obvious, is the most important
distinguishing mark of the human. But, equally obviously, it is
everywhere abused, often to cruel and terrible ends. Jane Austen
enacts and dramatises the difficulties, as well as the necessity, of
using language to proper ends. Just as thoughtless or perverse
use of language can be the most insidious destroyer of the
human, so the most responsible employment of language (and at
times silence) not only makes for the dignity of the human but has
powers and strengths of salvation. When Fanny Price – 'the
lowest and last' as Mrs Norris insists – defies all the powers
seeking to persuade or coerce her to marry Henry Crawford,
finally even defying the awesome patriarchal authority of Sir
Thomas Bertram by saying, 'I – I cannot like him, Sir, well enough
to marry him', she is refusing a false discourse and a false
economics of affection whereby marriage was subject to the
prevailing ethos of market values. She is a true speaker. And all of
Jane Austen's novels portray a movement towards true seeing
and true speaking. This movement is more difficult for some than
others – Fanny Price seems to have these gifts from the beginning
even in her most unprivileged situations. 'I was quiet but I was
not blind', she says, and it summarises her stance and position
for much of the novel. Emma on the other hand is an arrant
'imaginist' and has to be tutored, by experience and by Mr
Knightley, into correct vision and responsible speech. Anne
Elliot has to move, painfully, from an excessive prudence (and
arguably repression) to a fuller degree of articulateness and a
more comprehensive confrontation of her true feelings. But one
way or another all the heroines achieve the desired end. Those
characters who do not either disappear into misery or continue

blindly on in their confident unseeing and their empty words and meaningless stereotypical utterances.

To return, briefly, to the quotation from *Shirley*. It is generally agreed that Charlotte Brontë's attempt to broaden the landscape of her novel, to provide a larger social context for the love stories, in many ways did not succeed nor did it make the novel more successful than, say, *Jane Eyre*. The almost documentary amplification of the passional interests and intensities of the novel, though not without its interest and relevance, does not finally have that kind of almost obsessive life and intensity which we associate with the best of her work. We cannot say that Jane Austen's work is the poorer for lacking such overtly topical passages of social history and comment. Let me quote one more passage, from a novel actually contemporary with Jane Austen:

A mild romantic gentle-tempered youth, bred up in dependence and stooping patiently to the control of a sordid and tyrannical relation, had suddenly, by the rod of oppression and the spur of injured feelings, been compelled to stand forth a leader of armed men, was earnestly engaged in affairs of a public nature, had friends to animate and enemies to contend with, and felt his individual fate bound up in that of a national insurrection and revolution . . . even, his love seemed to have assumed a character more manly and disinterested, as it had become mingled and contrasted with other duties and feelings.

These words refer to Henry Morton in Scott's *Old Mortality*. This was published in 1816, the same year as *Emma*, and we can recognise how inconceivable it would be to find these words in any Jane Austen novel. It is not just a matter of the difference between a male and a female author – though that surely comes into it. Jane Austen's fiction just does not include or examine a hero or heroine whose 'individual fate' becomes 'bound up' with matters and movements of wide public and historical significance. (As usual, *Persuasion* provides an exception – Captain Wentworth is just back from the wars, but of course Jane Austen's novel does not aspire to contain that part of his life.) For all her wealth and independence, even Emma's life remains intensely parochial and domestic.

At this point let me bring forward two quotations, which in their different ways point to the apparent narrowness and restrictedness of Jane Austen's fictional range of reference. First, Henry James in a letter to George Pellew written in 1883 (Pellew had written a dissertation on Jane Austen's novels on which James comments):

> I could have found it in me to speak more of her genius – of the extraordinary vividness with which she saw what she did see, and of her narrow unconscious perfection of form. But you point out very well all that she didn't see, and especially what I remember not to have seen indicated before, the want of moral illumination on the part of her heroines, who had undoubtedly small and second-rate minds and were perfect little she-Philistines. But I think that is partly what makes them interesting today. All that there was of them was feeling – a sort of simple undistracted concentrated feeling which we scarcely find any more. In of course an infinitely less explicit way Emma Woodhouse and Anne Elliot give us as great an impression of 'passion' – that celebrated quality – as the ladies of G. Sand and Balzac. Their small gentility and front parlour existence doesn't suppress it, it only modifies the outward form of it. You do very well when you allude to the narrowness of Miss Austen's social horizon – of the young Martin in *Emma* being kept at a distance, etc.; all that is excellent.

For James there *was* 'passion' in the 'front parlour existence' of Austen's heroines, though he regards them as having 'small and second-rate minds' and as being 'perfect little she-Philistines'. Which is perhaps a little hard on, say, Elizabeth Bennet to go no further. And 'want of moral illumination'? That surely is a rather surprising judgement if we think of Emma, Anne Elliot, even Fanny Price. Perhaps, indeed assuredly, 'moral illumination' does not come to them in the way it comes to, say, Isabel Archer, or Strether; but that it comes, whatever James might have meant by 'moral illumination', there can be no doubt. Indeed, while we all agree that James could scarcely have written as he did without George Eliot and Balzac (not to mention Hawthorne) behind him, it seems to me quite as arguable that James learned as much from

Jane Austen as Jane Austen did from Richardson. Which is to say, a great deal.

James is surely exaggerating when he maintains that Jane Austen's heroines are composed exclusively of 'feeling', for while he is absolutely right to point to the undistracted and undistractable intensity of feeling of which they are capable (we might remember the 'undiverted heart' of Catherine Sloper in James's *Washington Square*, who loves intensely, silently and unrequitedly in the 'front parlour existence' which is finally her fate and doom – she is a Jamesian version of one kind of Jane Austen heroine), this hardly does justice to the wit, ironic reflectiveness and moral intelligence which, to varying degrees, characterises them. It is true that, even by Jamesian standards, there are very few significant events in their lives (no visits to Italy – or even London), but even apparent event*less*ness can be an event of cardinal importance in those parlours in which what James took to be those mentally second-rate and Philistine heroines had too often to eke out – and make out – their politely but cruelly constricted lives. How little relevant this may have seemed to someone coming to the parlour room of English society of the time may be instanced by the second quotation, from Emerson's journals (1861):

> I am at a loss to understand why people hold Miss Austen's novels at so high a rate, which seem to me vulgar in tone, sterile in artistic invention, imprisoned in the wretched conventions of English society, without genius, wit, or knowledge of the world. Never was life so pinched and narrow. The one problem in the mind of the writer in both the stories I have read, *Persuasion* and *Pride and Prejudice*, is marriageableness. All that interests in any character introduced is still this one, Has he (or she) the money to marry with, and conditions conforming? 'Tis the 'nympholepsy of a fond despair', say, rather, of an English boarding-house. Suicide is more respectable.

Emerson is of course not all wrong. 'Marriageableness' *is* a key consideration, and as for the 'pinched and narrow' aspects of contemporary English social life with the imprisoning effect of its 'wretched conventions' – well, who made us more aware of those than Jane Austen, often through the silent agonies which her aware, and distinctly *not* vulgar, heroines often have to suffer? They would not have found much to quarrel with in Emerson's rather crude diagnosis. But America – particularly America as Emerson conceived or dreamed of it – was simply not an available alternative. There is not a Jane Austen heroine who even begins to aspire to the imaginative condition of a Walt Whitman. At the same time we might add that it was quite beyond Emerson's capabilities, and doubtless his desires, to write a social novel, or indeed a novel of any kind. Whatever else he knew, he simply did not understand what was involved, by way of pleasure and pain, in the intricate and potentially abrasive reciprocities involved in living with – having to live with – other people within those 'wretched conventions' which were (and are) so often the condition of both the curses and blessings of whatever we choose to call civilised existence. And, while Emerson was quite ready to quit his family and house in order to commune with nature and the Over-Soul, for Jane Austen 'marriageableness' is indeed the key to existence as she knew it. While it is true that her novels depict many ill-suited couples and marriages which are prisons of *ennui* if not of torment – machines for the 'production' of misery – this is all the more reason why it is so imperative for her heroine to struggle for the right kind of marriage, which is so central to society that it cannot be written aside as Emerson seems to wish to do by making it seem a marginal and even petty concern. It is, for Jane Austen, *the* metaphor for the most desirable kind of relationship, which can both 'ground' and situate her heroines (and their husbands) and allow them more fully to live out their proper *telos* or end as women. The good marriage is also indispensable for the renewal of society. That there are so many bad, or bleakly empty marriages in Jane Austen, revealing different degrees of failed mutuality, non-reciprocation and myopic egotism or frivolous self-gratification, only underlines the imperative of finding a good marriage no matter what the obstacles, in the form of the different fragments of authority, prohibition, interdiction and coercion which circulated in that small – at times claustrophobic – society, or the difficulties and risks of opportunities and gestures of initiation and approach which were not within the power, or under the control, of the heroine. Once the full significance of a true 'marriage' in Jane Austen's works has been grasped then we will see that, Emerson to the contrary notwithstanding, 'suicide' is hardly more 'respectable' than the concerns, anxieties and hopes which can surround (or precede) such an important matter – a matter, precisely, of *life* or a kind of death-in-life which may indeed tempt one to think that Emerson's preference for suicide might be understandable. But the Jane Austen heroine wants to live and so marriage must necessarily be her concern. (I write this in the full awareness that Jane Austen never married. That fact does not in any way invalidate the tenor or verdict of her imaginative works.)

'Why shouldn't it be argued against her that where her testimony complacently ends, the pressure of our appetite presumes exactly to begin?' asked James in 'The New Novel'. James is indirectly alluding to the fact that many of the great nineteenth-century novelists found that it was more challenging, more rewarding, more interesting to explore what happens to relationships *after* marriage than to concentrate on the delights and difficulties, the privations and problems, which precede it, the obstacles and triumphant negotiations which lead up to it. For novelists such as Flaubert, Tolstoy, George Eliot, James himself, the most serious, significant and profound (often tragic) problems *begin* with that union and contract which for Jane Austen seems to terminate and resolve all problems. This major shift or development in the scope and focus of the novel is a subject in itself. Here we can admit that we can see what James means: Jane Austen regularly avails herself of the convention of marriage-as-felicitous-closure, leaving unanswered – and unaskable – any number of potentially fascinating questions which each novel may prompt (what *will* become of Emma as Mr Knightley's wife?). But there is less 'complacency' of testimony, and more irony and covert inconclusiveness (and even overt uncertainty) in Jane Austen's novels and conclusions than James suggests by his observation. The confidence and satisfaction in 'social unions' and marriage which many critics have found in her work is by no means always unequivocal or unqualified. There is an increasingly large part of her main characters which is not so easily or happily accommodated to 'social systems' as some critics assert. Indeed, by the end of her work social systems themselves are called in question and found increasingly inadequate to satisfy her heroines' needs. Social novelist Jane Austen certainly is, but, if she does not quite envision a life in a 'world elsewhere', she certainly sees that alternative modes of social organisation – or even extra-social forms of life – may have to be canvassed. Her novels never simply, complacently celebrate the social *status quo*. At its best, society has to be purged and reconstituted. At its worst it has to be rejected and abandoned. Jane Austen's novels do not 'perennialise' society: they problematise it.

## JANE AUSTEN AND SOCIETY

In the unfinished manuscript of *Sanditon*, the phrase 'social order' is crossed out and replaced by the more general formulation 'the common wants of society'. We could see this hesitation and erasure as indicative of Jane Austen's growing uncertainty that, by the time she came to write her last work, there *was* any meaningful 'social order' left to refer to so confidently. Just what 'society' meant for Jane Austen, it is difficult to establish. Indeed, it was a major difficulty for many eighteenth-century writers who specifically addressed themselves to this topic. David Hume, for instance, uses both 'society' and 'company' without any stable differentiation between the words. Society, company, community: it was not easy to fix the differences between them. Society as 'company' could mean a small, self-sufficient 'community', happily cut off from, or impervious to, the more anonymous conglomerate of society at large. In its more inclusive sense, 'society' could refer to the whole body of institutions and relationships which organise and maintain the whole nation state – or fail to do so. (For Hume 'company' has served to 'introduce the rules of *Good Manners or Politeness*', while 'society' has constrained mankind to 'establish the laws of justice'.) Clearly, for Jane Austen, society was much more a matter of 'company' and 'community' (face-to-face relationships) than the whole state system of institutions and relationships. She concerned herself with the 'rules of good manners or politeness' and not with questions concerning 'the laws of justice'. Yet it would be wrong to infer from this that she had no interest in, or awareness of, the larger 'society' which surrounded and contained the 'community' she wrote about. What I think we can say is that she hoped that what she had depicted as happening to the 'community' of her novels, its potentialities for self-destruction, its possibilities for self-restoration, its values and vulnerabilities, was in some way parabolic of what was happening to 'society' at large. If you like, she saw 'community' as a microcosm of 'society'.

The consensus would seem to be that Jane Austen was in one sense the most 'social' of novelists (almost always seeing people in the context of 'company' and 'community' or the unhappy – or desired – lack of these), and in another sense one of the least 'social' of novelists, since apparently she showed no interest in the historical and political changes of her period, and 'of organized society she manifests no idea' (Richard Simpson, in the *North British Review*, 1870). It seems clear to me that this last assertion is inadequate, indeed erroneous. Jane Austen was well aware of such phenomena as the French Revolution, the Industrial Revolution, the wars, and many actual and incipient changes in English society as a whole – even if the allusions to these phenomena are sometimes so discrete or subtle that many generations of readers and critics did not notice them, or eluded or occluded them in their own socially determined readings of her work. There has been a tendency to privatise her work and to miss the wider implications of seemingly local events. Yet some of these take us well beyond what are sometimes thought to be the blinding enclosure within which she worked in happy (and privileged) ignorance of what was going on in the world outside. One social factor that Jane Austen is very aware of is money, and to some (significantly limited) extent the sources of income of many of her characters.

*materialism*

We can get some idea of what money was 'worth' in Jane Austen's time if we consider some figures provided by Douglas Jay in a book written in quite another context: *Sterling: A Plea for Moderation*. He draws up a Retail Price Index for the years 1264–1983. His Index stood at 1146 in 1830, and at 1146 again in 1931. Since then it has risen to 4454 in 1960, 12,104 in 1975, and 29,260 in 1983. *Emma's* famous £30,000 would thus have been worth almost exactly the same in 1930; but by 1983 more like £900,000 and by the time this book is published no doubt over £1 million. Such figures, however, do not perhaps give us a very specific sense of what prices, incomes and wages were in Jane Austen's period. For a vivid contemporary document which incidentally does just that, one can hardly do better than read *The*

*Diary of Benjamin Newton: 1816–1818.* Newton was just such a clergyman as might have figured, with approval, in Jane Austen's work. Rector of a rural parish in Yorkshire, he was pious (but definitely not an 'enthusiast'), well-educated, civilised, polite, with a proper care for community and love for family. He liked his books, his food and wine, his horses, his dogs. He appreciated pretty and witty women and valued society and rational conversation. He did his duty, cherished his family, looked after his parish, enjoyed his hunting and relished his pleasures. His diary, indeed, provides an excellent historical document concerned with recording daily details of exactly the area of English life about which Jane Austen was, for the most part, writing. In the course of his diary some interesting sums are mentioned. His post bill for one year was £40; he is offered £2900 for 69 acres of woodland (he refused – remember the enclosure and sale of land in *Sense and Sensibility*); a gig and harness is for sale at £20; meat is 6½d. per pound, coal 12s. per ton; a family which inherits £40,000 is considered very rich (the members squander their money and 'make beasts of themselves . . . some by drink and the rest by dirt'); £2000 per annum is a very handsome income for a 'gentleman' with a large family; a single woman with a bastard child is paid 4s. per week for the maintenance of the child and 16s. per annum is paid to the house in which she resides; a bushel of wheat is sold for 19s.; Newton pays £95 for a 'pipe of Port' (which gives him 60 dozen bottles); a 'plowboy' is hired at £7 per annum ('if he behaves himself and 6 guineas if he is not obedient'); a 'maid servant' is hired by a gentleman in the parish 'after the rate of 2/8 per week whereas he ought to have paid somewhat less than 2/– per week' (we might bear this in mind when we recall how absolutely inaudible and invisible the servant class is in Jane Austen: no doubt they received their keep but, like the ploughboy, as salaried human beings they hardly exist – underpaid out of the social landscape, as it were); a 'taylor's' bill amounts to £13 18s.; Newton buys 'a drill, a bull and a mare' for £13; the Duke of Marlborough leaves his sister £5000 and 'a small annuity'; Newton buys a horse for £22, a piano for £12 12s.; one of his annual tithes brings him £150; a painting by Ibbetson is valued at 60 guineas; there is a distribution of the New Year 'Sacrament money' to the poor families of the local parishes, each family receiving 15s. each;

Newton sells two cows for £30 9s.; wax candles are 4s. 6d. per pound, wine glasses 14s. 6d. the dozen; Newton agrees to pay £140 for a barouche (a four-wheeled carriage for four people and a driver); the owners of Ripon are considering 'improving the estate' – 'they talk of expending 7 or 8000 pounds on a range of hothouses and greenhouses' (remember *Mansfield Park* and, again, *Sense and Sensibility*); on holiday the Newtons are surprised to be charged 4s. per day to live with a family, until they learn that that includes four meals a day (!); a blacksmith's boy is paid 10s. for 'twenty dishes of mushrooms'; a leading lawyer and politician, Sir Samuel Romilly, earned 'between £16,000 and £17,000 per annum' – he committed suicide after the death of his wife. I leave this range of figures to speak for itself.

As has often been pointed out, Jane Austen is careful to state just how much many of her characters have or can expect. Sometimes the money is inherited, more often it comes from the land or trade (where the sums involved are usually left imprecise). The confused and changing relationship between these figures in society who owe their wealth to land and those who derive it from trade is often made clear by Jane Austen. Yet in her work there is as much mystification, vagueness or silence concerning the origins of wealth as there is sharp-eyed specificity. She does not always inquire too curiously about the sources of income – just as she can, when she wants to, distribute to her deserving but needy characters money which comes from nowhere but her sense of what is morally merited – and fictionally fitting. Fairy gold, clean of all trace of any possible origin in the economic realities of the time. Similarly, she never traces back the origins of wealth or revenue from the land to the actual work which produced it. Nor, having pointed to 'trade', does she explore what was actually involved in the making of profits from it. Nevertheless we can say that she was much more aware of what was going on in the part of society on which she concentrates than many people think. On this matter Raymond Williams, in his indispensable work, *The Country and the City* (see in particular ch. 11, 'Three around Farnham') makes the following succinct comment:

> it must be clear that it is no single, settled society, it is an active, complicated, and sharply speculative process. It is indeed that

most difficult world to describe, in English social history: an acquisitive, high bourgeois society at the point of its most evident interlocking with an agrarian capitalism that is itself mediated by inherited titles and by the making of family names.

Granted that Jane Austen does concentrate on a *relatively* stable section of society – a 'community' still adhering in some ways to a traditional and settled way of life, this is not to say that she did not have intimations that it was under such strains as might lead to its transformation or supersession.

It is important to stress that the society (in the sense of community, but with larger implications) Jane Austen was writing about – and of which she was a loyal and critical member – was one which was essentially based on landed interests, the sacredness of property. At least since John Locke affirmed that 'Government has no other end but the preservation of property' (in *The Second Treatise of Government*, 1690), the 'rights of property' were continually stressed until they no longer appeared as the arbitrary and repressive ideology of the ruling propertied class but rather as a law of nature – 'that law of property, which nature herself has written upon the hearts of all mankind' (William Blackstone, 1793). Throughout the eighteenth century the general order and stability of society and the 'rights of property' were not only inseparably linked: they became regarded as identical. Dr Johnson, for example, stressed the importance of 'property' as 'a great principle in society', just as he upheld the privileges of 'old family interest: of the permanent property of the country'.

In an essay discussing 'Property, Authority, and the Criminal Law' in the eighteenth century (in *Albion's Fatal Tree*) Douglas Hay examines the various ways in which the populace was persuaded, or forced, to assent to 'the rule of property'. Capital statutes concerning offences against property grew from about fifty to over 200 between the years of 1688 and 1820, and yet the number of hangings for such offences hardly increased at all. Clearly terror was not the most important – or successful – way of maintaining the structure of authority which arose from property and protected its interests. The bonds of 'obedience and deference' had to be maintained and perpetuated in other, subtler ways. What could never be exacted by legalised brutality might be won by a paternalistic mode of behaviour on the part of the landed class, by graciousness, justice, generosity, mercy. In this way – ideally at least – social control in the eighteenth century might appear as a 'spontaneous, uncalculated and peaceful relationship of gratitude and gifts' and the whole system 'a self-adjusting one of shared moral values, values which are not contrived but autonomous'. To maintain that this ideal was in fact how society worked and was bonded together necessarily involved a great deal of mystification, varying degrees of self-deception and inter-colluding habits of seeing – or not seeing – and selectively distorting and censoring aspects and conditions of society as they actually were. And of course the façade of harmonious relationships between the ruling propertied class and the populace was often a very thin and transparent one. There *was* social order and stability, but it was always precarious and insecure. Just as there *were* regular hangings, there were frequent if often ineffectual riots. But above all of course there was the frightening example of the French Revolution. The Gordon Riots of 1780 in London indicated the existence of plenty of easily-inflammable latent violence and discontent. (In a riot in October 1795, a window of the royal coach was broken, to the accompaniment of cries of 'No King!') The dream of an unshakeable, 'natural' social order composed of benevolent propertied authority and loyal deferential populace came to seem increasingly threatened, increasingly unreal (to Jane Austen among other people). It was impossible complacently to assert that anything like the French Revolution couldn't happen here. It all too obviously could.

This is why, for one thing, there was an increasing emphasis on the importance of property, in maintaining social peace and order in late eighteenth-century England. (An example of this intensification of emphasis is the way in which Burke reversed Adam Smith's assertion that property was dependent on social order and made social order dependent on property – thus further 'naturalising' and prioritising property.) To this extent Jane Austen is in agreement with the dominant ideology: her proper heroes all have landed property and her heroines need a propertied man (*Persuasion* as always the significant exception). But in addition, and equally important, there was a new emphasis on the need for good manners and morals among the propertied class. Since they did not rule by police and force but rather by a system of deference and obedience, they had to be exemplary – in every sense. 'Restraint, control and propriety were vital if society was not to blow up in their face' (Roy Porter, *England in the Eighteenth Century*). The title of a work by John Bowdler, 'Reform or Ruin' (1798) catches the sense of the new urgency that was felt – exemplary conduct in manners and morals was necessary, not for religious reasons, nor primarily for aesthetic reasons. They had become a political necessity as essential as property to the maintenance of order and peace in society. Property was a necessary, but not sufficient, basis for a stable and orderly society. Decorum, morality and good manners – in a word, 'propriety' – were equally indispensable. The one without the other could prove helpless to prevent a possible revolution in society. This is one reason why Jane Austen constantly sought to establish and demonstrate what was the necessary proper conduct in all areas of social behaviour, why she scrutinised so carefully any possible deviance from, or neglect of, true propriety – in her own writing as well as in the behaviour and speech of her characters. To secure the proper relationship between property and propriety in her novels was thus not the wish-fulfilment of a genteel spinster but a matter of vital social – and political – importance. That is why it is in many ways irrelevant to argue whether she was a relatively mindless reactionary or an incipient Marxist. She did believe in the values of her society; but she saw that those values had to be authentically embodied and enacted if that society was to survive – or deserve to survive. She indeed saw her society threatened, but mainly from inside: by the failures and derelictions of those very figures who should be responsibly upholding, renewing and regenerating that social order. Bad manners were not simply a local and occasional embarrassment to be laughed at: they could be symptoms of a dangerous sickness in her society which could ruin it from within – through neglect, transgression and omission rather than by mobs and the guillotine. That there are so few of her characters who seem fully qualified to act as the necessary maintainers of the society of her novels is a measure of her concern and incipient pessimism, a pessimism actualised and visible in her last work.

The convergence of the importance of 'property' and 'propriety' is clearly marked by a shift in etymology – and here I am indebted to a student at King's College, David Badiell. He pointed out to me that 'propriety' was defined by Dr Johnson as 'peculiarity of possession: exclusive right', that F. S. Cohen in his 'Dialogue on Private Property' defines 'property' as 'the essence of all that is proper'; and that, while the *Oxford English Dictionary* gives the first meaning of 'propriety' as 'the fact of owning something', the seventh meaning is given as 'conformity with good manners' and the date given for the first example of that usage is 1782 – in the work of Fanny Burney! The meaning of 'propriety' had shifted from ideas of ownership to notions of correctness of behaviour – perfectly illustrating the newly felt importance of exemplary manners after the French Revolution. As Badiell noted in an essay, this shift in meaning 'shows how economic structures can demonstrate themselves as correct and universally valid. Ideology represents itself as social morality. Property means propriety – because property is proper.' The two terms have become interdependent. Thus it is that Jane Austen's heroines often have the requisite sense of 'propriety' but – being women – no property. Propriety without property is relatively impotent in society – as Fanny Price is in the chaotic impropriety of her Portsmouth home. The proper heroes should have both, but must marry if the conjunction is to become active and regenerative. Thus the ideal marriage at the end of a Jane Austen novel is not simply a conventional happy ending, an easily available tactic of narrative closure. It offers itself as an emblem of the ideal union of property and propriety – a model to be emulated, a paradigm for a more general combination of the two on which the future of her society depends. Marriages in her work which lack either or both are, by the same token, admonitory failures.

From this point of view it would be fair to say that Jane Austen seems more concerned with the dangers of impropriety than with the deprivations of poverty. But we should also beware of thinking that she had a simple unproblematic notion of property and propriety. There are ambiguities and latent contradictions or instabilities in the 'property' some of her characters own (Sir Thomas Bertram's neglected Mansfield Park and his dubious West Indies money, for example); while 'propriety' may be mixed with – or indistinguishable from – related but more egotistical (and thus potentially socially less constructive and cohesive) motives or characteristics – as for example, when we read that Emma 'had feelings, less of curiosity than of pride or propriety'. It is a mark of Jane Austen's scrupulous awareness of such fine distinctions and necessary differentiations that we are made to recognise the importance of a tireless vigilance over the nuances of motivation and intention. Jane Austen knew as well as anyone that feelings do not come pure and motives unmixed. But as far as possible we should be aware of which feeling or motive is dominant. Pride – or propriety? Which? It matters – even if any final and conclusive disentanglement is impossible. No more than Emma should we allow ourselves to act in a motivational mist or an emotional blur. And for Jane Austen it was essential to strive for as great a clarification of – and adherence to – true notions of propriety as possible. If property is proper, propriety is primary. For Jane Austen, 'society', whether viewed as a 'community' or taken in a wider, more inclusive sense, ultimately depended on a genuine understanding of, and commitment to, propriety; not simply a propriety expressed in a code of etiquette, or signalled by rank, or manifest in property – although all these factors could be of varying degrees of importance. The ultimate propriety on which all other proprieties depended was a true propriety of language, and all that implied. That, and what Goethe called a 'politeness of the heart': 'There is a politeness of the heart; it is related to love. It gives rise to the most comfortable politeness of external behaviour' (*Elective Affinities*). Given that true propriety of language and that 'politeness of the heart', 'society' may well take other forms than the ones with which Jane Austen happened to be most familiar. She clearly allows of that possibility. Without them there could not be anything worth calling society at all. 'Social order' would indeed be totally erased.

As a coda to this section let us compare three women, acting for one reason or another as observers, of a street scene (or a scene through a window) in which they play no part. The comparisons are not trivial: they reveal much about the problems of the relationship between the woman and the possibility of a felt sense of community – or lack of it.

Here, first, is a passage from chapter 27 of *Emma* (1816): it occurs while Emma is waiting for Harriet to do some business and shopping:

Emma went to the door for amusement – Much could not be hoped from the traffic of even the busiest part of Highbury; – Mr Perry walking hastily by, Mr William Cox letting himself in at the office door, Mr Cole's carriage horses returning from exercise, or a stray letter-boy on an obstinate mule, were the liveliest objects she could presume to expect; and when her eyes fell only on the butcher with his tray, a tidy old woman travelling homewards from shop with her full basket, two curs quarrelling over a dirty bone, and a string of dawdling children round the baker's little bow-window eyeing the gingerbread, she knew she had no reason to complain, and was amused enough; quite enough still to stand at the door. A mind lively and at ease, can do with seeing nothing, and can see nothing that does not answer.

Now a passage from Dickens's *Dombey and Son* (1846–8), chapter 33, describing Harriet Carker's feelings as she periodically looks through her window:

She often looked with compassion, at such a time, upon the stragglers who came wandering into London, by the great highway hard by, and who, footsore and weary, and gazing at the huge town before them, as if foreboding that their misery there would be but as a drop of water in the sea, or as a grain of sea-sand on the shore, went shrinking on, cowering before the angry weather, and looking as if the very elements rejected them. Day after day, such travellers crept past, but always, as she thought, in one direction – always towards the town. Swallowed up in one phase or other of its immensity, towards which they seemed impelled by a desperate fascination, they never returned. Food for the hospitals, the churchyard, the prisons, the river, fever, madness, vice, and death – they passed on to the monster, roaring in the distance, and were lost.

And this famous passage from *Middlemarch* (1871–2), which

comes from near the end of chapter 80. It occurs when Dorothea, suffering over what she thinks is going on between Will and Rosamond, realises that 'the dominant spirit of justice had once overcome the tumult and had once shown her the truer measure of things'. The key moment of realisation – or epiphany if you like – comes when she looks out of her window:

> She opened her curtains and looked out towards the bit of road that lay in view, with fields beyond, outside the entrance gates. On the road there was a man with a bundle on his back and a woman carrying her baby; in the field she could see figures moving – perhaps the shepherd with his dog. Far off in the bending sky was the pearly light; and she felt the largeness of the world and the manifold wakings of men to labour and endurance. She was a part of that involuntary, palpitating life, and could neither look out on it from her luxurious shelter as a mere spectator, nor hide her eyes in selfish complaining.

Apart from noting the obvious difference that two of the passages refer to rural scenes and the other to an urban – or suburban – one, it is worth remarking a few other distinctive and distinguishing aspects of the three pieces. In Jane Austen's piece there is an implicit sense of community: three of the people concerned in the scene are named (and thus known, at least to Emma), while the butcher and the old woman ('tidy'), the dogs and the children fit well enough into a scene which can contain them with no resultant incongruity or dissonance. Emma, the spectator, is 'amused' – a rather neutral term suggesting a sufficiency of distraction with no threat of anything disturbing. Her mind is 'lively and at ease' – but what is it thinking, what is it doing? We do not know; instead we are only assured that such a mind 'can do with seeing nothing, and can see nothing that does not answer'. Answer to or for what? Again, it is not made clear. As far as we can know, Emma does not learn or infer anything from the scene. She is not bored, not elevated, not outraged, not depressed. She is 'amused enough'. She in no sense feels her relationship to the local community – or locality – to be problematical. She moves within a very small circle (socially but also geographically – she has never seen the sea) and, as far as she knows, she is content to do so. Just how totally content she is with this small social scene we shall consider later on; but in this scene there is surely not a trace of alienation, difference or radical detachment.

By contrast Harriet Carker looks out at a scene with which she has no connection and cannot have any. There are no names here; nothing and no one is familiar. There is no community – only transience. It is only thirty years since *Emma* but we are now well into the sense of 'two nations' which was to dominate Victorian writing. Dickens's London, drawing the helpless and deracinated into its devouring maw, is a world away from Emma's Highbury. There are only 'travellers' – not inhabitants. The scene is ultimately a 'monster'; the spectator, outside her own room (and arguably within it) is nobody. Everything bespeaks alienation and *anomie*. There is nothing here to 'amuse' Harriet Carker. Her feelings can only run to compassion, while the tone of the author – and we can fairly note a distinction between character and author which was not immediately detectable when considering the Jane Austen passage – fairly fumes with indignation. *Middlemarch* looks back to the 1830s (though it is fair to add that it also takes in aspects of the 1860s and 1870s), and, while Dorothea does not experience the almost vacuous amusement and untroubled content of Emma as she looks out through her window, she is not all but annihilated by the sense of alienation registered by Harriet Carker. In effect what she experiences is a kind of epiphany. The world is not random and selfish, contingent and meaningless. It does offer the spectacle of a kind of community. In its typological generality – the shepherd, the woman and baby – the scene has the qualities of a timeless, religious, biblical scene, rather than conveying the sense of a specific, historical locale. The community is not one of the sort known by Emma (again no names appear – no one is recognised), but an archetypal community of shared endeavour, not perhaps to one known common end, but of the more general obligation to work, to do the job to which, however, mysteriously, you were appointed – in a word (one of George Eliot's favourites), to do your 'duty'. 'That involuntary, palpitating life' is not perhaps as known and knowable, as comfortable and mentally untaxing as Highbury. But it is also not the London seen by Harriet Carker. It *is* a kind of community from which one may not withdraw either as a 'mere spectator' or as a selfish complainer. The question then becomes, what is the most appropriate mode of participation? How George Eliot dealt with this question is not, here, our concern. But how Emma does is very much to our point. She is certainly not at all given to 'selfish complaining', and being a 'mere spectator', amusing as it may be for brief moments, will hardly satisfy her energy and spirits. So we come to the question, what will Emma, who, as the first sentence informs us, 'seemed to unite some of the best blessings of existence', actually *do*? We are also told that while growing up Emma got into the way of 'doing just what she liked'. One of the questions, then, posed by the novel from the start is, what will this privileged, overindulged, remarkable young woman now like to do? Emma's problem is a paradigm of the larger problem of the position, role, and scope of action of women in Jane Austen's society. Which is another way of describing what her novels are all about.

## JANE AUSTEN AND EDUCATION

A concern with education is central to Jane Austen's work, though not the kind of education we might associate with schools or any pedagogic curriculum. In chapter 2 of *Mansfield Park* Fanny Price is mocked for her lack of education (mainly her ignorance of textbook geography and history, it would seem) by her cousins, and both Sir Thomas and Mrs Norris decide that she is 'far from clever'. But of course she has more real moral intelligence than anyone else in the book and finally turns out to be the 'teacher' of them all – apart from those who are, morally speaking, irredeemably ineducable. In this more comprehensive sense of education, all of Jane Austen's heroines have to be educated or tutored – by men, an older woman or sister, experience, or themselves (never a parent). Or they in turn act as educators. Emma has to be tutored and guided by Mr Knightley; Fanny Price educates Mansfield Park. Elizabeth Bennet and Darcy, we may say, educate each other. Anne Elliot has to educate herself, after being miseducated by Lady Russell. (The risk and dangers of miseducation and diseducation are, needless to say, always present in various forms.) Education for Jane Austen was much more a matter of proper conduct and truly good manners than any range of skills or information. In this connection I want to refer briefly to three works, directly addressed to matters and problems of education, that would certainly have been known to Jane Austen. (For a good general book on this subject, see *Jane Austen and Education* by A. Devlin.)

In John Locke's *Some Thoughts Concerning Education* (1693, running into twenty-five editions by 1777), we find many pronouncements which come close to Jane Austen's way of thinking. Locke asserts from the outset that 'of all the men we meet with, Nine Parts of Ten are what they are, Good or Evil, useful or not, by their Education'.

His emphasis is continually on internal qualities rather than external attributes. Young minds should be 'principled with inward Civility'; first instil 'the Principles of good Nature and Kindness the Ornaments of Conversation, and the out-side of fashionable Manners, will come in their due time'. Indeed, Locke refers to 'the Dangers of Conversation' as tempting young people to aim for a superficial cleverness and to cultivate an ostentatious display of factitious brilliance. ''Tis Virtue then, direct Virtue, which is the hard and valuable part to be aimed at in Education; and not a forward Pertness, or any little Arts of shifting.' We rightly think of Jane Austen as a supreme artist of conversation and probably correctly infer that she herself was notable both for the wit and intelligence of her own conversation. Yet in her novels she can mark very clearly and subtly the uses and abuses of conversation. Some of the most seemingly clever talkers are notably deficient in 'virtue' – though the apparent cleverness may reveal itself as mindless froth or more or less vapid self-aggrandising display (and banality; meanness or downright nastiness are immediately audible for what they are). Often a Jane Austen heroine finds herself, Cordelia-like, having to maintain an honourable silence when surrounded by the noise of meaningless or duplicitous talk. Yes, for Jane Austen too there were discernible 'dangers of conversation'. Locke would have approved of her heroines when a sense of virtue and honesty reduces them to silence. Locke also praised the virtues of 'steadiness' as opposed to anything that smacked of what he calls a 'Sauntring Humour', just as he was against anything 'which serves only to teach the Mind to wander after change, and superfluity; to be unquiet, and perpetually stretching itself after something more still, though it knows not what'. He was suspicious of 'the unquiet mind'. Just so, for Jane Austen, 'steadiness' and at times a literal stillness are invariably signs of virtue, while restlessness, dissatisfaction, 'sauntering' humours, and 'unquiet' minds (and desires) may well be signs of incipient dereliction or even latent vice. (In this book see in particular the chapters on *Mansfield Park*, *Persuasion* and *Sanditon*.)

Similarly she would have echoed Locke's elevation of 'Civility' over 'Ceremony'. In Locke's words, 'Civility' is 'a Christian duty' and leads to 'the true art of living in the World', while *'excess of Ceremony'* could be a fault in good manners. Just what true 'good manners' are is of course a matter of major importance for both Jane Austen and her heroines – the term is labile (even at times volatile). There are good manners (plausible) and good manners (an authentic index of deeper moral qualities) and it is not always easy to make the requisite distinction. Good manners can mean different things to different characters and different things at different times to the same character.

For instance, Lord Chesterfield in *Letters to his Son* (1779), promotes the idea of 'pleasing' as the main quality to aim at. It all becomes a matter of surface, of one's appearance to, and effect on, others. This ability to please manifests itself as 'good breeding', for, as Lord Chesterfield asserts, 'with nine people in ten, good breeding passes for good nature'. There are many of Lord Chesterfield's 'sons' in Jane Austen – the Willoughbys, the Wickhams, the Churchills – but their 'pleasing' manners and appearance are deceptive and have to be discerned as such (by us, by the properly educated heroine) no matter how attractive they may initially appear. Like the attractive–deceptive Crawfords, they lack true inner moral goodness, strength and stability. They may glitter and shine – even coruscate – but they are without the true 'inner light'. As is the case with the evil Mr Elliot in *Persuasion*, their seemingly perfect manners can absolutely not be trusted.

Some words of Burke give an indication of the high importance that was attached to 'good manners' during Jane Austen's period.

Manners are of more importance than laws. Upon them, in a great measure, the laws depend. The law touches us but here and there, and now and then. Manners are what vex and soothe, corrupt or purify, exalt or debase, barbarise or refine us. . . . They give their whole form and colour to our lives. According to their quality, they aid morals, they supply them, or they totally destroy them.

'First Letter on a Regicide Peace'

Note that first sentence: 'Manners are of more importance than laws.' During this period the number of laws passed making offences to property a capital offence increased exponentially – but it was clearly felt that draconian laws alone would not suffice to preserve social stability and peace. The French Revolution and the ensuing war with France served, of course, to increase the anxiety among the ruling class quite immeasurably. Pitt's government passed some extremely repressive laws (the Treason and Sedition Act in 1795; the suspension of Habeas Corpus in 1794 and 1798) as well as instituting a widespread network of informers. But 'Manners are of more importance than laws.'

It was not a matter of decorum for its own sake: good manners and morals were seen as essential to the preservation of order in society. They alone could or should do what excessive laws, an often recalcitrant militia, and the absence of any properly organised police force were (it was felt) unable to do. It was as if the security and stability of the nation depended on good manners. To put it as bluntly as possible, good manners were no longer regarded merely as a seemly adjunct to the life-style of the upper classes: they became England's answer to the French Revolution. Whereas in the earlier part of the eighteenth century the ruling class had often been associated with libertinism, moral laxity and varying degrees of coarseness and boorishness, it was now felt that only by reforming their principles and conduct could they preserve their position, their property, and secure the peace of the country as a whole. Jane Austen's profound concern with good manners was thus not simply a reflection of a cloistered gentility: it was a form of politics – an involvement with a widespread attempt to save the nation by correcting, monitoring and elevating its morals. (The desire to conflate the ethical and the social, morals and manners, can be seen in other eighteenth-century writers of course; perhaps most importantly in Shaftesbury, who declared that the purpose of his essays was 'to recommend morals on the same foot with what in a lower sense is called manners, and to advance philosophy (as harsh a subject as it may appear) on the very foundation of what is called agreeable and polite'. That is from his *Characteristics*, a work which may well have been known to Jane Austen.) There is ample evidence from documents of the time of the very rigid etiquette which prevailed at social occasions – as if order in the ballroom or at the dinner table would somehow help to preserve order in society at large. There was perhaps an element of wishful, or even magical, thinking here; but it is clear that to a large extent Jane Austen shared it. Care for civility meant care for civilisation – as she knew it. In her work there is a vigilant attention paid to the detailed etiquette required on social occasions and a matchlessly sharp eye for any infractions of the tacit rules of etiquette, subtle or crude. Here indeed is an important source for the drama in her novels – a drama concerning the problematics of good manners which was a crucial part of a much larger drama: the drama of the salvation and regeneration – or damnation – of the social order of her time.

One can get some sense of the nature of that drama if one considers the social occasions on which 'manners' – the enactments or the infringements of the tacit codes of proper conduct – were most conspicuously visible. I shall call this drama the hermeneutics of manners. Consider a ball or a formal dinner, for example. If you subtract the very basic purpose of such occasions – to enjoy the pleasures of dancing and eating – you are left with a large superstructure of the occasion which is in effect simply concerned with manners. Apart from the minimal 'utilitarian' purposes (or excuses) for such occasions – and there are characters who hardly eat and refuse to dance – they are primarily occasions at which manners are demonstrated and celebrated – and tested. They are performances of communal decorum in which society mimes its codes and signs of behavioural values. In themselves they are morally and politically neutral, as the simple act of eating is. Their real importance lies in their being meta-events. Society forgathers to see how society forgathers. They are social occasions about themselves. They are society's meta-theatre. There key problem – and drama – arises from the fact that a skilful or well-educated person can, if he or she wishes, deploy and manipulate the signs in such a way that it can become very difficult, if not impossible, to distinguish 'true' good manners from adroitly 'simulated' ones. Since it is all a kind of theatre anyway, how can you tell who is 'acting' his acting? Jane Fairfax's defensive answers to Emma's probing questions about Frank Churchill offer an example of this problem, even though she is only pretending that she has only met Churchill on relatively public occasions. Emma is trying to find out 'what he truly was'. Jane replies, 'At a watering-place, or in a common London acquaintance it was difficult to decide on such points.' 'Manners were all that could be safely judged of under a much longer knowledge than they had yet had of Mr Churchill. She believed every body found his manners pleasing.' Never mind Jane's understandable evasion – Emma's curiosity and Jane's answer sum up the key problem–drama. The unmarried woman (above all) when confronted by a hitherto unknown unmarried male (who is thus always a *potential* mate) desperately wants and needs to find out 'what he truly is'. But by the rules of etiquette prevailing in that society unmarried women almost only meet new males at organised social events, and there 'manners were all that could be safely judged of'. Except that manners are just the most 'unsafe' or potentially misleading signs to judge. In a meta-theatre how can you tell the 'true' actors from the 'acting' actors? Or, to put it another way, how can you tell a person with Lord Chesterfield's good manners from one with Locke's? An acute observer, such as Jane Austen, can. But then, she has privileged knowledge as the creator of her characters. Her heroines often find it extremely difficult and indeed can make potentially serious mistakes (hence, often, much of the ensuing drama). We can say – because Jane Austen educates our perception more quickly than some of her heroines lacking our advantages – that her truly good men (significantly rare) are more notable for their 'civility' than for their 'ceremony'. They do not study or seek to please. But precisely that may mislead an entirely proper and intelligent young female. They may strike her – and us (for, of course, we can make initial errors of judgement as well, if like the heroine we only have his 'manners' to judge of) – as too serious, humourless, severe, haughty, perhaps a little pedantic, a little lugubrious (and – even if this is not articulated – somewhat de-eroticised, prematurely middle-aged). This may indeed be the price paid for striving to adhere to steady moral principles and true decorum from which the world is all too prompt and potent to divert or deflect people. But if 'manners' are all that can be 'safely judged by' it may well be impossible to see this and difficult to find ways and occasions of coming to discern it. Who can say that Emma is initially obviously 'wrong' about Frank Churchill? How could she be initially 'right' about Knightley (as her obvious mate) when he treats her with what seems like avuncular fondness and censoriousness, as if she were a younger sister or niece? The crucial paradox is this: when manners are the *only* signs that can be 'safely judged by' they are, at the same time, the only signs that *cannot* be safely judged by. To the extent that society's welfare and well-being depend on 'good manners', this is a potential predicament of tolerably far-reaching implications.

Turning to two writers who were contemporary with Jane Austen, I want to consider some of the advice – and implications of the advice – contained in two works specifically concerned with the upbringing of young girls, one by a man, the other by a woman. In his *Enquiry into the Duties of the Female Sex* (1796) Thomas Gisborne reveals all the assumptions (or prejudices) concerning both the nature of woman and the proper sphere of her activities which were dominant in Jane Austen's period. Primarily woman is formed for domesticity:

> The sphere of domestic life, the sphere in which female exertion is chiefly occupied, and female excellency is best displayed, admits far less diversity of action, and consequently of temptation than is to be found in the widely differing professions and employment into which private advantage and public good require that men should be distributed.

From this initial premise–prejudice the familiar repressive exhortations and admonitions all too predictably (and tediously) flow. Gisborne's stereotyped image of the woman is both boringly, and disturbingly, familiar. (It is against such bland, and only apparently benign, repressive and negating stereotyping that Jane Austen's heroines often have to struggle.)

More interesting is Gisborne's rather ambivalent attitude to conversation. 'Conversation is an index to the mind' – fairly said.

Gisborne then asserts that 'female fluency in discourse is greater and more persevering than that of the other sex', which leads to the danger of female conversation 'babbling along, shallow and frothy'. Well, there are certainly some shallow babblers in Jane Austen, male as well as female. But, while Gisborne seems in part to blame an inborn (or cultivated) disposition in women for mocking and frivolous 'prattle' habitually given to assailing 'knowledge and learning' with 'a volley of brilliant raillery and sparkling repartee', he also blames men for talking to women as though they were nearly 'devoid of understanding'. All too often it appears that

> a man of sense, when conversing with a woman he deemed to possess a cultivated mind, would study, as it should seem, to shun every subject of discourse which might afford scope for the exercise of reason; that his whole aim would apparently be, to excite noisy gaiety founded on nothing; to call forth a contest of puny witticism and flippant repartee . . . such is the sort of conversation daily to be heard. . . .

Since men effectively dominate the discourse of conversation even when they seem not actually to dictate it, men must be held to a large extent responsible for the 'female conversation' which they both provoke and solicit. It is no wonder that sometimes Jane Austen's heroines have positively to struggle to speak their own words – to own their own voices.

It is hardly surprising that Gisborne (a clergyman) should constantly stress the importance of inculcating religion and the imperatives of duty. Indeed, he has a good deal to say about the struggle between 'duty' and 'amusement'. It is interesting to note that one solution he sees to the problem of counteracting a tendency to contract 'a habit of excessive fondness for amusement' depends on locale and place of residence:

> To the daughter of a country gentleman, though her heart should be fixed on company and diversions, the paternal mansion, insulated in its park, or admitting of no contiguous habitations except the neighbouring hamlet, seldom furnishes the opportunity of access to a perpetual circle of amusements.

Perhaps that is true enough. But the paternal mansion and the protective park in themselves constitute no guarantee of a sound education. Mansfield Park alone is evidence enough for that, and Emma needs a better education than the paternal mansion in the country gives her. The metropolis may be a 'vortex' of 'giddiness and dissipation', but an apparently protected and privileged life in the country may have its voids and moral vacancies.

To some extent a quiet rural life as outlined by Gisborne *was* an ideal for Jane Austen, but it is one that is often only won after varying degrees of travail, error and distress. True, Gisborne is aware of a problem which Jane Austen must also have seen very clearly: namely, 'how are well-bred women to support themselves in the single state through the dismal vacuity that seems to await them?' This is a question not of economics but of employment. Literally, since 'work' as we now understand it (labour, crafts, professions, and so on) was precisely what the 'well-bred woman' was debarred from. Gisborne offers the solution of serious and instructive occupations but the prescription is somewhat too general to be very helpful. Jane Austen, when she wasn't being a good daughter, sister, and a prodigiously solicitous and affectionate aunt, wrote. Her heroines do not – and we may say that the problem of meaningful occupation is potentially as serious as the problem of a right education in her work. Emma, for example, nearly contrives to damage or ruin a number of other peoples' lives because of her radical lack of a real occupation – and the boredom that comes of that negative condition.

The real answer to the problem for Gisborne, and indeed for Jane Austen's heroines, is of course marriage and domesticity. To settle, to be steady, 'to guide the house' (Gisborne quotes St Paul) – this is really what a woman must be trained and prepared for. 'Home is the centre round which the influence of every married woman is accumulated.' To that end we once again encounter admonitions against the dangers of wandering – really, of moving around too much. He warns against 'the interruption of domestic habits and occupations . . . the acquisition of an unsettled, a tattling, and a meddling spirt; evils which spring from the custom of "wandering" from place to place, no less from that of "wandering from house to house" '. He warns of the bad consequences of 'the immoderate indulgence of a propensity to roving' and the dangers which follow 'when the rage of rambling has seized a woman'. Jane Austen was aware of the various possible bad effects of 'roving' and 'rambling' (on men as well as women) and she would perhaps have echoed Gisborne in his exhortation, 'Let the cheerful tranquillity of domestic pleasures stand forward to supply the place of trifling and turbulent festivity abroad.' But she knew that such an ideal domestic tranquillity was not always so easy to achieve. Some Jane Austen heroines have to learn their true 'duties'. They all have to find their proper homes.

Hannah More's *Strictures on the Modern System of Female Education* (1799) is indeed a 'strict' work, more emphatic perhaps even than Gisborne's work in its insistence on the crucial and dominant role which should be played by religious instruction and meditation in the upbringing of a young woman. Indeed, one can get the impression that Hannah More's solution to the problems posed by all those blank and unoccupied spaces which inevitably recur in the ideally pure (and ideally empty) life of a well-bred young woman is to fill them with prayer. There are many chapter titles like 'A Scheme of Prayer'; indeed, the last chapter of the book is entitled 'On the Duty and Efficacy of Prayer' – as if an almost uninterrupted converse with, or monologue to, God was the best way to occupy the female mind and keep it out of touch with, and hearing of, the wicked, contaminating world. Many of Hannah More's 'strictures' are familiar enough in this context of education for young females. Novels are bad; she is emphatic about the dangers of 'an ill-directed sensibility' or 'an ungoverned sensibility'; she is against that part of society which calls itself 'the fine world' and the lowering and homogenising effect of its 'plastic fashion' (which leads to a loss of whatever might have been the natural character of the individual). Once again we encounter warnings about the adverse effects of wandering abroad or moving around: the 'inability of staying at home . . . is one of the most dangerous symptoms of the reigning mania'. More detected – and abhorred – what she called the 'revolutionary spirit in families'. Certainly some major changes were taking place in the family and its patterns of dominance and obedience during this period. Many of Jane Austen's heroines manifest a 'spirit of independence' when subject to varying degrees of coercion or 'persuasion'. Even

Fanny Price, who might seem to qualify as one of Hannah More's ideal women 'who have meekly sat down in the humble shades of prose and prudence', shows a powerful spirit of independence when it comes to being universally urged into what she knows would be a wrong marriage. Here again, for all her real and apparent conservatism, Jane Austen does not simply follow the most reactionary prescriptions. Just as, while she was undoubtedly pious, she does not chooose to show her heroines filling up much of their spare time with prayer and religious meditation. Hannah More affirms that for a woman true Christian piety consists in '*subduing* the spirit of the world . . . even while her duty obliges her to live in it'. It was this duty – of how to live in the world (rather than renounce it) – that preoccupied Jane Austen.

In general we should have to admit that Jane Austen's *ideal* of what a young woman should be – and what the most important qualities in a woman were – comes close to Hannah More's prescriptions. As when Hannah More asserts that the best kind of woman is 'one who can reason and reflect, and feel and judge and discourse, and discriminate', and that the most important quality or ability in a woman is the power to direct 'the faculties of the understanding . . . and all the qualities of the heart, to keep their proper places and due bounds, to observe their just proportions and maintain their right station, relation, order and dependence'. A whole eighteenth-century tradition – including Locke and Dr Johnson – can be discerned behind all this hierarchisation and pattern of order and obedience ('proper places', 'due bounds', 'just proportions', 'right station' and so forth), and it was behind Jane Austen as well. It is as if the young woman were to internalise the properly monitored order of society, thus contributing to its preservation rather than being in any way a disruptive or subversive presence or a potential force for challenge and change. Hannah More would seem to want to make young women almost mute and immobile upholders – and incarnations – of the most conservative and Christian *status quo*. (She will allow a 'chastised wit' but '*humor*' is very sparingly to be ventured on.) *Some* of Jane Austen's heroines *partly* fulfil this role – but the facile and lugubrious prescriptions of a conduct book are hardly adequate to contain their often complex needs and desires, or to cope with the difficult situations and predicaments they often face. And the *status quo* is not uncritically or mindlessly upheld. Indeed it is often shown to be in a bad state of disrepair if not actually degenerate, and may have to be redeemed and renewed (as in *Mansfield Park*) or, in some cases in some places, actually abandoned (as it is to all intents and purposes in *Persuasion*). Jane Austen's heroines may, in the course of the novels, be 'educated' for an ideal society – on the lines laid down by writers like Gisborne and Hannah More. But the actual society they find themselves in is often far from ideal and it is often a major part of their struggle not only to learn how to be their best selves but also to find some almost private form of small society in which they can be themselves most authentically.

Of course, when it comes to the all-decisive matter of marriage, all the education in the world is as nothing if the relationship is not informed by – suffused with – 'love': 'nothing can be compared to the misery of being bound without Love', wrote Jane Austen to her niece in 1815. But, as always, the prescriptive use of the word 'Love' leaves everything to be asked. Just what 'love' might or could mean, might or ought to be, in the convergence and conflict of considerations and forces concerning money and manners, property and propriety, decorum and desire, is necessarily a constant matter of interest, a primary problem and concern throughout the novels of Jane Austen.

## JANE AUSTEN AND LANGUAGE

In *A Room of One's Own* Virginia Woolf refers to what she regards as a typical male use of the sentence and then turns to Jane Austen.

Jane Austen looked at it [i.e. the male sentence] and laughed at it and devised a perfectly natural, shapely sentence proper to her own use and never departed from it. Thus with less genius for writing than Charlotte Brontë she got infinitely more said. Indeed, since freedom and fullness of expression are of the essence of the art, such a lack of tradition . . . must have told enormously upon the writing of women. Moreover . . . there is no reason to think that the form of the epic or of the poetic play suits a woman any more than the sentence suits her. But all the

old forms of literature were hardened and set by the time she
became a writer. The novel alone was young enough to be soft
in her hands . . . yet who shall say that even now 'the novel'
. . . this most pliable of forms is rightly shaped for her use?

To what extent one can confidently ascribe gender to a particular
sentence or habitual sentential structure is debatable unless you
happen to regard the whole grammar of language – if not
language itself – as shamelessly and irremediably phallocentric. It
would, I think, be hard to demonstrate that some of Jane
Austen's sentences are more (or less) 'natural and shapely'
(meaning feminine?) than some of Dr Johnson's. Jane Austen
was not seeking for 'freedom and fullness of expression' in the
way that Virginia Woolf was. Virginia Woolf exploited the 'soft
. . . pliable' form of the novel and developed her own particular
kinds of sentence for her own ends – as did James and Proust, to
go no further afield. The sentence itself – if we can hypostatise
such a protean entity – is gender-neutral. Which is not to say that
there are not certain ways of forming and using sentences which
are    recognisably    aggressive,    domineering,    pompous,
monolithic, assertive, and so on, and which may thus seem
characteristically male. One might want to characterise the
opposite qualities as likewise characteristically female. But this
line of speculation would not help us very much in considering
Jane Austen's particular use of English. There are certain
characteristics of her written prose which could be related to the
fact that she was a woman, but these are also related to the fact
that she was a woman of a certain class at a particular time in
history.

It is for instance certainly true – and has not gone unnoticed –
that her language is marked by a minimum of physical action.
Vigorous transitive verbs are rare, and for the most part (there are
of course some deliberate and significant exceptions) her
language tends to record movements governed by considerations
of decorum and etiquette – composed and controlled (one might
say constricted and confined). Of course people move – they
dine, they dance, they promenade, and so on (Elizabeth Bennet
will even run across a field) – but reckless or involuntary
movement, movement for its own sake, is often mocked or
reproved or signalled as subtly dangerous. Stillness (and that

controlled movement called grace) is the ideal; excessive or surprising motion is the deviant, and potentially disruptive and threatening. Part of this is of course explained by the position of women in Jane Austen's society: they were ideologically pinioned, as it were, tacitly coerced into very controlled movements, if not actually 'arrested'. Unpredictable mobility was errancy in more than one sense. Thus the 'activity' which is recorded by Jane Austen is largely an activity of seeing and saying, thinking and feeling, wondering and assessing, hoping and fearing, conjecturing and interpreting. The movements are predominantly movements of the mind and heart. There is a much larger vocabulary of meditation and response than of proposition and initiation. Not surprisingly, 'the passive voice, which insists on the static, is frequent, as is its equivalent, the impersonal construction' (Howard S. Babb, *Jane Austen's Novels: The Fabric of Dialogue*). Rather than offering the reader an irregular or unrestrained morphology of individual emotions, Jane Austen tends to subsume strong feelings into a formal – even formulaic – structure. The prose tends to balance out into patterns of antithesis and parallelism. Emotion is thus not denied but contained by her rhetoric. In general she mutes, excludes or eludes any kind of violence in her discourse. If she avoids over-direct expression, excessive and potentially distracting particularity, striking metaphors, too markedly arresting peculiarity and idiosyncrasy of individuation, and tends always towards the conceptual, the general, the communal, the sense and values which should be held 'in common', this is because she is constantly enacting and re-creating a requisite decorum and propriety in her language. Although dialogue is of course crucial, there is a tendency to move away from the abruptions and abrasions of direct speech (it has been maintained that her dialogue only clarifies issues and events which are already to be inferred from her own narrative voice – this is excessive but it does point to a discernible tendency). There are dramatic scenes and events in her work but these are significantly rare – indeed, significant because they are rare. (The 'drama' put on by the characters in *Mansfield Park* is utterly disruptive and its effects have to be exorcised: in itself this 'dramatises' a more general exorcism or disavowal of 'drama' in general.) With again significant exceptions, her language – like her plots – tends to avoid all violence, anything that might shock, surprise, or 'alarm'. (It is one symptom of how different the world of *Persuasion* is from that of the earlier novels that in the very last sentence we read that Anne has to pay for the new kind of felicity she finds – new for a Jane Austen heroine – with 'the tax of quick alarm'.) For the most part Jane Austen's novels offer no radical surprises; expectations are raised which are usually satisfied, not frustrated. Usually we know who will marry whom – the suspense resides more in the question of 'how' than in that of 'whom'. (The intimation that Fanny Price might have married Henry Crawford is a notable exception.) Jane Austen's novels work more by deferral of gratifications – not disappointment or deflection of them. We, the readers, like the main characters, are, after no matter what trials and tribulations, erroneous expectations or misplaced hopes, usually rewarded and reassured. Disappointments and sufferings there are but, finally, no shocks.

In general the language of Jane Austen's novels excludes not only the unassimilable roughness and dissonance of working-class speech but also any of the potential discordance of colloquial or vernacular discourse. *Vulgarities* of speech and egregious lapses of tact and failures of tone there are in plenty (we need think no further than Mrs Elton) – but they are not violences. They usually signal a misplaced ambition to excel in what is ignorantly mistaken to be the proper discourse of the dominant society. They reveal a profound unawareness of, and gross insensitivity to, the true spirit of that discourse. They make us wince even while they make us laugh – exactly the response Jane Austen wants; for thus unwittingly and indirectly such vulgarities and rudenesses reinforce our sense of just how important the maintenance and upkeeping of the true spirit of her dominant discourse is. (It is a measure of Jane Austen's awareness of how precarious – and essential – that maintenance is that Emma herself should be guilty of a cardinal rudeness, a disturbing betrayal of that proper discourse which she should be among the first to uphold.) What all such vulgarities – perversions and transgressions – of the privileged discourse (or the discourse of the privileged) are *not* is the breaking-in or disruptive rebellious penetration of fragments of a completely other, potentially hostile discourse from some socially dangerous elsewhere. The threats to Jane Austen's society and her language – and they are many and increase throughout her work – are essentially all from within. We can see this borne out if we just consider two examples of what might appear to be, or offer, threats from the external or excluded areas of society. The gipsies who briefly begin to terrorise Harriet in *Emma* could indeed represent a threat from that vagrant impoverished and desperate area of society (or non-society) of which we hear so little in Jane Austen's novels. And indeed we do not actually 'hear' anything from them in this episode. Her discourse precisely denies them a *voice*. Instead, that discourse describes their speech in its own terms – terms which are general, disindividuating and, in effect, dispersive. 'Harriet was soon assailed by half a dozen children, headed by a stout woman and a great boy all clamorous, and impertinent in look though not absolutely in word.' The 'whole gang' surrounds Harriet. They are 'loud and insolent'. But in Jane Austen's text they are completely inaudible. She has translated them into silence. It is some indication of the power of class at that time that the 'whole gang' flees in terror at the mere approach of Frank Churchill. One senses here, briefly, the confident sense of omnipotence of Jane Austen's discourse which can conjure up such a potentially dangerous 'gang' and then swiftly make them vanish, leaving not a trace on the novel and its language. Just what latent anxieties such a display of discursive power might be concealing is another – and too speculative – matter.

The other example is Fanny Price's 'home' in Portsmouth. In the chapter on *Mansfield Park* I shall have more to say about this crucial episode – it is notable for being arguably the most violent passage of prose in Jane Austen's work. Here I just want to point out that in this 'abode of noise, disorder, and impropriety', while we are told of a mode of speech which is utterly alien to the ideal of discourse which Mansfield Park *should* uphold – as the novel itself *does* – we actually hear very little of it. We read of 'noise rising upon noise', of people 'all talking together', of 'hallooing', of general confusion and shouting. But very little of it is transcribed. In particular the father – an admonitory negative of what a true father should be – is described as being one of the veritable dregs of society: 'he swore and drank, he was dirty and gross'. But such speech of his as is transcribed as it were verbatim, while it is rambling, insensitive and inconsequential, and includes the occasional 'by G—', it is hardly horrendously indecorous or notably improper or violent. Here the discourse of a potentially dangerous other, while not being totally silenced, is muted and transmuted into a discourse which, while being distressing to Fanny and somewhat offensive, does not radically challenge or threaten the author's supervising discourse. In such episodes Jane Austen has recourse to a protective and sanitising diegesis (narrative summary in and on her terms) rather than risk a possibly contaminating and encroaching mimesis (simulation or reproduction of the terms and terminology of the alien other). Such potential threats – discursive if not political – as the gipsies or the Portsmouth house of chaos and noise, are distanced and disarmed (if not actually silenced) by an authorial discourse which is still, however precariously, able to contain and control them. Just because people may run wild – and talk wildly – on the peripheries of her social world (or outside it altogether), Jane Austen's language usually feels no obligation to follow them: on the contrary, for the most part it demonstrates a capacity for implicitly exhorting her readers to abjure such 'wildness' in the interests of a requisite decorum and propriety. It radiates a stable and stabilising influence. It is powerfully 'unmoved'.

To a large extent this changes in her late work when the threats from within seem to be no longer containable. In *Persuasion*, where the vulgarities are compounded by serious betrayals of trust, abdications of responsibility, even downright evil, there are significant changes in the tone, style and vocabulary of Jane Austen's language – what I have been calling her discourse – and there is a corresponding radical change in plot structure (there is even an unprecedented physical shock in Louisa's accident on the Cobb). The changes are even more marked in the unfinished *Sanditon*. It is still unmistakably Jane Austen but the discourse is radically changed as she discerned changes, derelictions, delinquences and deteriorations, in her particular class; an increasing inability or disinclination to uphold, embody and enact the values which Jane Austen saw as the only protection, salvation and, possibly, justification of the particular privileged landed class of which she wrote, and to which in many ways she was committed. She is critical – often bitterly – because she saw that class contributing to its own accelerating demise. Where she is 'subversive' it is largely by an acute discernment of the ways in which that class was subverting itself. To return to the opening point: there is much in Jane Austen's use of English which may be attributable to the fact that she was a woman – her angle of vision, her area of knowledge, her grammar, must all be influenced by that fact. But it is more important to see her particular way of writing as that of a person who feels engaged with and embattled on behalf of the values of a particular class in a particular phase of history. That the shifts in tone and atmosphere move from celebration to renovation, from confidence to defensiveness, from upholding to replacing, from attempts at restoration to rejection and self-banishment – in general, from optimism to pessimism – is partly (perhaps largely) a reflection of what she felt was a regrettable but unavoidable historic change in the structure of society. If the narrative voice of the earlier works seems to assume an important degree of unity and agreement between author and audience, in the later works that confidence markedly decreases. The putative reader may be ironised as well as, and as much as, some of the characters, as if Jane Austen can no longer quite rely on overt or tacit appeals to values and beliefs held in common, shared assumptions, an identity of discourse. It is as though she became increasingly unsure of her audience (even as she became more popular), uncertain and distanced from whomever her readers might be. For whom, beyond herself, was *Sanditon* being written?

Communication is, of course, a central concern both *for* Jane Austen as a writer, and *in* her novels; how she will communicate to her readers is inseparable from how her characters communicate – or fail to – with each other. So dialogue is as crucially revealing in her novels as her own voice. For if it does not, in general, serve to advance the narrative plot in the simplest sense (though of course it does do just that on occasions – the Box Hill episode in *Emma*, for instance) it certainly serves to reveal the true character of her characters (and thus, indirectly, the character of language itself). Almost exclusively the characters define themselves in their speech – or free indirect speech, which Jane Austen uses so often and so brilliantly (an example of an exception to this would be Frank Churchill's going to London to get his hair cut). It may be a simple matter of diction. What occupies their minds, what is the scope and reach of their intelligence, imagination and sympathy? Do they indulge in ostentatiously self-advertising figurative language, or do they reveal a suspicion of its latent tendency to theatricalisation and factitious self-dramatisation? Do they deploy abstract concepts and value terms scrupulously and reliably, or do they exploit them to give a façade of rationality and morality to purely egotistical intentions and desires? Does a character speak too much or say too little given the tacit requirements of the situation? Is a character mindlessly loquacious or gracelessly taciturn? Are characters given to facile agitations and exaggerated emotionalism or are they capable of a tactful adequacy of utterance and an appropriate reserve? Are their generalisations reliably founded in experience and reflection or do they emerge as inert and inapposite clichés, mere repetitions of the accepted terminological currency of their social tribe? Do they merely echo the sociolect or do they employ it in such a way as to give it renewed force and relevance? Are they given to a true propriety of speech or are they only capable of fumbling approximations to it, lapsing into more of less subtle failures of propriety – or out-and-out vulgar parodies of it? Do they 'speak' or are they 'spoken'?

'Communication' is of course absolutely indispensable in making any society possible, and we should be alive to all the strains and difficulties, the painful importunities, as well as the vital and vitalising opportunities, it can entail; all those aspects most eloquently and economically alluded to in a phrase from *Emma* – 'the necessary penance of communication'. In emphasising this phrase I wish to keep in view, as I think Jane Austen did, not simply the indisputable joys, pleasures and enrichments, but also the arduousness, the unsleeping vigilance, and unremitting care, the inescapable obligations – the sheer hard work – involved in, and incurred by, our inescapable linguicity, our unavoidable status as communicators. For us, no less than for Jane Austen, communication is both a privilege and a penance, a penance *because* a privilege, an ordeal as well as an opportunity. Necessarily. And necessarily necessary.

# 2

# Anger in the Abbey: *Northanger Abbey*

The Gothic aura attached to the name 'Northanger Abbey' – at least for Catherine Morland – is soon dissolved. She first hears the name in what was originally published as the second volume (ch. 17) when she is invited there by General Tilney (important to note, since it is he – the *father* – who finally ejects her, a very gross transgression of hospitality and emanating from the patriarchal centre of power). That invitation allows Jane Austen to tease Catherine's unexpressed rhetoric of internal excitement and desire in a way which seems central to the intention of the book. 'Northanger Abbey: – These were thrilling words and wound up Catherine's feelings to the highest point of ecstasy. Her grateful and gratified heart could hardly restrain its expressions within the language of tolerable calmness.' A 'language of tolerable calmness' is no bad phrase for what Jane Austen worked for. (What is 'tolerable'? Should one always remain totally 'calm'?). 'Abbey' – we have to remember the quite significantly calibrated notions of domicile that were clearly operative in those times. Thus Catherine after her invitation to the Abbey: 'With all the chances against her of house, hall, place, park, court, and cottage, Northanger turned up an abbey, and she was to be its inhabitant.'

The nomination 'Abbey' was what had worked on Catherine's mind and her naïve imagination blooms in response. But within a comparatively short time (by ch. 26 – some sixty pages later) Catherine feels that 'the Abbey itself was no more to her than any other house'. What turns the Abbey into simply a 'house' but at the same time seems to turn the benevolent owner into an incomprehensible monster? It is as though, as the building loses its 'evil', the owner gains it. The relationship between people and habitations is both crucial and paradoxical for Jane Austen – as is absolutely clear from this early novel. It is one of Catherine's

*Jane Austen*

mistakes, or understandable naïveties, that initially she tends effectively to identify place and person. Thus she is surprised that the Tilneys are not more 'elated' by the possession of an Abbey: 'Their superiority of abode was no more to them than their superiority of person.' Not only does she come to perceive the Abbey as a house: she has to confront the fact of the inferiority of its owner (in terms of what might be expected both of a gentleman and of a host).

Because of her book-fed imagination (and no other novel by Jane Austen is so concerned with reading and its effects), Catherine of course expects traces of past crimes, hidden evidence of some unspeakable transgression, various modes of concealment of past acts, a general sense of guilty secrecy, all amid the – by then – conventional stereotype of what a 'Gothic' setting would be, and a pervasively ominous atmosphere. (For details about the books which are read in the novel, by Catherine and others, see Marilyn Butler, *Jane Austen and the War of Ideas*: also the Introduction to the Penguin edition of the novel by Anne Henry Ehrenpreis. I should just like to draw attention to a conversation in chapter 14 during which Catherine expresses her distate for 'real solemn history'. Compared with the Tilneys' liking for 'history' this might seem to indicate a certain shallowness or callowness of mind on Catherine's part. Yet she does make one telling point which is usually overlooked. One reason why 'history', as then written, does not appeal to her is this: 'the men all so good for nothing, and *hardly any women at all* – it is very tiresome' [emphasis added]. A little silly, perhaps. But her off-hand complaint 'hardly any women at all' anticipates a complaint which has become much more articulate in our own times: namely, that 'history' has been traditionally written from an almost exclusively male point of view. See, for example, the well-known book by Sheila Rowbotham, *Hidden from History*, subtitled 'Women's Oppression and the Fight Against It', which examines precisely why, in the works of 'history' that have come down to us, there are 'hardly any women at all'.)

There is a good deal of defence of novels and reading in this novel, so that it is in part a self-justifying artefact. At the same time there is ambivalence. Reading can deform reality in advance so that the avid reader, living with an inflamed imagination, might well not only 'see' things which are not actually there in the external world, but also *not* see what *is* there. In this way reading may lead to a misreading of the actual non-fictional given world. It is clear from the start that Jane Austen is going to subject Catherine to a fair amount of irony in this connection. We read, for instance, that 'she read all such works as heroines must read to supply their memories with those quotations which are so serviceable and so soothing in the vicissitudes of their eventful lives'. 'Eventfulness' is a notion (and a problem) I shall come back to. But we can see straightaway that in effect Catherine wants to turn life into a prolonged series of quotations. In this way she quite literally is in danger of perverting reality, and one of the things she has to learn is to break out of quotations, as it were, and discover the complex differences (as well as the complex connections) between reading a book and reading the world. I emphasise the 'complexity' because, of course, when it comes to the prospect of a hidden evil or horror in Northanger Abbey, Catherine is, as it were, wrongly right. She has to address herself to the problem of General Tilney's behaviour – 'what could have provoked him to such a breach of hospitality, and so suddenly turned all his partial regard . . . into actual ill-will'. This is a much more problematical and painful phenomenon than anything that might be found by groping around in old cupboards and drawers. The fact – not the 'fancy' – is that General Tilney 'had acted neither honourably nor feelingly – neither as a gentleman nor as a parent'. I should stress again that the General is *the* figure of the father in the book – the one with all the powers of summons and dismissal, promotion and prohibition. Catherine's actual father is by contrast, though a clergyman, both weak and permissive: not a force in the book.

(References to the diminished authority, responsibility, and effectuality of the figure of the heroine's father will recur throughout this account of Jane Austen's novels. In anticipation I shall note here, taking the novels in chronological order, that Mr Morland is weak and passive; Mr Dashwood is dead; Mr Bennet has withdrawn from all responsibilities into his library and his negating cynicism; Sir Thomas grievously neglects the upbringing of his children, fails to appreciate Fanny, and for much of the time is absent pursuing profits in the West Indies; Mr Woodhouse is a hopeless hypochrondriac, feeble, infantile and inert; Sir Walter Elliot is simply the worst father of the lot, totally absorbed in his own vacuous vanity, utterly neglectful of all his duties, and positively malign in his treatment of Anne. In general this means that the heroine lacks the guidance and support – the directive and constructive authority – which she, as any child, needs. She must find these things elsewhere: either from within or through a learning process which involves her interaction with, and reaction to, others. In a very important sense she has to find and make her own way. How she does this provides much of the drama of the novels. It might also be noted that the fathers of most of the main men in the novels have died; thus Willoughby, Darcy, Bingley, Crawford, Mr Knightley and Captain Wentworth are all free – perhaps too free – to do what they like and marry, or seek to marry, whom they choose. This extra freedom of the male stands in contrast to the female's relatively abandoned and often doubly precarious and vulnerable condition – even Emma's financial independence confers a very ambiguous 'freedom'. This asymmetrical relationship between what we may roughly designate as male power and female plight, allowing of course for marked individual variations, is at the centre of Jane Austen's novels.)

So the General's failure both as host and parent is potentially a very serious threat to the decent and rational orderings and reciprocities and continuities of society. Catherine is of course wrong in her belief that the General killed his wife; but the wrongness deviously arrives at rightness. 'Catherine, at any rate, heard enough to feel, that in suspecting General Tilney of either murdering or shutting up his wife, she had scarcely sinned against his character, or magnified his cruelty.' The secret which Catherine discovers has no actual blood stains on it, but it is lethal none the less, for it consists of putting money (and social advancement) first with complete disregard for the feelings of others – indeed, without respecting and recognising them as persons at all. Catherine is taken up by the General when he has been given reason to think of her as 'being handsomely legacied hereafter': for the General she simply *is* the money that might come with her. When he is disabused of his expectations, Catherine realises that 'she was guilty only of being less rich than he had supposed her to be'. Catherine is of course in no way responsible for his delusions about her prospective wealth: that is all due to the false intimations put about by the Thorpes, 'a forward, bragging, scheming race'. But, when the General discovers that he has been deceived about Catherine's wealth, his reaction is not shame (that he should only have regarded her as a potential financial source) but rage that he has been misled. 'Enraged with almost every body in the world but himself, he set out the next day for the Abbey, where his performances have been seen.' These performances including the instant and crudest possible dismissal of Catherine from the Abbey. The degradation and negation of the role – and obligations – of host could hardly be more complete. And, when Henry makes it clear that he intends to ask Catherine to marry him anyway, the reaction is, again, rage. 'The General was furious in his anger, and they parted in dreadful disagreement.' It is this irrational ruthless unfeeling anger in the Abbey which Catherine has to encounter – arguably more sinister and frightening than anything in the Gothic novels which so engaged her imagination. For this is the real thing: the utter egotism, hardness, cruelty and insensitivity of the human heart, and the frightening power of the enraged figure of parental authority. To stress it again: it is the anger in Northanger Abbey which is the real hidden horror.

When Catherine is driven to the Abbey by Henry the approach is literally devious or sinuous: 'every bend in the road was expected with solemn awe to afford a glimpse of its massy walls of grey stone'. But she is riding within the carriage of her quotations and the entrance to the Abbey is both disappointingly and surprisingly direct. Fiction has, as it were, been bypassed: 'there was a something in this mode of approach which she had certainly not expected'. This literal difference between the journey of her imagination or dreams and the actual journey anticipates the process of disabusal and learning she will have to undergo. This process, incidentally, is central to Jane Austen's novels and the conclusions often involve a final coinciding of the heroine's knowledge and the reader's knowledge, so that, although they start off at quite a distance from each other – this goes for Emma as much as for Catherine – by the end the heroine and the reader occupy the same cognitive space. They finally know what is what, and we know what is what, and we know that they know. Of course, this posits or presumes the possibility of arriving at a corrected and accurate perception of reality. This is part of Jane Austen's eighteenth-century cast of mind, though it is not to be construed as a complacency. But how different from, say, a twentieth-century novel such as Ford's *The Good Soldier*, in which the recurrent refrain from the narrator, is, 'I don't know'. He doesn't know as narrator, and we don't know him as readers. There is no assured and ascertainable cognitive space to share. Or compare Chekhov's comments in a letter stating that he wanted 'truthfully to depict life and in passing to show how much life deviates from a norm': 'This norm is not known to me, as it is not known to any of us. We all know what is a dishonourable act, but what is honour – we do not know.' I do not want to suggest that Jane Austen was so fatuously confident that she could always 'know' and could always produce a distinct definition of ethical 'norms'. But her work does give the sense that it is possible to work towards them, that some sure knowledge can be arrived at, that some 'norms' may be comprehended and uttered.

Catherine of course, besides going through the courting-process which is essential to all Jane Austen's novels, also goes through a learning-process, both discarding fantasies and facing facts. This kind of double process of disillusion and enlightenment is one which many Austen heroines experience (Fanny Price is a notable exception). First of all Catherine has to be disabused of her naïve and foolish 'Gothic' expectations. Here I think Jane Austen has a special bout of fun both with Catherine and the reader. When Catherine, in fear and trembling, rummages in the old chest she finally finds 'a white cotton counterpane, properly folded'. And when she gropes around in the drawers of the old black cabinet – the first four of which are 'entirely empty' – she finally finds a manuscript which in the clear light of day turns out to be 'an inventory of linen'. For 'linen' we may read 'sheets' and say that, in searching for some gory or ghoulish inscribed story, Catherine has indeed come across a 'blank' – neatly folded sheets with nothing written on them. The second object – expected to provide a satisfying terror and suspicion – is the epitome of domestic routine and ordinariness, 'a washing bill'. Clearly the two objects are meant to go together: linen and 'inventory of linen'; non-text and banal commentary. Just good housekeeping. Scarcely the appurtenances of *The Mysteries of Udolpho*. Catherine soon abandons this realm of foolish expectations. 'The visions of romance were over. Catherine was completely awakened.' She realises that she 'had been craving to be frightened'. Without wishing to deviate into the follies of would-be psychosexual criticism, I think it is legitimate to recognise that in an impressionable adolescent girl the desire – craving, indeed – for some kind of intense excitation may easily be sexual even if it takes another form. To be aroused by fear is still to be aroused. And while I am tentatively following this line I would draw attention to the phrase used when Catherine is looking into the cabinet at all the (empty) drawers: there is 'in the centre, a small door, closed also with a lock and key (which) secured in all probability a cavity of importance'. This suggests to me a thinly veiled image of virginity, and if that seems far-fetched and perverse just let me suggest that there were more mysteries and possible problems and terrors in the transition from virginity to marriage – indeed, in that 'cavity of importance' – for a young girl such as Jane Austen was writing about than in *Udolpho* or any other novel, 'Gothic' or not, which Catherine may have read.

(The potential psychological significance of such enclosed spaces in the furniture of the house was considered by Gaston Bachelard in his *Poetics of Space*, in which he offers an 'examination of the images of intimacy that are in harmony with drawers and chests, as also with all the other hiding-places in which human beings, great dreamers of locks, keep or hide their secrets'. We may recall that when Catherine is trying to 'penetrate' the secret of the cabinet she has much trouble with the lock, and then becomes uncertain whether it was in fact unlocked and she unwittingly locked it. Bachelard asserts, 'Wardrobes with their shelves, desks with their drawers, and chests with their false bottoms are veritable organs of the secret psychological life. . . . A wardrobe's inner space is also *intimate space*, space that is not open to just anybody.' See in particular his chapter entitled 'Drawers, Chests and Wardrobes'. It offers many suggestive comments which, with caution, one might bear in mind in considering the significance of Catherine's intensely troubled negotiations with drawers and the cabinet.)

So Catherine is 'awakened'. Here is anticipated what will become a crucial theme for the novel (I am not just thinking of specific novels with such titles – such as Kate Chopin's *The Awakening*). For it is not entirely unproblematical what 'awakening' exactly is – awakening from what to what? From illusion to reality, might be the answer one feels immediately prompted to give. But it is clearly not quite so easy, since it is not always entirely clear which of our illusions are 'real' and which of our realities are 'illusory'. And then we may awaken to what Tolstoy called 'the dream of life'. Catherine is awakened from one kind of dream or fantasy, but she is about to enter a 'real' nightmare more puzzling and initially more fantastical and frightening than anything in the transparent fictions on which she had fed herself. One thing was obviously clear to Jane Austen: that you do not just 'wake up' once, ever afterwards living in the translucent and instantly knowable world of the 'real'. On the contrary, it is a process which may have to be undergone repeatedly – unless one opts for the dream of life, as many of her minor characters seem to have done. Thus, shortly after her 'awakening' Catherine is having to struggle with the incomprehensibility of the General's behaviour: 'the inexplicability of the General's conduct dwelt much on her thoughts . . . why he should say one thing so positively, and mean the other all the while, was most unaccountable! How were people, at that rate, to be understood?' How indeed – unless one has fathomed the unfathomable depths of the complications and complexities of human motivation. And not even Freud managed that. There will be further awakenings for Catherine.

She has what James often referred to as the 'blessed capacity to be bewildered': she experiences 'the pressing anxieties of thought' and the turmoil and turbulence of inexplicable behaviour in other people. She also has to undergo the shock and degradation of sudden banishment and a humiliating homecoming. The 'homecoming' is of course one of the oldest of literary subjects. The *Odyssey* is probably only one of the many oral epics based on the *nostoi*, and *Robinson Crusoe* basically a later version of the same theme. Horkheimer and Adorno (in *Dialectic of Enlightenment*) make the point that 'both Odysseus and Crusoe, the two shipwrecked mariners, make their weakness (that of the individual who parts from the collectivity) their social strength'. Catherine is hardly 'shipwrecked', though what happens to her has all the aspects of a quite unexpected sudden disaster, and she is indeed 'cast away'. Nor is she so obviously able to make her isolated weakness her 'strength', though she does finally achieve what she had wanted after the 'wreckage' of her hopes, which briefly soared while she felt she was the welcome guest at the Abbey. But there is a faint echo of the *nostoi* theme here, though the nature of the return inverts the ancient classical version. Jane Austen asserts that 'I bring back my heroine to her home in solitude and disgrace.' Hardly Odysseus coming back to Ithaca. But there is a crucial aspect to what happens to Catherine – her high hopes and her humble homecoming: at the beginning of her adventures she was 'looking forward to pleasures untasted and unalloyed, and free from the apprehensions of evil as from the knowledge of it. Three months ago had seen her all this: and now, how *altered* a being did she return!' (emphasis added). Here we have a phenomenon which is crucial for the novel – *alteration*. Not only must something happen (eventfulness) but there must be some change – development, enlightenment, disillusion, increase in self-knowledge, deepened moral awareness, a rise or fall in society, a change in economic position (the possibilities are endless) – and this we call alteration. Without eventfulness and alteration it is hardly possible to conceive of the novel (the eventfulness and alteration can of course be, and often are, internal). (If I don't bother to add 'or the epic or drama' it is because action in the external world and resultant changes are inherent to those genres; it was much less certain what the novel was going to be, or how it would 'move'.)

But before someone returns home he or she has to leave it, and this brings us to an interesting aspect of the whole question of how the novel should – or can – begin. 'Men can do nothing without the make-believe of a beginning.' Thus George Eliot starts *Daniel Deronda*. And, if, as James famously asserted, relationships really stop nowhere, nor can anyone really say with any certainty that they start anywhere. Edward Said (in *Beginnings*) has given us a profound account of the problems which surround all ideas of origin and beginning and we can no longer ignore that truth succinctly expressed by George Eliot that a 'beginning' is an indispensable 'make-believe' (we might say 'fiction') – in science, in poetry, and indeed very notably in the novel. Without that initial 'make-believe' the narrative – any narrative – could not get started, the sentence or the voice could not get moving. There may still be, to alter Dr Johnson's formulation, everything to be endured, but there could be nothing to be told. In the case of the novel there must be some initial act of severance and departure. There are of course exceptions to this, to which I shall refer, but in general the 'make-believe' of the beginning involved some form of separation from the parental home. We may take Robinson Crusoe's words as a kind of archetype of this. He sees what happens to him as an exemplary warning, starting with his going against the word of his father, 'the Opposition to which, was, *as I may call it*, my ORIGINAL SIN'. Again he regrets the life he finds himself involved in 'for which I forsook my Father's House, and broke thro' all his good advice'. That 'Original Sin', that *breaking through* the parental advice, a desire for travel as opposed to the repetitious life offered by staying within the orbit of home – these are often the necessary points or initiatives of commencement on which the resultant novel depended. To some extent we may say that narrative depends on this 'Original Sin', that breaking-through, which is a breaking-away into a world – geographic, experiential – as yet unseen, unread, unwritten. It is an adventure into 'difference'. And *that* does produce something to be told.

(Compare one of the main ideas in the work of Gilles Deleuze, which privileges what he designates the 'nomad' figure over the 'sedentary' members of society. The tension or contest between these two generic types is obviously in varying forms basic to most societies. It is certainly central to the novel, in which the 'nomad' figure in one form or another – the possible guises it may assume are legion – is arguably essential. Jane Austen would never elevate the nomad at the expense of the sedentary so extremely as Deleuze – in, for example, *Mille plateaux*. She preferred the sedentary, in certain forms, just as she valued 'stillness'. But the nomads are there in her fiction – sometimes just as unexpected visitors who threaten to disrupt an established orderliness – and are essential to it.)

But of course we must make some distinctions. Men can travel, adventure, explore, set out to make their fortunes, and so on. But for most women, certainly till past Jane Austen's time, such options were quite closed. Yes, we have a Moll Flanders but she is an exception proving the rule. All Defoe's main characters are male-type adventurers. Richardson's three heroines do in fact leave their fathers' houses, but they are either forcibly abducted or sent to another house for one reason or another. Fielding's male characters spend a good deal of time having adventures on the road, but when it comes to the angelic Amelia in his novel of that title we find a clear example of the problem. The first sentence reads, 'The various accidents which befell a very worthy couple after their uniting in the state of matrimony will be the subject of the following history' – but in fact almost without exception the 'accidents' happen to the not entirely worthy Mr Booth: he goes to the wars, he gets involved in fights, drinks and gambles too much, goes to prison, even (an early hint of what was to be the key 'event' in the nineteenth-century novel) indulges in adultery. The accidents which befall Amelia – pattern of all Christian and domestic virtues – are all concerned with housekeeping or worrying about the sickness of her children. She is, as the vast majority of women were then (and later), effectively housebound. For her, no news is good news, no 'event' is itself a desirable event. For her the ideal life would effectively be without narrative. There is simply not enough *alteration* in *Amelia* to make it a memorable or successful novel.

This raises a crucial problem for the novel as a genre, a problem which Fielding notes, light-heatedly enough, in such recurring comments as 'Nothing, as I remember, happened in this interval of time', 'Nothing happened between the Monday and the Wednesday worthy a place in this history', 'Nothing, I think, remarkable happened'; and such comments are repeated so often that one wonders what exactly qualified something to be 'worthy a place in this history' – or, indeed, in any other 'history'? What constitutes the 'remarkable'? What happens to narrative when 'nothing happens'? When Booth describes his married life to Miss Matthews the problem is brought into sharp focus: 'I scarce know a circumstance that distinguished one day from another. The whole was one continued series of love, health, and tranquillity. Our lives resembled a calm sea.' 'The dullest of all ideas', cries the lady. ' "I know", said he, "it must appear dull in description. . . ." ' But not in life, we infer. Do we then draw the moral that only when life somehow goes wrong (when the sea gets rough) can a narrative somehow go right – or even get started? The problem is even more starkly visible in Richardson's *Pamela*. There, after some 300 pages of erotic hide-and-seek, we get 700 more pages of – what? After Pamela has successfully engineered her marriage to the feebly licentious and easily converted Mr B., the novel effectively disappears. We are never taken out of that 'family calm' into which Pamela 'subsides' so contentedly. Which is fine for Pamela, but what about for us, the readers? All traces of physicality disappear under Pamela's writing, as she celebrates a closed world almost entirely free from 'events' and 'alteration', a clockwork world of unfailing regularity, surprise and suspense reduced to degree zero. There is nothing to hide; there is nothing to seek. There is – nothing. There is Pamela's writing, which offers us 700 pages of what Roland Barthes aptly described as 'the tedium of foreseeable discourse': no rupture, intervention or radical disturbance. Nothing, I think, remarkable happened. The 'novel' is transformed into a tract as the narrative drive is slowed down to the inertia, even to the absolute stasis, of timeless moralising. That is how Pamela's writing effectively destroys the novel, by telling her story and then denovelising it; the novel is emptied of its 'novel' contents by being so completely filled by her interminable, barely motivated writing. After the somewhat guilty, illicit 'pleasure' of the novel of sexual foreplay (300 pages), there are 700 pages of all-too-licit and sententious instruction (I except a brief flurry caused, significantly, by a masquerade), tending to smother everything which had been alive in the novel, so that the book ends up, indeed, as a kind of *scripture*. This was perfectly in line with Richardson's intentions and did not prevent the book from becoming a bestseller. But for the novel it represented a complete cul-de-sac.

Indeed, by the end *Pamela* demonstrates negatively what is indispensable for the novel to exist. Her house, the site of her perfect domestic bliss, is 'a heaven of a house: and being wound up thus constantly once a week, at least, like a good eight-day clock, no piece of machinery that was ever made is so regular and uniform as this family is'. It is a rather chilling picture, with all that it implies of mechanisation, reification and general dehumanisation. A novel (say, by Dickens) could be written to criticise or expose such a 'happy family' – but not simply to celebrate it. Indeed, Pamela writes explicitly condemning novels – all novels – and the moral of her book is, precisely, that ideally one should live a life about which no novel could be written. 'The dullest of all ideas.' By the end Pamela has returned to the conduct books (or more exactly the book of 'Familiar Letters' – a manual of moral advice, instruction and exhortation) from which she originated. And her aspiration is for a yet more remote place. She shows a growing appetite for transcendence, as in remarks such as the following: 'this world is not a place for the immortal mind to be confined to; . . . there must be an hereafter where the *whole* soul shall be satisfied; where there is no mixture, no unsatisfiedness; and where all is joy, peace, and love, for evermore!' And there are no more novels. For the novel – indeed, all narrative – emerges from, is dependent upon, 'mixture' and 'unsatisfiedness', the maculate conditions of life in which nothing is 'for evermore', except death. Pamela's dislike of the body, her yearning for an immaculate world in which there is no change, no 'mixture', no unsatisfied desire, does indeed point to a realm beyond this life altogether – not just 'a heaven of a house', but the house of Heaven itself. Pamela wants to return to the house of her immortal Father, whither the novel most certainly cannot follow her. For the novel is necessarily involved with the mixed and the mundane; mortal and fallible fathers, imperfect and confusing houses, ambiguous departures, uncertain journeyings, and arrivals and returns which are never – really – any more than temporary terminations, provisional stabilities, apparent fulfilments, incomplete completions. 'Evermore' and 'ever after' are only conventional signs signalling an arbitrary cessation of narrative which in reality signifies only a pause, an interruption, a hiatus. Happy endings are only the dream of narrative. In truth, they are simply indefinitely extended intervals. But after this digression about the non-novels generated by Amelia and Pamela, those perfect wives, let us return to Jane Austen's not quite so perfect heroines, who, being unmarried, must somehow engage with the extra-familial world. Wherein lies – for Jane Austen – the novel.

If we now just think of her two most famous heroines we note that Elizabeth Bennet really only leaves her father's house to go to her husband's house; and Emma makes a point of never leaving her father's house at all – not even to get married. We may set her against the male Robinson Crusoe as the woman who will not commit the 'Original Sin' and who reveres or at least respects every word of a singularly feeble and impotent hypochondriac father. What kind of novel Jane Austen wrote about her we shall have to consider. Yet clearly she was aware that in some way or another it might be necessary or advantageous for the young heroine to leave the parental home if there was to be a story to tell, and that is what happens to Catherine, though she does not exactly run away to sea! She is invited to Bath by the friend of her parents, Mrs Allen – 'a good-humoured woman, fond of Miss Morland, and probably aware that if adventures will not befall a young lady in her own village, she must seek them abroad'. 'Adventures' here certainly does not refer to the kind of thing to which Robinson Crusoe exposes himself. It refers more to what Fanny Burney wrote as the sub-title of her *Evelina*: 'A Young Lady's Entrance into the World'. The words 'entrance' and 'world' may be variously construed and redefined from novel to novel, but in general the 'world' would be the social world of varying extent (a small village society or the dangerous metropolis of London itself – as in *Evelina*) and the 'entrance' may involve a learning-process, the problems of avoiding the wrong kind of 'courtship', or seduction, and the waiting for the right kind. Ideally it will conclude with marriage – which should mean that the world is safely entered. It was in that transitional period between the parental home and marriage that Jane Austen found her subject, and in the young lady who had to enter the world that she found her heroines.

The question of what it was to be a heroine is really posed, ironically, by the first sentence of the book: 'No one who had ever seen Catherine Morland in her infancy, would have supposed her to be born to be a heroine.' The ironies continue. We learn that her mind is 'unpropitious for heroism'. She prefers cricket to 'the more heroic enjoyments of infancy, nursing dormouse, feeding a canary bird, or watering a rose-bush'. We are told explicitly that Catherine had 'by nature nothing heroic about her' and that, for instance, she only likes books that contain no information and that 'were all story and no reflection'. In general 'she fell miserably short of the true heroic height'. One problem is that there are no unusual families – and not even a lord or a baronet – in the neighbourhood. 'But when a young lady is to be a heroine, the perverseness of forty surrounding families cannot prevent her. Something must and will happen to throw a hero in her way.' Her chances of being a 'heroine' only begin when she goes to Bath (incidentally referred to as 'this terrific separation' – 'Terrific' may well be taken as ironic, but it is that key act of separation I referred to). There is one famous moment when Jane

Austen defends the kind of novels which Catherine reads with Isabelle.

> Yes, novels; – for I will not adopt that ungenerous and impolite custom so common with novel writers, of degrading by their contemptuous censure the very performances, to the number of which they are themselves adding. . . . Alas! if the heroine of one novel be not patronized by the heroine of another, from whom can she expect protection and regard? I cannot approve of it.

And the spirited defence of 'the novel' continues.* But so does the irony, as Jane Austen continues to refer to 'my heroine'. Yet there are moments when Catherine is described in a different

---

\* By Jane Austen's time there was developing a clearer sense of the difference between the novel and the romance or at least an attempt to make a clearer differentiation between genres that were to a varying extent becoming inextricably interwoven. Thus, for example, Clara Reeve, writing in 1785 (when Jane Austen was ten), has the character of Euphrasia attempt to clarify the distinction in *The Progress of Romance*:

> The word *Novel* in all languages signifies something new. It was first used to distinguish these works from Romance, though they have lately been confounded together and are frequently mistaken for each other . . . the Romance is an heroic fable, which treats of fabulous persons and things. The Novel is a picture of real life and manners and of the times in which it is written. The Romance in lofty and elevated language, describes what never happened nor is likely to happen. The Novel gives a familiar relation of such things as pass every day before our eyes, such as may happen to our friend, or to ourselves; and the perfection of it, is to represent every scene, in so easy and natural a manner, and to make them appear so probable, as to deceive us into a persuasion (at least while we are reading) that all is real, until we are affected by the joys or distresses, of the persons in the story, as if they were our own.

It may seem a little naïve to us but it is a good enough distinction to start from, though Jane Austen would hardly accept such a relatively simple and stable-sounding distinction. Of course, in Clara Reeve's terms she writes novels and not romances. And *Northanger Abbey* has often been seen as a novel ironising romance. But looked at in another way it could be seen as a *kind* of romance slyly ironising a *kind* of novel. We cannot ever be *quite* sure how to read Jane Austen – or how to read her reading of other novels and romances. I doubt if she felt that the genres were quite so clear-cut and disjunct as Clara Reeve suggests. The 'novel' was always a mixed and never a pure form and arguably it constantly admits some energising admixture of romance – in one form or another.

way, as for example during one miserable episode at the theatre: 'Feelings rather natural than heroic possessed her.' As Catherine indulges the 'luxury of a raised, restless, and frightened imagination' while she reads *Udolpho*, she is imagining herself to be one kind of 'heroine'. But, when we read that, during a moment of surprise at seeing Tilney with another woman, 'Catherine sat erect, in the perfect use of her senses, and with cheeks only a little redder than usual', or when she is described, on a surprise visit to her home by Henry Tilney, as 'the anxious, agitated, happy, feverish Catherine', then we are dealing with a 'natural' heroine – in Jane Austen's terms. The point should be now clear. Catherine is of course no 'heroine' according to the stereotypes and clichés of the popular Gothic novels and romances of the day. But she *is* the 'heroine' of Jane Austen's novel, prey to all the anxieties, agitations, embarrassments, disappointments – and hopes and happinesses – which would 'naturally' beset a young lady entering the world.

But in terms of actual action in the external world (as opposed to the controlled activity of the imagination and living mentally on and by novels) what is such a heroine to do? The discrepancy between the uncurbed ranging of the internal world, where no reality principle need operate, and the unchangeable constraints and limited options for action in the given external circumstances inevitably leads to frustration. For what a girl such as Catherine can actually, effectively do is – nothing. There are the usual distractions available to young girls within the house, and a few very circumscribed ventures into the external world – a walk, perhaps a ball or a visit to a theatre. When Jane Austen writes that Catherine was about to be 'launched into all the difficulties and dangers of a six weeks' residence in Bath' we detect an irony. That there can be 'difficulties and dangers' turns out to be true, but they are not of the kind that Catherine (as self-conceived 'literary' heroine) anticipates. Society outside the home – the 'world' to be entered – turns out to be, not an area which offers a rich extension of experience, stimulating new contacts, enhancing conversations which nourish new consciousness, but, rather, 'a mob'. In the Upper Rooms or the Pump Room where 'everyone' goes to 'meet' there is the reverse of true social encountering. Rather we are given the impression of the stifling crowdedness of 'a struggling assembly'. 'Every creature in Bath . . . was to be seen in the room at different periods of the fashionable hours; crowds of people were every moment passing in and out, up the steps and down; people whom nobody cared about, and nobody wanted to see.' 'The crowd was insupportable' – and so on. The 'conversation' tends to be the circulation of thoughtless formulations and meaningless noise – loud but 'empty'. Dancing may offer a temporary distraction and pleasure, but that involves a partner (there is a significant exchange in which Henry Tilney compares dancing to marriage, suggesting that the former is an 'emblem' of the latter). And, being a girl, Catherine can only sit and wait – she cannot move her body any more than she can pursue her desires as she wants. Often she shares 'with the scores of other young ladies still sitting down all the discredit of *wanting a partner*' (emphasis added). In one sense that plight at a dance figures the whole situation of the young girl waiting to 'enter the world'. Catherine – and the girl – can only be passive. She can only wait, and hope. John Thorpe with his crass talk of 'horses and dogs' may indeed point to the crudity and mindlessness of much male 'activity' and discourse (and it is worth remembering that Jane Austen never describes a scene when men alone are present – as though the male world were indeed a 'closed book' to her), but a typical female conversation will concern itself with 'dress, balls, flirtations, and quizzes' (this last referring to picking out odd-looking people to laugh at). That there may be rare exceptions to this vapid chatter, Catherine learns from her acquaintance with Eleanor Tilney – and the conversations that finally lead to her marriage with Henry Tilney. But for much of the time she has to endure, and participate in, the trivial kind of discourse described above. (It should be remembered how difficult it was, or could be, to find a space or place to engage in sincere, private, conversation. Jane Austen was writing of a society in which everything – and every word – was more or less 'public'. Privacy was hard to come by. In her letters she refers to the 'pleasures' of 'unreserved Conversation' but even in this novel she notes the difficulty experienced by her heroine and others of getting together 'for any confidential discourse'. It is a difficulty which can become a form of purgatory for some of her heroines who at crucial times want and need 'confidential discourse' or 'unreserved Conversation' but instead have to participate in the public circulation of empty words and meaningless inanities.)

From that list of common topics of conversations I want to concentrate for a moment on the matter of 'dress'. First let us remember that Northanger Abbey is not mentioned, let alone entered, until some way into the second half of the book. Before that we mainly read of Catherine enduring the 'dangers and difficulties', or rather the boredom, of unpartnered life in society (it is hardly surprising that at one point we read of Catherine 'vainly endeavouring to hide a great yawn': it is the 'great yawn' of the female trapped in immobility and triviality by a predominantly insensitive – and boring – male world). So through deflection and displacement by way of compensation we find a notable obsession with dress. Mrs Allen is exemplary in this: 'Dress was her passion. She had a most harmless delight in being fine; and our heroine's entrée into life could not take place till after three or four days had been spent in learning what was mostly worn, and her chaperon was provided with a dress of the newest fashion'. Harmless, perhaps, but it can involve an inversion of values. A small example would be when Mrs Allen takes Catherine to the Upper Rooms – as they struggle through 'the mob' Mrs Allen shows 'more care for the safety of her new gown than for the comfort of her protegée'. More serious – at least as a symptom of misplaced concern – is Mrs Allen's reaction when Catherine reappears after her cruel treatment by the General. Mrs Allen comments vaguely that she has 'no patience with the General', then immediately adds, 'Only think my dear of my having got that frightful great rent in my best Mechlin so charmingly mended, before I left Bath, that one can hardly see where it was. I must shew it you some day or other.' She is more genuinely concerned with her lace garment than with the 'frightful great rent' that has just been made in Catherine's experience of the world – of men in particular. Torn garments move her more than torn lives. Given the relative impotence of the woman, this displacement of concern is perhaps understandable enough. But it does involve some perversion of affective energy.

In the course of the novel, Jane Austen herself makes some very pertinent comments on the female obsession with dress. She is referring to Catherine, who is thinking about a ball at which she will meet the Tilneys again:

> What gown and what head-dress she should wear on the occasion became her chief concern. She cannot be justified in it. Dress is at all times a frivolous distinction, and excessive solicitude about it often destroys its own aim. Catherine knew all this very well; her great aunt had read her a lecture on the subject only the Christmas before; and yet she lay awake ten minutes on Wednesday night debating between her spotted and her tamboured muslin, and nothing but the shortness of the time prevented her buying a new one for the evening. This would have been an error in judgment, great though not uncommon, from which one of the other sex rather than her own, a brother rather than a great aunt might have warned her, for man only can be aware of the insensibility of man towards a new gown. It would be mortifying to the feelings of many ladies, could they be made to understand how little the heart of man is affected by what is costly or new in their attire; how little it is biased by the texture of their muslin, and how unsusceptible of peculiar tenderness towards the spotted, sprigged, and mull or the jackonet. *Woman is fine for her own satisfaction alone.* No man will admire her the more, no woman will like her the better for it. (Emphasis added)

(It is worth noting that Jane Austen herself seems to have shared this obsession with dress. There is hardly one of her letters which does not refer to some article of clothing or material – stockings, gowns, gloves, handkerchiefs, silk, muslin, shifts, caps, frills, sleeves, belts, mittens, nightcaps, frocks, silk gowns, petticoats, 'fashion'. These are just some examples, and she is capable of revealing some of that displacement of feeling which was discernible in Mrs Allen, as, for example, when she is going into mourning:

> pray tell Elizabeth that the new mourning gown is to be made double *only* in the body and sleeves. . . . *I* am to be in bombazeen and crape, according to what we are told is universal *here*, and which agrees with Martha's previous observation. My mourning, however, will not impoverish me, for by having my velvet pelisse fresh lined and made up, I am

sure I shall have no occasion *this winter* for anything new of that sort.

Jane Austen is the last person one would expect to be sentimental or morbid about death, and at times of grief such a distraction is more than understandable. But still – it is part of that preoccupation with clothes which she notes in the discourse of many of her female characters. Allowing for that irony which plays over much of what she writes, the following statement nevertheless has a curious aptness: 'We live entirely in the dressing-room now, which I like very much. I always feel so much more elegant in it than in the parlour.' Elegant. Elsewhere she writes, 'What dreadful Hot weather we have! – It keeps one in a continual state of Inelegance.' Why and whence the concern for 'elegance' if 'woman is fine for her own satisfaction alone'? Fashion and elegance seem to be games – or compensations – for their own sake. Yet we do not need to read Roland Barthes on 'Fashion' to realise that all dress is part of a code, constantly conveying signals and being deciphered. But Jane Austen, who most certainly must have realised this, seems not to be inclined to explore this aspect of dress. And the fact that the inherent ambiguity of dress is that it at once reveals and conceals is a paradox which, again, she chooses not to explore, although I believe it can tell us something important about her writing. I shall return to this later.

Of course this is all partly related to the limitations on what she could write about. Critics writing about Jane Austen's letters often concern themselves with the problem of how cool or even malicious they are. But that is not really the point. For, while it would be quite inaccurate to say that they are really about nothing – there are references to births, marriages and deaths, news about her brothers, comments on balls, card games and food, for example – still they often give the impression of being written mainly out of a desire or a need simply to *write*. As she often indicates herself: thus there are references to 'the nonsense I have been writing', of 'having really nothing to say'; 'we are doing nothing ourselves to write about'; 'I am not at all in a humour for writing; I must write on till I am.' Compare *Mansfield Park*: 'Every body at all addicted to letter writing, without having much to say, which will include a large proportion of the female world at least. . . .' When she writes, 'I flatter myself I have constructed you a smartish Letter, considering my want of Materials', we may perhaps suggest – with no facile pun intended – that her constant preoccupation with dress material is partly substituting for a larger 'want of Material'.)

We might immediately follow Jane Austen's generalisation with the following assertion by Nietzsche from *Beyond Good and Evil*: 'Comparing man and woman in general one may say: woman would not have the genius for finery if she did not have the instinct for the secondary role.' I am not here concerned to attempt to assess the truth of such assertions – particularly the one by Nietzsche, with its highly tendentious use of the word 'instinct'. What does interest me is that Jane Austen does not seem to see woman's obsession with dress as part of the mating- or courting-game. The emphasis is on narcissism not on seduction. One may then ask, 'What is it then that does affect "the heart of man"?', and here of course we immediately come up against the absence of any reference to the body in any real sense in Jane Austen. I should perhaps say the sexual body. There is indeed a vocabulary of the 'figure' in her work but no explicit reference to sexuality or sexual attraction (just as the terms used for establishing identity do not include the individual's sense of her – never mind his – sexuality). In this connection it is worth noting the reason which Jane Austen gives for Henry Tilney's decision to marry Catherine. It is anything but physical – or passional.

> I must confess that his affection originated in nothing better than gratitude, or, in other words, that a persuasion of her partiality for him had been the only cause of giving her a serious thought. It is a new circumstance in romance, I acknowledge, and dreadfully derogatory of an heroine's dignity; but if it be as new in common life, the credit of a wild imagination will at least be all my own.

The key words are 'gratitude' for her 'partiality' for him. This could be seen as a form of narcissism on the male side as well. In the 'dance' of such a marriage, it seems to a certain, perhaps a large, extent that the partners are dancing with themselves.

I have noted that dress at once reveals and conceals, and in this it bears comparison with Jane Austen's writing. (In the past language was more than once referred to as 'the dress of thought'.) We quickly notice how very few metaphors Jane Austen uses. This is not the place to go into a discussion on the significance of writing which employs an abundance of metaphor, as opposed to the kind of writing which seeks to eschew it. Wellek and Warren, writing about Jakobson's ideas, refer to his notion 'that metonymy and metaphor may be the characterising structures of two poetic types – poetry of association by contiguity, of movement within a single world of discourse, and poetry of association by comparison, joining a plurality of worlds' (*Theory of Literature*). Without venturing into the by-now familiar discussion concerning the relationship and difference between predominantly metonymic writing and predominantly metaphorical writing, we can see that Jane Austen's works do seem to aim at establishing a 'single world of discourse' (though there are many fragmented and imperfect – even nonsensical – partial discourses contained *within* her 'single discourse') and that she is not at all concerned to 'join a plurality of worlds'. Such a 'plurality' could lead to a potentially uncontrollable proliferation of ambiguities and possible meanings, whereas the drive of her writing seems to aim at a 'single' sense, with the defaulters, perverters or incompetent users of the one true discourse either finally extruded or corrected, educated and assimilated. Metaphor may blur and confuse by its overabundance and excess of possible references and other 'worlds'; Jane Austen, it seems, aims at a total transparency – so that, while her characters may move and speak in a blur of confusion (cf. Sarah who 'indulged in the sweets of incomprehensibility' and even Catherine who, when surprised by Henry Tilney, falls into a 'perplexity of words', and the various empty and meaningless exchanges between people 'in what they called conversation') or may use language to delude and mislead, the authorial discourse invites us to repose confidence in its absolute clarity and openness.

But, while I have said that we do seem to arrive at a point of cognitive certainty and settled – clarified – social arrangements and pairings, it is perhaps not quite so simple as that. We may recall the windows in Northanger Abbey, which disappoint Catherine and her expectations of Gothic gloom, penumbral uncertainties, hidden mysteries: 'but every pane was so large, so clear, so light! To an imagination which had hoped for the smallest divisions, and the heaviest stonework, for painted glass, dirt and cobwebs, the difference was very distressing.' It might seem to Catherine that the General had replaced Gothic darkness with modern light; but in fact it is simply a change in surface adornment/concealment. For the Gothic he has substituted 'all the profusion and elegance of modern taste'. (That 'elegance' is a misreading by Catherine – in fact his taste is revealed as inherently vulgar, as we easily learn from his pride in his fuel-efficient Rumford fireplace, the 'elegant' breakfast set, and so on. He justifies, or rationalises, his compulsive acquisitiveness by maintaining that 'he thought it right to encourage the manufacture of his country', but in fact it is a symptom of the new consumer urge of the age and the crass material instinct for competitive emulation it spawned. In an indirect way the General is a typical – and nasty – 'product' of the exponential increase of consumer products which the Industrial Revolution was making available. His chivalric, military title is as misleading as everything else about him: it conceals a most unheroic, monomaniacal, greedy, ruthless, dehumanised consumer–acquisitor. His only code is a mindless attachment to commodities – and the money to buy more.) Things are not 'clear' and 'light' in the Abbey, as they are not in the General.

Now we tend to think of Jane Austen's writing as being as open and lucid and transparent as those windows – 'so clear, so light'. And so, in a sense, it is. But we should be aware that there is such a phenomenon as the opacity of the illusion of total clarity and transparency, and that truth is intimately bound up with concealment. (Just as, to belabour the point, dress may at once reveal and conceal the 'truth' of the body beneath it.) And of course there is much concealment in the novel. Not just the simple concealment of objects in drawers and cabinets – as I have intimated, Jane Austen turns that into a joke. But there is concealment of motive and intention (the General), and, perhaps more insidious and widespread, the concealment of knowledge – particularly by women:

Where people wish to attach, they should always be ignorant. To come with a well-informed mind is to come with an inability of administering to the vanity of others, which a sensible person would always wish to avoid. A woman especially if she have the misfortune of knowing anything, should conceal it as well as she can.

This authorial assertion is of course ironic, potentially bitterly so, but it does point to a society which operates, in part, by 'concealment', not just concealment of the body but also the concealment – repression, obfuscation – of knowledge; a society, therefore, in which people – particularly women – collude, *have to* collude, in an unspoken conspiracy to conceal truth.

But, it may be objected, Jane Austen's own prose reveals and illuminates all these concealments. It lays things open, it 'deconceals'. And this is true – up to a point. But we should be aware of the potential ambiguity of the truth which even the most apparently transparent discourse – perhaps particularly such discourse – seems to reveal. Heidegger recalls us to the earlier, Greek meaning of the word for truth: 'The Greeks call the unconcealedness of beings *aletheia*. We say "truth" and think little enough in using this word.' It may seem almost absurd to refer to Heidegger in discussing Jane Austen, but he focuses on this problem in a way which I think can be helpful if we are to appreciate the real nature of Jane Austen's prose. I shall run together a few quotations from the same essay ('The Origin of the Work of Art'):

> There is much in being that man cannot master. There is but little that comes to be known. What is known remains inexact, what is mastered insecure. . . . And yet – beyond what is, not away from but before it, there is still something else that happens. In the midst of beings as a whole an open place occurs. There is a clearing, a lighting. . . . Only this clearing grants and guarantees to us humans a passage to those beings that we ourselves are not, and access to the being that we ourselves are. Thanks to this clearing, beings are unconcealed in certain changing degrees.

We may rightly say that Jane Austen's work is such a 'clearing'. But Heidegger continues,

And yet a being can be *concealed*, too, only within the sphere of what is lighted. Each being we encounter and which encounters us keeps to this curious opposition of presence in that it always withholds itself at the same time in a concealedness. The clearing in which beings stand is in itself at the same time concealment.

The notion of the 'clearing' as being at the same time a 'concealment' may seem a good deal too curious for those not particularly fond of German metaphysical speculation. And yet it is close to what I said about dress. And I should be prepared to stand by a description of Jane Austen's writing as a 'clearing' which is at the same time a 'concealment' – the one being the condition of the other. Much of the following passage is surely relevant both to Catherine's experience and to the reader's experience:

> We believe we are at home in the immediate circle of beings. That which is, is familiar, reliable, ordinary. Nevertheless, the clearing is pervaded by a constant concealment in the double form of refusal and dissembling. At bottom, the ordinary is not ordinary; it is extra-ordinary, uncanny. The nature of truth, that is of unconcealedness, is dominated by a denial. Yet this denial is not a defect or a fault, as though truth were an unalloyed unconcealedness that has rid itself of everything concealed. If truth could accomplish this, it would no longer be itself. *This denial, in the form of a double concealment,* belongs to the nature of truth as unconcealedness. Truth, in its nature, is un-Truth.                                             (Italics as in original)

If that last proposition seems unacceptably oxymoronic we should perhaps remember that 'reveal' and 'reveil' have the same etymology. To un-'veal' is to 'veil' again. If I may stretch the words a little, we can say that 'revelation' is always, in some way, 'reveilation'. In any case, we can surely admit the force and relevance of Heidegger's argument. 'Refusal and dissembling' do take place *within* the clearing of 'truth', and the 'ordinary' is indeed – as Catherine discovered – 'extra-ordinary'. Jane Austen's writing is indeed 'clear'. But that clarity depends on all that is concealed within it, and all that is excluded from it. This is emphatically *not* to return to the old and fatuous complaint of the narrowness of her range of reference, or the smallness of the society she describes, or whatever along those lines. It is to attempt to point to a profound and important apparent paradox by which the high degree of clarity and truth (unconcealedness) which her writing attains is dependent on, and inseparable from, concealment and denial (like her society – see the next chapter, on *Sense and Sensibility*). The 'clearing' is also, and necessarily, opaque.

Jane Austen's heroines want explanations and 'truth' – about others, about themselves – as much as they want the right marriage and a good and stable social situation, and Jane Austen indeed shows them moving towards these things so that they often achieve cognitive certainty, the desired partner and a fixed and stable position in society almost at the same time. For them the narrative is finished – closed. But Jane Austen is aware that complete truth is unattainable just as 'perfect felicity' is a fiction. She would have understood Conrad's assertion that 'no explanation is final'. Conclusion – and novels must end – is not finality. And even *Northanger Abbey* ends on a note of teasing – but potentially troubling – uncertainty: 'I leave it to be settled by whomsoever it may concern, whether the tendency of this work be altogether to recommend parental tyranny, or reward filial disobedience.' This is somewhat of the order of Swift turning on us and asking us if we would rather be knaves or fools. Are tyranny and disobedience the only alternatives? Jane Austen is being at least half ironic, of course – though the conclusion does point to the potential conflict within the family between generations. And the fact remains that, while Catherine is left with the partner and enlightenment she wants, we are left with a question so formulated that we would perhaps rather not have to answer it. Everything in the narrative is cleared up; but not everything in the 'clearing' is clear.

Catherine, via literature, imagines atrocities taking place in contemporary England. In fantasising that General Tilney may have killed his wife she is – in literal terms – wrong. But there are various ways of denying and destroying life, and in his brutal and repressive way the General does work to block the budding life, not only of Catherine, but also of his children (he 'seemed always a check upon his children's spirits', and again, as Miss Tilney is beginning to befriend Catherine: 'The entrance of her father put a stop to the civility'). There are atrocities and atrocities and they can take on domestic and social forms without thereby ceasing to be atrocities. Thus Henry Tilney's famous reproach to Catherine – in a passage Jane Austen inserted at a later date – has to be read with an alert wariness:

> Dear Miss Morland, consider the dreadful nature of the suspicions you have entertained. What have you been judging from? Remember the country and the age in which we live. Remember that we are English, that we are Christians. Consult your own understanding, your own sense of the probable, your own observation of what is passing around you – Does our education prepare us for such atrocities? Do our laws connive at them? Could they be perpetrated without being known, in a country like this, where social and literary intercourse is on such a footing; where every man is surrounded by a neighbourhood of voluntary spies, and where roads and newspapers lay everything open? Dearest Miss Morland, what ideas have you been admitting?

Catherine responds with tears of shame; but the reader may note that the speech is heavy with unintended (by Henry Tilney) ironies. The age they lived in was fraught with anxiety following the French Revolution and the Terror – indeed, the atmosphere has been called 'paranoid'; foreign plots were suspected and signs of Jacobin sympathies were almost hysterically sought for. 'Observations of what is passing around you' precisely excludes the widespread neurotic fear of what might be 'passing around' outside or beneath the area of immediate observation. As for 'education', it no more prepares anyone for atrocities than atrocities prepare one for education – 'atrocious' comes from *ater* meaning black, while education is premised on light and illumination. Of course 'atrocities' could be perpetrated in England, for there is no predicting where 'blackness' and cruel deviance from and transgression of Christian norms or legal proscriptions might erupt. And what a female's education might 'prepare' a girl for in those days is hard to say. As for the state of 'social and literary intercourse', the novel itself offers sufficient example of how much such 'intercourse' might exclude, how little of the political and economic realities of the day it might engage. With reference to those 'voluntary spies', which have attracted a variety of critical comment, I can do no better than quote Warren Roberts in *Jane Austen and the French Revolution:*

> We have seen that Pitt took severe measures to stifle the radical opposition, such as suspending the Act of Habeas Corpus, the passage of the Seditious Meetings Act and Treasonable Practices Act, and censorship of the press. Related to these actions was a widespread use of spies, which began in 1792. . . . Austen was referring to actual spies who were serving or trying to serve Pitt and the government and whose purpose was to crush the various agents of radicalism and subversion. . . . Austen wrote the novel during the very period when the activity of spies was at a peak and the atmosphere was highly charged with fear and suspicion.

If England has become a land of 'voluntary spies', it is not the secure and calm place Henry Tilney seems to be trying to evoke. And, while 'roads and newspapers' may seem to facilitate speed and increase of exposure and information, so far from laying everything 'open' they may equally well serve to foster and accelerate rumour, obfuscation and fear. Paradoxically they may, indeed, lay things 'closed'. It is Catherine who, perhaps unwittingly enough, has laid an 'atrocity' open in provoking the General into showing his venal and cruel nature.

We might compare, or rather contrast, Marlow's words to his socially respectable English listeners as he tries to evoke the reality of Kurtz for them in Conrad's *Heart of Darkness*:

> You can't understand. How could you? – with solid pavement under your feet, surrounded by kind neighbours ready to cheer you or to fall on you, stepping delicately between the butcher and the policeman, in the holy terror of scandal and gallows and lunatic asylums – how can you imagine what particular region of the first ages of man's untrammelled feet may take him by way of solitude – utter solitude without a policeman – by way of silence – utter silence, where no warning voice of a kind neighbour can be heard whispering of public opinion? These little things make all the difference.

I am not suggesting that General Tilney is comparable with Kurtz (!), but Marlow's cutting words indicate that he perceives the structure of society and the nature and modes of operation of its restraints and constraints in a way which seems to be quite unavailable to Henry Tilney. Henry tries to evoke an England which is a kind of phantasm of peaceful life from which the possibility of horror and violence has been eradicated. 'It could not happen here.' But there is violence and violence, and, as the novel reveals, in a sense it can and does occur – in Gloucestershire, as well as in France.

Another crucial passage relates to this problem – of whether certain things are possible or plausible in England – and it needs to be quoted in full:

Charming as were all Mrs Radcliff's works, and charming even as were the works of all her imitators, it was not in them perhaps that *human nature, at least in the midland counties of England*, was to be looked for. Of the Alps and Pyrenees, with their pine forests and their vices, they might give a faithful delineation; and in horrors as they were there represented. *Catherine dared not doubt beyond her own country*, and even of that, if hard pressed, would have yielded the northern and western extremities. But in the central part of England there was surely some security for the existence of a wife not beloved, in the laws of the land, and the manners of the age. Murder was not tolerated, servants were not slaves, and neither poison nor sleeping potions to be procured, like rhubarb, from every druggist. Among the Alps and Pyrenees, perhaps, there were no mixed characters. There, such as were not spotless as an angel, might have the disposition of a fiend. But in England it was not so; among the English she believed, in their hearts and habits, there was a general though unequal mixture of good and bad.     (Emphasis added)

In the eighteenth century it was becoming a problem for some thinkers as to whether 'human nature' was everywhere the same, allowing for obvious surface differences of customs and *mores*. If God created man, then, in essence, he should be the same everywhere (compare Hobbes's reference to 'the similitude of *Passions*, which are the same in all men' in *Leviathan*; and Hume's 'every human creature resembles ourselves', in the *Treatise of Human Nature*). But if human nature was *not* the same everywhere then that opened the possibility of having to allow for absolute differences in moral systems and codes of conduct – a genuine cultural relativism which meant that ethical norms and laws might be local, and thus perhaps arbitrary – and thus perhaps provisional. The great authority of absolute imperatives and prohibitions – such as seems to be behind, say, the Decalogue – could be endangered and start to melt away, ending who could say where? We notice that in Catherine's thinking about 'human nature', after her 'awakening', there is a distinct sense of shrinkage concerning the possible area in which her notions of 'human nature' might obtain. Perhaps not in Europe, perhaps not even in the 'northern and western extremities' – 'human nature' thus defined and located threatens to dwindle to what is permitted and prescribed (and proscribed) by the laws and manners of 'the central part of England'. Elsewhere she is prepared to admit the possibility of the existence of a dualist, even Manichean, model of human nature whereby people simplify out into 'angels' and 'fiends' so that what is 'romance' in Gloucestershire might be 'realism' in France (particularly bearing the Revolution in mind). As though only in the extremely small sphere of her actual experience was human nature to be found 'mixed'. Proximity and contiguity and contact bring an apparently 'realistic' assessment of the composition of human nature. Any distance beyond that might be the site of unmixed 'extremities' in human disposition and behaviour. But clearly the drawing of such a circle or perimeter, an invisible boundary within which people are mixed but controlled and there is security and no slavery or murder, and beyond which they fall into polar extremes of good and evil, is impossible. That possibility of 'shrinkage' which her thinking admits can know no limits. This is to say not that there is no validity in her sense that there may be distinct *differences* in the way people manifest their dispositions in central England and in the Alps, but rather that morality does not follow topography and that her sense of a protected circle of security immune to the 'fiendish' (and thus the 'angelic'?) is an illusion – albeit an understandable one. The opposition in her thinking is really between the known and the unknown. But the known has proved to be the unknown – the unpredictable – and thus, in a profound sense unknowable. As she thought she 'knew' the General and could read his conduct correctly – and discovered she did not and had not. The apparent familiarity and stability and reliability within the circle of security give way with no warning at an entirely unpredictable moment (there is no education which could have prepared her for the General's behaviour). Geography and manners indeed change from place to place, country to country (and one might add, from class to class within the same area), but human nature is of course 'mixed' everywhere. Iago and Desdemona are 'extremes' which might occur anywhere, any time. But they are also in a sense aberrations. The 'norm' is nothing which can be defined or delimited – but it is invariably mixed. There is no fixed or determinable circle of security, and the 'extreme' – in the form of good and bad, benevolence and malevolence – may occur anywhere, even in the heart of the heart of England. For instance, in Northanger Abbey.

It is shortly after this passage that we read, 'The anxieties of common life began soon to succeed to the alarms of romance.' It sounds like a Johnsonian distinction, and in terms of the novel we can undertand what it implies. Yet it is hardly a stable distinction. 'Common life' has proved to be capable of producing surprising uncommonness; anxiety may be a form of controlled alarm, while alarm can be the result of a suddenly exacerbated anxiety. 'Common life' is as much a mixture as 'human nature' – things cannot be so lucidly separated out as Jane Austen's prose seems to suggest. To be sure, the book is a comedy, and the appropriate couples are brought together at the end and adequate money is dispensed, somewhat ironically, by Jane Austen – as when she observes in the last chapter that the 'anxiety' felt by Henry and Catherine (waiting for the 'consent' of the General, not his 'money' – Jane Austen will give them that) will not be felt by 'my readers, who will see in the tell-tale compression of the pages before them, that we are all hastening together to perfect felicity'. The book starts to reveal itself as a book, and that 'perfect felicity' is, in its way, as much a form of 'romance' as anything in Catherine's reading (compare Hobbes, again from *Leviathan*: '*Continual successe* in obtaining those things which a man from time to time desireth, that is to say, continuall prospering, is that men call FELICITY; I mean the Felicity of this life. For there is no such thing as perpetuall Tranquillity of mind, while we live here; because Life it self is but Motion, and can never be without Desire, nor without Feare, no more than without Sense'). But without wishing melodramatically to turn the novel into something darker than it is, we can note that there has been a distinct shadow cast across the comedy. And, if General Tilney is unique in Catherine's experience, he would most surely not be unique in even as small an area as the English Midlands. His 'anger' is there until almost the very end, to shock even his son:

> The General, accustomed on every ordinary occasion to give the law in his family, prepared for no reluctance but of feeling, no opposing desire that should dare clothe itself in words, could ill brook the opposition of his son, steady as the sanction of reason and conscience could make it. But, in such a cause, his anger, though it must shock, could not intimidate Henry.

When he *does* give his 'consent' – he has to, there aren't many pages left – it is meaningless: 'his consent, very courteously worded in a page full of empty professions'. By pointing up the 'empty' words which make possible the 'perfect felicity' of the ending, Jane Austen is not only revealing her own contrivance of the perfunctory neatness of the conclusion. She is also indicating that the General has not changed, and that, while there may be satisfactory arrangements and joining of couples and at least a temporary satisfaction of 'desire', the irrational cannot be truly eradicated (if temporarily mollified), and total stability and security are not – not really – ever finally attainable. There is always the possibility of anger in the Abbey – or, indeed, in any structure in the social edifice. The novel ends with a truce between anger and desire. But the war can always be rejoined elsewhere.

# 3

# Secrecy and Sickness:
## *Sense and Sensibility*

---

*Sense and Sensibility* is, of course, about sense and sensibility, but it is also about secrecy and sickness. It opens with considerations of property and concludes with the symmetries of marriage, the two phenomena which determine the territorial divisions and the familial continuities of society, and this is entirely characteristic of what we take to be the Jane Austen world. But there is a muffled scream from Marianne at the heart of the novel (almost literally at the centre, in the twenty-ninth of fifty chapters), and the cause and subsequent suppression of that scream are quite as important in the book as the more or less delicate jostling for partners, property and power, which would seem to occupy the foreground of the action. That the scream is a symptom of the sickness, and the sickness intimately connected with the prevailing secrecy, is an aspect of the complex meaning of the novel which I shall try to indicate. In attempting to approach the novel in this way I am not trying to be merely, or perversely, original. But some extension of the customary vocabulary used in assessing this novel by Jane Austen seems to me to be necessary if we are to comprehend some of the most important issues of a book which seems to hold little interest for many of Jane Austen's most perceptive critics. For example, Walton Litz, who has written what is surely one of the best books on Jane Austen (*Jane Austen: A Study of her Artistic Development*), maintains that 'most readers would agree that *Sense and Sensibility* is the least interesting of Jane Austen's major works'. He sees it as being caught uneasily between burlesque and 'the serious novel' and graciously half exculpates it by saying that 'many of the difficulties in *Sense and Sensibility* can be explained, if not excused, by an examination of its evolution'. It is true that we know that there was an early version of the novel called *Elinor and Marianne* written some time around 1795–6 as a series of letters (like *Lady*

*Susan*, which it followed in order of composition); that *Sense and Sensibility* was started in November 1797; that, however much of the novel was finished then, it was worked on or considerably reworked in the next decade, finally to be published in the form we now have in 1811. There is no doubt that certain manifest unevennesses of technique may be ascribed to this prolonged evolution and one can see the point of Litz's summary that the novel is 'a youthful work patched up at a later date, in which the crude antitheses of the original structure were never successfully overcome'. What Litz means by 'crude antitheses' is the schematic separation of qualities indicated by the title, a fictional strategy which lingers on in *Pride and Prejudice* and which looks back to such eighteenth-century moralistic fictions as Mrs Inchbald's *Nature and Art*. (Litz also points to Maria Edgeworth's *Letters of Julia and Caroline*, published in 1795, in which two sisters also speak up in turn for sense and sensibility.) The use of antitheses as an instrument for separating out qualities to achieve ever greater clarification through ever finer differentiation is a predominant feature of eighteenth-century prose at least from the time of Locke, and it provides much of the energy of the dominant poetic form of the Age of Reason, the heroic couplet, which was made to yield its full analytic potential by Pope. Antitheses were a source of strength for much eighteenth-century literature, but, so Litz would argue, something of a hindrance for the emergent novelist Jane Austen, because, as a habit of mind, the use of antitheses tends to produce polarised abstractions, the confrontation of stereotypes, and the automatic opposition of extremes. These make against the flexibility, and that sense of the unclassifiable in people and their actions, which are desirable in the novel. To achieve that flexibility and that sense, Jane Austen has to move beyond antitheses.

Clearly much of this is true and we could note a comparable development within a genre by recalling how the bold schematic bareness of the morality play gave way to the dense dramatic richness of Shakespeare's mature works. Jane Austen's later works, to say nothing of the novels of such a writer as George Eliot, when compared with eighteenth-century moralistic fictions, clearly mark a great extension and deepening of the possibilities of the novel form. But in regarding *Sense and Sensibility* as an eighteenth-century matrix containing, as it were, the embryo of a nineteenth-century novel which struggles but fails to be born, I think we miss a lot that the book actually contains (Litz gives it some ten pages in a 180-page book, which is tantamount to a dismissal). Admittedly the title and the use of the two sisters does seem to indicate a fairly primitive schematisation, but the stuff of a novel may well belie the apparent simplicity of its structuring. The fact that Marianne has plenty of sense and Elinor is by no means devoid of sensibility should alone convince us that Jane Austen was already enough of a novelist to know that nothing comes unmixed, that qualities which may exist in pure isolation as abstractions only occur in people in combination, perhaps in confusion, with other qualities, in configurations which can be highly problematical. Indeed, the drama precipitated by the tensions between the potential instability of the individual and the required stabilities of society is in some ways as much the subject of this novel as it is of more celebrated fictions concerned with the opposition between individual energy and social structures. Which is another way of saying that, besides looking back to Maria Edgeworth's *Letters of Julia and Caroline*, *Sense and Sensibility* may be said to look forward to Freud's *Civilisation and its Discontents*. This is not to suggest – rare thought – that Jane Austen was an early Freudian, but rather to insist that *Sense and Sensibility* touches on some matters of perennial importance which tend to be obscured if we regard it as an early casualty in an evolving genre.

(To trace the history of the deployment of the word 'sensibility' – and the words 'sense' and 'Sensible' – in eighteenth-century literature would be to trace the history of the evolution of changing attitudes to, and evaluations of, a whole cluster of feelings and attitudes and dispositions which became a major preoccupation and concern of many eighteenth-century writers. Many books have been written on the subject. The only point we need to note here is that the connotations of the words, and the relationship between what they referred to, had become exceedingly problematical and labile by the time Jane Austen was writing. Their meanings were the reverse of fixed. Briefly we may say that for Richardson, and for Henry MacKenzie, 'sensibility' was to be equated with virtue. It denoted a fineness of feeling and disposition which took one out of the arena of more brutal and abrasive appetites and desires which constituted 'the world', or society at large. It was a privileged sign of superior delicacy and morality. However, it was not only too sensitive and fine to operate in the world, too frail to engage in its crude competitive struggles: it also carried with it its own potential dangers. Even in Richardson it can become destructively – or self-destructively – excessive, as in the figures of the demented Clementina and the suicidal Laurana in Jane Austen's favourite novel, *Sir Charles Grandison*. That is to say that from the start of the cult of 'sensibility' – particularly in the tradition we think of as comprising the 'sentimental novel' – sensibility was always potentially, and often actually, ambivalent. It might permit of dangerous affective excitations as well as promoting the most refined virtue. Taken to excess – and how or where to draw the line? – it could lead to hysteria instead of exquisite morality, physical and mental collapse instead of an almost other-worldly composure. It was a mark of privilege always capable of turning into an affliction or ailment. That is to say it could signal a positive desocialisation – too exalted and committed to exquisite emotional integrity to function in the base world; or a negative desocialisation – too sick, uncontrolled and disordered to engage in any sane, sustained relationships. Almost exclusively, of course, the main ambivalences of 'sensibility' were localised and displayed in the figure of the – usually unmarried – woman. The story of 'sensibility' and the 'sentimental novel' has been told many times. One of the best recent accounts of it I know is by Dr John Mullan in an as-yet-unpublished thesis, 'Sentiment and Sociability'; and see also *Sex and Sensibility* by Jean Hagstrum. But it is enough for our purposes to have a sense of how shifting and ambivalent – and how important – the notion of 'sensibility' was when Jane Austen came to explore it, and its cognate terms, in her fiction.)

Seen in bare outline the plot displays a good deal of geometry. Elinor and Marianne move gradually towards desirable marriages with worthy men, Colonel Brandon and Edward Ferrars. This progress is variously complicated by the unscrupulous behaviour of two selfish people – Lucy and Willoughby. In pursuing their self-advancing ends these two remove themselves by opportunistic marriages which will provide suitable punishments in the form of domestic misery. At the end two parallelograms are formed which demonstrate on the one hand true harmony (Elinor and Edward, Marianne and Brandon), and on the other a merely apparent, superficial harmony (Lucy and Robert, John and Fanny Dashwood); as is often the case, Jane Austen helps to make us appreciate the value of the real thing by juxtaposing a travesty or parodic version of it. It is this geometry which provides the formal resolution to the novel, and we shall return to it. But the body of the novel concerns itself with those things which complicate and cloud the emergence of that or any other geometry and it is in this connection that I want to consider the secrecy and sickness which, I suggested, are matters of some importance in the book.

'Come, come, let's have no secrets among friends', cries the incorrigibly inquisitive Mrs Jennings, and her less than courteous demand takes an added significance when we consider just how much secrecy there is among the few, and closely related, characters in the book. Colonel Brandon has to take a sudden departure, thus disrupting the planned excursion to Whitwell, but he cannot give any explanations. Lucy only lets Elinor know about her secret engagement to Edward Ferrars to silence her as a potential rival – 'it was always meant to be a great secret'; while Willoughby's inexplicably cruel conduct to Marianne begins to fall into place when his plan to marry Miss Grey is made known – 'it was no longer to be a secret'. Concealment obviously befits the calculating designs of these two cool self-seekers, but there are more secrets than the unavowed deeds and previous commitments of the main eligible males in the novel. For one thing, the idea of secret relationships was built into the social banter as a sort of game – thus the good-hearted but insensitive Sir John goes out of his way to create 'secrets' to bring a somewhat vulgar piquancy to his dinner table. ' "His name is Ferrars", said he, in a very audible whisper; "but pray do not tell it, for it's a great secret." ' One can imagine that the motives behind such social games as the masked ball were similar: if a society finds itself too utterly illuminated and everyone too boringly familiar, it may well seek to reintroduce some shadows, masks and screens if only to restore the stimulus and *frisson* of a rudimentary sense of mystery – or, at least, the titillating atmosphere of erotic conspiracy. But there is a much more important kind of secrecy which Jane Austen makes us aware of: the secrecy of everything the heart may not enforce with the hand, display with the face, or express with the voice; that is, the secrecy of those things within, which are struggling to get out and meet with different kinds of restraints or suppressions. Such concealments may be admirable, or sly, or simply all that is possible in the circumstances, but in one form or another they recur throughout. There is the 'extraordinary silence' and 'strange kind of secrecy' maintained by Marianne and Willoughby; and later, in London, Marianne is secretive even to Elinor, manifesting 'a privacy that eluded all her watchfulness'. Elinor herself, when she hears of Lucy's engagement to Edward, manages 'a composure of voice under which was concealed an emotion and distress beyond anything she had ever felt before'. The phrase 'the necessity of concealing' gives some indication of Elinor's sense of responsibility towards the codes of formal behaviour; as a result no one would suppose 'that Elinor was mourning in secret over obstacles which must divide her for ever from the object of her love'. When Colonel Brandon seeks confirmation from Elinor that his love for Marianne cannot be returned he feels that 'concealment, if concealment be possible, is all that remains'. Examples could be proliferated, but the recurrence of such phrases as 'ill-judged secrecy', 'the appearance of secrecy', 'promise of secrecy' suggests how prevalent is the vocabulary of all kinds of concealing, whether the secrets are those kept by the individual from society or those the private self must try to keep from the public self. Elinor, who is made the repository of other people's secrets without anyone to whom she can tell her own, experiences to the full the burden and torments of secrecy: 'For four months, Marianne, I have had all this hanging on my mind, without being at liberty to speak of it to a single creature.' And, if silence is often required in the interests of honour and dignity, there may be another justification for secrecy, something more like self-survival. This is hinted at in the revealing letter written by Mr Dashwood after Lucy has been secretly married to Robert Ferrars. 'The secrecy with which everything has been carried on between them was rationally treated as enormously heightening the crime, because had any suspicion of it occurred to the other, *proper measures* would have been taken to *prevent the marriage*' (emphasis added). In this instance no one will suppose that the scheming Lucy married for love – love of Robert, at least; but the italicised phrases which come so easily to the heartlessly respectable Mr Dashwood hint at the cruel coercive powers of society and the ruthlessness with which many of its members were willing to manipulate or 'correct' the aberrations of individual passion in the interests of wealth or some illusory hierarchical propriety. So, if secrecy is often a painful obligation imposed by the forms of a rigid society, it may also be a strategy against or around them.

By the end all the secrets have come to the surface and, with no more mysteries to cloud the emergent geometry of the book, the appropriate marriages can all be solemnised. But not before Marianne has been very ill indeed. As a person who believes in letting the emotions use the body as an expressive vehicle, it is hardly surprising that she cultivates tears as often as Elinor strives for composure. But what happens after Willoughby first leaves her and then treats her with such incomprehensible cruelty goes beyond the affectations of an emotional girl. Jane Austen traces the progress of her illness with such detail that we get some idea of the language of symptomatology and diagnosis of the time. She suffers from melancholy and has 'headaches, low spirits, and over fatigues'. Later she is 'wholly dispirited, careless of her appearance, and seemingly quite indifferent whether she went or starved'. For a while she is almost catatonic, 'without once stirring from her seat, or altering her attitude'. When she shows Elinor the letter which Willoughby sends disclaiming any understanding between them, she 'almost screamed with agony'. After this Marianne gets worse. 'Faint and giddy from a long want of proper rest and food'; 'an aching head, a weakened stomach, a general nervous faintness'; 'she moved from one posture to another, till growing more and more hysterical, her sister could with difficulty keep her on the bed at all'; so it goes on at intervals until she contracts the fever which nearly kills her. Here we are given a whole chapter describing the course of the illness from the time the doctor pronounces 'her disorder to have a putrid tendency', through the accelerations of her pulse, the incoherence of her mind, her 'rapid decay' and 'stupor', until the crisis is past, the pulse slows down, and Elinor, when 'Marianne fixed her eyes on her with a rational though languid gaze', knows her sister is better. We may note that it is precisely at this point when her long illness has passed its peak and Marianne is returning to health and reason that Willoughby suddenly appears at the house – not as a threat but as a penitent; no longer the swaggering huntsman with a gun as he first appeared, but cowed and full of recriminations and regrets. It is as though, exactly at the moment when Marianne finds the reserves to rally from her fever, Willoughby's potency is vanquished and he appears out of the night to concede not only his mistake but also his defeat.

I have stressed the detailing that goes into Marianne's illness because it seems to me to be something much more serious than the amazing burlesque on excessive sensibility to be found in such pieces as *Love and Friendship*. For Marianne's illness is clearly psychosomatic and in many of its symptoms – the incoherence of mind, the catatonic trances alternating with restless demands for 'continual change of place', her periods of complete absence from and unawareness of the immediate world around her – her behaviour is pathological in a way which for the late eighteenth century could have been construed as madness. (Many of the early Romantic poets went mad, including Cowper, one of Marianne's – and Jane Austen's – favourites.) I want here to introduce some quotations from Michel Foucault's *Madness and Civilization*. He gives evidence to show how in the later part of the eighteenth century there was a great increase in 'nervous diseases': of the causes of these diseases Tissot wrote, 'I do not hesitate to say that if they were once the rarest, they are today the most frequent.' And Foucault quotes another contemporary physician, Matthey, to show the growing sense of the precariousness of a reason which may at any moment be undermined by some inward disorder.

> Do not glory in your state, if you are wise and civilized men; an instant suffices to disturb and annihilate that supposed wisdom of which you are so proud; an unexpected event, a sharp and sudden emotion of the soul will abruptly change the most reasonable and intelligent man into a raving idiot.

It is interesting that Foucault has occasion to record that at this time the English were thought to be unusually prone to madness and melancholia. This was partly ascribed to the fact that they were a nation of merchants, anxiously preoccupied with financial speculations, which not only led to more tyrannical families but in general to a state 'in which man is dispossessed of his desires by the laws of interest'. (These observations are extremely relevant to *Clarissa* as well.) It was also related to the equivocal liberty enjoyed by the English ('every man is left to his own uncertainty'), of which Foucault writes, 'liberty, far from putting man in possession of himself, ceaselessly alienates him from his essence and his world; it fascinates him in the absolute exteriority of other people and of money, in the irreversible interiority of passion and unfulfilled desire'. Still writing about this period, Foucault continues (in a section aptly entitled 'Madness, Civilization, and Sensibility') to give his account and explanation of the high incidence of nervous–mental disorders of the time. 'It is not only knowledge that detaches man from feeling; it is sensibility itself: a sensibility that is no longer controlled by the movements of nature, but by all the habits, all the demands of social life.' In particular those women who nourished themselves on literature (particularly novels) were prone to nervous disorders: 'it detaches the soul from all that is immediate and natural in feeling and leads it into an imaginary world of sentiments violent in proportion to the unreality, and less controlled by the gentle laws of nature'. (One contemporary cure for nervous disorders was to expose the sufferer to landscape so that the tendency to subjectivity might be somewhat corrected by a sense of those 'gentle laws': this is what Elinor tries with Marianne in, for example, chapter 16.) Foucault concludes this particular section of his book with the following somewhat sweeping but suggestive generalisations:

> In the second half of the eighteenth century, madness was no longer recognized in what brings man closer to an immemorial fall or an indefinitely present animality; it was, on the contrary, situated in those distances man takes in regard to himself, to his world, to all that is offered by the immediacy of nature; madness became possible in that milieu where man's relationships with his feelings, with time, with others, are altered; madness was possible because of everything which, in man's life and development, is a break with the immediate.

I have gone to some lengths to introduce Foucault's

imaginative perspectives on the later eighteenth century, not to advance the absurd theory that Marianne is actually a raving lunatic, but to invite the consideration that 'sensibility', besides being a psychological phenomenon connected with the early Romantic movement which was sometimes characterised by the kind of unironic excess easily ridiculed by satirists, should also be seen as symptomatic of a certain kind of society and as such an indirect comment on it. It is clear, for instance, that Marianne is well aware of, or perhaps we should say suffering from, that condition characterised by Foucault as a sense of 'the absolute exteriority of other people' and the 'irreversible interiority of passion and unfulfilled desire', and much of her later behaviour does indicate a 'break with the immediate'. She is indeed sick, sick with the intensity of her own secret passions and fantasies. What is the nature of the society in which this sickness breaks out, at least as Jane Austen depicts it? It is a world completely dominated by forms, for which another word may be screens, which may in turn be lies. For Marianne forms are equated with falsity; she will not join in the social masquerade. Her 'usual inattention to forms' is noted throughout. Society is for her as trivial as the endless whist that others delight to play; characteristically 'she would never learn the game'. A typical moment occurs when an insincere compliment to a cold lady invites corroboration. ' "What a sweet woman Lady Middleton is," said Lucy Steele. Marianne was silent; it was impossible for her to say what she did not feel, however trivial the occasion; and upon Elinor, therefore, the whole task of telling lies when politeness required it always fell.' The astringent realism of Jane Austen's vision is clearly in evidence in the latter part of the sentence for society is indeed maintained by necessary lies. Marianne is one who demands that outward forms exactly project or portray inward feelings; this is that demand for sincerity, that loathing of hypocrisy, which is one of the most sympathetic characteristics of the Romantic movement. The difficulty here is that, while every individual may have a different inner world of feelings and thoughts, there is only one concrete external world in which we must cohabit. No one knew better than Jane Austen that people who were as remote foreigners to each other mentally might very well be very close neighbours physically. And, while she saw with unsparing clarity just how much cruelty, repression and malice the social forms made possible, how much misery they generated, she knew that a world in which everyone was totally sincere, telling always the truth for the sake of their own feelings and never any lies for the feelings of others, would be simply an anarchy, everybody's personal 'form' cancelling out everybody else's.

More subtly Jane Austen perceived that it was often those people who claimed to be impatient of forms who were in some ways most reliant on them. Willoughby at first seems like a daring young lover, 'slighting too easily the forms of worldly propriety' in Elinor's sober eyes; yet he readily abandons his passional sincerities to secure the wealth and social position which will maintain him in his idleness and self-indulgence. Marianne's feelings go much deeper, yet it is worth noting that all along she expects more opulence and comfort from marriage than the supposedly too prudent Elinor (she calls £2000 a year a mere 'competence', while Elinor would regard £1000 as 'wealth'). In many ways both these lovers live at the expense of other people: Willoughby very literally, and Marianne more subtly in that, while she indulges every mood, making few concessions to social forms, she is in fact leaving Elinor with the task of covering up for her. It is one of Jane Austen's deft touches that Elinor should be very good at screen-painting, for she it is who is constantly trying to smooth and harmonise potentially abrasive and discordant occasions, giving the raw social realities a veneer of art. It is also an example of the complexity of Jane Austen's vision that, when Elinor's painted screens are being so cruelly insulted by the unspeakable snob Mrs Ferrars, Marianne refuses to 'screen' her personal outrage and anger and expresses her contempt for such malicious manners. We cannot fail to sympathise with her outburst if not positively applaud it, which means that Jane Austen has brought us to the point of feeling some positive approbation and appreciation for both the maintainer of screens and the discarder of screens. Clearly no very simple verdicts are being invited in this early novel. (It is interesting to compare Virginia Woolf's use of the word 'screen', for she also saw it as crucial in the description of life-with-others, but in a notably different way from Jane Austen. In her diary she refers to the 'screen-making' habit of the human personality, and goes on to acknowledge that 'this habit is so universal that probably it preserves our sanity. If we had not this device for shutting people off from our sympathies we might perhaps dissolve utterly; separateness would be impossible.' Nevertheless she adds, 'the screens are in the excess, not the sympathy'. A part of Virginia Woof wanted to break down all the screens and discover and affirm the fluid interrelatedness and unity of all our separate-seeming lives. The 'screens' erected by the personality to preserve a sense of identity – and thus separateness – were an unfortunate social necessity: ideally the all-penetrating tides of 'sympathy' would break them down. Jane Austen envisaged no such ideal possibility. For her, for Elinor, the 'screens' are necessary to conceal and mitigate some of the ugliness and abrasiveness of society. At its best 'screen-making' was a form of social decorum. Virginia Woolf's characters put up screens to preserve the self; Elinor paints and makes screens to preserve society. Yet Jane Austen too might have felt that, if society were composed of more sensitive people, it would be a relief to do away with some of the screens, in the interests of a more direct interchange of sympathies. But, given the society she knew and depicted, Elinor's screen-making *is* a form of sympathy – and 'selflessness'.)

At one point Marianne cries out with some 'energy' to Elinor, 'Our situations then are alike. We have neither of us anything to tell; you, because you do not communicate, and I, because I conceal nothing.' This is not in fact fair to Elinor, who has to keep silence because she has promised to honour a secret, but the remark does point to a crucial difference between Marianne, who 'abhors all concealment', and Elinor, who is willing to contain private feelings in the interests of preserving some order among the necessary social coverings. Where Marianne seeks to express herself, Elinor works to compose herself, and Jane Austen has caught this difference between them even in contrasting their figures. Marianne's 'form, though not so correct as her sister's . . . was more striking'. I shall add some more comments on the two sisters later, but at this point I think one can see that through them is brought into focus a problem right at the heart of that, or indeed any other, society: namely, how much of the individual's inner world should be allowed to break out in the interests of personal vitality and psychic health; and how much should the external world be allowed to coerce and control that inner reality in the interests of maintaining a social structure which does provide meaningful spaces and definitions for the lives of its members? When Elinor says to her mother of Marianne and Willoughby, 'I want no proof of their affection . . . but of their engagement I do', she is showing her awareness of this problem. 'Affection' is a personal disposition, and 'engagement' is a social act – the one a matter of unsocialised inwardness, the other a subscribing to the fixed impersonal symbolisms of the public world. What Elinor wants is that Marianne's love affair should be brought out of the formlessness of feeling into the defining forms of society. Otherwise she fears it might have no real continuity – and in the event she is right, though we cannot by the same token say that Marianne is wrong. What I want to suggest is that much of the drama of the book (which includes the comedy) is concerned precisely with that point at which the energies, desires and needs of the private world impinge on, or are impinged on by, the public. When Edward Ferrars, that victim of his parents' social ambitions who has led a life of *'fettered* inclination' (emphasis added), finally comes to Elinor both free and determined to marry her, he reveals something of both his nervousness and resolution by an unconscious act which makes one begin to think that Jane Austen would not perhaps have been so very surprised by Freud's formulations as we may at first suppose. 'He rose from his seat and walked to a window, apparently from not knowing what to do; took up a pair of scissors that lay there, . . . spoiling both them and their sheath by cutting the latter to pieces as he spoke. . . .' There are times when the scissors will destroy the sheath just as there are times when the sheath will contain the scissors. Edward's feelings can break from the sheath at this point to some purpose because he is directing them towards marriage. Marianne's passions are stronger and less prone to be 'fettered'; it is not surprising that a characteristically disruptive vocabulary attaches to her upsurges of emotion – 'Marianne's feelings had then broken in, and put an end to all regularity of detail', 'Marianne's indignation burst forth': in her we see clearly an example of the instinct to annihilate the forms that constrict her – of the extreme impatience of the scissors with the sheath. And, because her strong feelings do not find the free play they desire, they disrupt and undermine her body until she utters that scream at the centre of the book in the centre of London. It is a muffled scream because the sheath is everywhere tight around her, but an inarticulate cry more eloquent than any language she might have used. And, between Marianne's compulsion to scream and Elinor's instinct to screen, Jane Austen brings home to us some of the problems and paradoxes involved in life in society as she knew it.

One of the paradoxes I have been suggesting is that it was a society which forced people to be at once very sociable and very private. Elinor withdraws to reflect in private as often as Marianne does to indulge her moods; and even in the company of others the 'effect of solitude' may be produced. 'Her mind was inevitably at liberty; her thoughts could not be chained elsewhere; and the past and the future . . . must be before her, must force her attention, and engross her memory, her reflection, and her fancy.' This mental solitude, which as often as not means mental suffering, is stressed in the last line of the Book I: 'Elinor was then at liberty to think and be wretched.' With this cameo Jane Austen is stressing how often interior freedom amounts to interior distress. At the same time it is clear that there are many people in this society who are all but devoid of any inner life. Sir John Middleton, for instance, is a good-natured man 'whose prevailing anxiety was the dread of being alone': such people are responsible for many of those organised contiguities which can be such a strain for sensitive people whose anxieties are of a much more inward and personal nature. The stress of being involved in private and social realities at the same time means that a lot of the important activity takes place in that small area where inner and outer realities meet – the eyes. Marianne 'turned her eyes towards Elinor, to see how she bore these attacks'; 'they all sat down to look at one another'; 'he eyed them with a curiosity which seemed to say . . .'; 'nothing escaped *her* minute observation and general curiosity; she saw everything'; 'Edward . . . gave her a look so serious, so earnest, so uncheerful, as seemed to say . . . '; 'Elinor . . . could not restrain her eyes from being fixed on him with a look that spoke all the contempt it excited'; 'she watched his eyes, while Mrs Jennings thought only of his behaviour'; 'even *her* eyes were fixed on him with the same impatient wonder': the whole vocabulary of vision is much in evidence throughout, indicating just how much goes on in that most sensitive organ which both connects and separates consciousness and world. And in a world of so many secrets and imposed suppressions the eyes have to be unusually busy, not only encountering surfaces but also having to penetrate them, not only deciphering the signs but also interpreting them.

Inevitably in a world of screens the information any one individual receives is likely to be imperfect, and the misreading of insufficient evidence can lead to confusion. People with good intentions may in fact work to secure bad ends: Mrs Jennings is happy to think that Colonel Brandon is proposing to Elinor, but in fact he is offering to help Edward and Lucy, quite unaware of the pain this must cause Elinor. Misleading signs can produce more direct pain too, as when Elinor takes the empirical evidence of Lucy's ring on Edward's finger as indicative of his true emotional attachment. One can share a good deal of Marianne's abhorrence for all forms of 'concealment' when one sees something of the mischief and misery that can ensue in a world where the truth of things is usually not to be found on the surface. And it is Marianne who perhaps suffers most from the false face which the social world can put on when she receives that devastating snub from Willoughby at the party in London. The setting is important: it is a crowded room 'splendidly lit up, quite full of company, and insufferably hot', and the two sisters mill in to 'take their share of the heat and inconvenience'. Then Elinor sees Willoughby, and the drama commences.

> She soon caught his eye, and he immediately bowed. . . . Elinor turned involuntarily to Marianne, to see whether it could be unobserved by her. At that moment she first perceived him, and her whole countenance glowing with sudden delight, she would have moved towards him instantly, had not her sister caught hold of her. 'Good heavens!' she exclaimed, 'he is there – he is there. Oh! why does he not look at me? Why cannot I speak to him?'

Marianne would move directly and candidly towards the man she loves and whom she thinks loves her. But direct movement in accordance with the emotions is not so easy in this society; there is the intervening crowd, the glaring light, the constriction of 'good manners' and decorum, the overall oppressive heat – in all a sufficient analogue of the society as a whole. This is the sheath at its most constricting. They are all in a sense trapped and immobilised and as a result all the activity goes into the eyes. And the severest indictment one can make of the social game is that at this point it lends itself entirely to Willoughby's designs – he can use the respected forms to compound a profound emotional falsity at the expense of Marianne. Marianne however cries out against this treachery of appearances. 'Her face crimsoned over, and she exclaimed in a voice of the greatest emotion, "Good God! Willoughby, what is the meaning of this?" ' No request for enlightenment could be more justified. Marianne, her face full of blood (and blushing here is as indicative of passion under pressure as it is in Racine), is protesting with bewildered outrage against the betrayal of all emotional integrity not only made possible but also concealed by the accepted rules of the social game. As such she is a self-authenticating figure of protest with a complaint which nothing and no one in the novel can ever really answer. She reveals her agony through symptoms of illness and faintness which she does nothing to hide, while Elinor, typically, 'tried to screen her from the observation of others'. There is a quintessential truth about the conditions of life in society expressed in that quiet struggle between screaming and screening. Meanwhile Lady Middleton, for whom the surface of society and its appurtenances are the only reality, carries on with her card game. The overall tableau at this point seems to me to be tolerably profound for such a supposedly deficient and unsatisfactory novel.

But, if the rules and forms of society inhibit much expressive action, particularly uncensored passional gestures, so that the eyes move more than the hands, that does not mean that action has been curtailed or completely banished to the inner world. It means rather that much of it has shifted to the more abstract but no less intense realm of language. Of all the defining structures erected by society, language is the most important, not only because we use it to transmit and inherit information, but also because it is with language that we give shape to our feelings and identity to our values. It is through language that the consciousness of man derives meanings and projects purposes from his encounters with otherness. And the quality of life in a society is dependent on its language – the way it has formulated its priorities and guiding concepts. But of course there is another aspect to this perfecting of a language. For one thing it is available to the unscrupulous person who wishes to project a completely false model of reality, to fabricate or invert any state of affairs. She 'talks very well, with a happy command of language, which is too often used I believe to make Black appear White'. That is said of Lady Susan, one of Jane Austen's supreme manipulators. It indicates how vulnerable we all are to any unscrupulous person who has a complete command of the terms of our language. And there is another kind of possible linguistic victimisation in that our conduct is always at the mercy of other people's interpretative descriptions. Thus Marianne makes a very heartfelt retort to Elinor's warning that she is 'exposing' herself to the risk of 'impertinent remarks': 'If the impertinent remarks of Mrs Jennings are to be proofs of impropriety in conduct, we are all offending every moment of all our lives.' This is not just a witticism at the expense of a trying but well-meaning gossip. It is a protest of the sincere heart against the distortions of social language, which continually threaten to submit the individual's feelings and actions to derogatory redefinitions. One of the most important aspects of the Romantic movement was the refusal of the intensely feeling individual to have the meaning of his experience settled by other people's language. Indeed, there is a notion running through Romantic thought that all language is to some extent a falsification, since it involves transposing unique inner feelings into public terms and forms: there is even the feeling that, just as the laws and taboos of a society determine how a man acts, so its language determines how he feels. When Marianne says at one point, 'sometime I have kept my feelings to myself, because I could find no language to describe them in but what was worn and hackneyed out of all sense and meaning', she is speaking like a Romantic, preferring to keep her feelings intact and silent inside her rather than have them betrayed by the stale forms of the available language of the world around her. The language she prefers is that of the early Romantic poets, a language of solitude rather than society, a language which is more set on lending itself to the expressing of emotions than addressing itself to the problems of conduct. And, in case we think that Jane Austen is setting up a simple opposition between social and 'poetic' speech, we should remember that Marianne's favourite writers were also Jane Austen's.

There is a great deal of sympathy, then, with Marianne's conviction that language should be used to express private feelings rather than to preserve social forms. But Jane Austen could see perfectly well that if everyone limited language to the expression of sincere emotions there would be an anarchy of speech comparable to the anarchy of behaviour which would result from allowing action to be wholly determined by honest impulse. If we are to live together (and Jane Austen does not conceive of the alternative of the 'world elsewhere' of the hermit, the expatriate, the recluse, and so on), then it is essential that there should be some agreement about conventions of speech as about conventions of behaviour. This is why there is so much stress in Jane Austen's work on the necessity to call things by their right names. She was well aware of the relativity of individual vision, how different people can take away a different impression and interpretation of the same scene according to their particular perspective and preoccupation (for instance, 'Mrs Dashwood, not less watchful of what passed than her daughter, but with a mind very differently influenced, and therefore watching to very different effect'), but she could see the danger of this relativism affecting language so that everyone might have his or her own definition of the same word. Much of the energy and effort, not only of Elinor but also of Jane Austen herself, is aimed at the attempt to arrive at a terminological exactitude which would be subtle, comprehensive and authoritative. A ready example of her concern can be found in the way the book opens. In chapter 1 she establishes a vocabulary adequate to describe and assess the various qualities and attendant excesses or possible weaknesses of Marianne and Elinor. In the next chapter there is the devastating account of the conversation between Mrs Dashwood and her husband, in which, with the most specious abuse of the language of 'reason' and balanced consideration, she persuades John to do absolutely nothing for his sisters – a complete inversion of the intention of his father's will. In this incomparable rationalisation of meanness and selfishness we have an unexcelled example of Jane Austen's comprehension of the power of language to make black appear white. So it is that a good deal of the struggle in the book is between the proper use and the misuse of language; among the things we can learn from this book is the subtle lesson that a good deal of our happiness can depend on what we call things and how we name our experience. Elinor's 'wealth' is much less than Marianne's 'competence' – one takes the point. Similarly Barton Cottage is a different thing according to what you call it: 'as a house, Barton Cottage, though small, was comfortable and compact; but as a cottage it was defective, for the building was regular, the roof was tiled, the window shutters were not painted green, nor were the walls covered with honeysuckles'. If we demand cottages when we are confronted with houses we have an endless capacity to secure our own discontent; a change of vocabulary may serve to bring our preconceived images more into line with the existing realities, and Jane Austen was sufficiently before our time to think that with an effort words could be made to coincide with things and that, moreover, a good deal of our dignity and peace of mind depend on making them do so.

Careful distinctions are thus being made throughout. 'Motives of interest' can be distinguished from 'prudence'; 'insipidity' is not to be confused with 'gravity'; 'calmness of manner' is not necessarily the same thing as 'sense'; the mere noise of a social evening is not to be confused with real 'conversation'. Characters who are foolish or worse give themselves away by their abuse of language. Robert Ferrars considers an individual 'valuable' only because 'her house, her style of living, all bespeak an exceeding good income' – a crass but common confusion of the commercial and the spiritual. John Dashwood regards his wife as having 'the fortitude of an angel', which is perhaps as inappropriate a simile as any in the book. Miss Steele thinks someone 'very genteel' because 'he makes a monstous deal of money', but of course the comparative vulgarity both of her and of Lucy's perceptions and values has been revealed by their grammatical lapses and conversational crudities. Willoughby is, like the traditional seducer, smooth of tongue and shows an effortless mastery of the appropriate persuasive modes of talking. Like Henry Crawford in *Mansfield Park*, he has a gift for role-playing which is indicated in a passing allusion to his prowess at reading parts in plays, though he doesn't stay long enough with Marianne to finish reading his part of *Hamlet*. (One guesses that he had perhaps arrived at the part where Hamlet inexplicably rejects Ophelia.) But even his fluent exploitations and improvisations can reach a point of dumbness, as he reveals when he admits to Elinor that, when he received a note from Marianne still avowing her affection and trust, 'I could not answer it. I tried, but could not frame a sentence.' His unconsidered dexterity with speech and his duplicity have brought him to the point where he forfeits the ability to speak truly. Where Marianne occasionally submits to the silence of sincerity, this is the silence of shame.

Elinor and Marianne are often having differences of terminological opinion, as might be expected, as each tends to give definitions based on the particular bias of her temperament. Elinor pronounces Brandon to be 'a sensible man, well-bred, well-informed, of gentle address, and, I believe, possessing an amiable heart'; Marianne prefers the negative mode: 'he has neither genius, taste, nor spirit . . . his understanding has no brilliancy, his feelings no ardour, and his voice no expression'. In this Marianne may be said to be not entirely just, yet, speaking as a young high-spirited girl, her comments cannot be entirely negated by Elinor's terms. Another example of how language changes with point of view is to be found in the exchanges between Marianne and Edward Ferrars on the local landscapes. Marianne responds to the whole panorama of hills, woods and plantations and speaks of 'grandeur'; Edward looks at the condition of the lane, thinks of winter and speaks of 'dirt'. Later Edward admits that his vocabulary is based on a sort of unemotional empiricism, neutrally descriptive: 'I shall call hills steep, which ought to be bold, surfaces strange and uncouth, which ought to be irregular and rugged; and distant objects out of sight, which ought only to be indistinct through the soft medium of a hazy atmosphere.' He sees and speaks more in terms of 'utility' than of natural beauty – 'I know nothing of the picturesque.' Similarly Elinor is rather dry about the 'passion for dead leaves' which can produce such enthusiasm in Marianne:

> with what transporting sensations have I formerly seen them fall! How have I delighted, as I walked, to see them driven in showers about me by the wind! What feelings have they, the season, the air altogether inspired! Now there is no one to regard them. They are seen only as a nuisance. . . .

The question may arise, should they be seen as anything else? But it would be wrong to think that Jane Austen's sympathies are wholly with Edward and Elinor in this linguistic debate.

Although the cult of effusing over the pictorial and aesthetic merits of natural scenery was responsible for some very affected responses by Jane Austen's time, she could see that there *was* 'grandeur' as well as dirt in that natural scene, and a delight in nature only slightly more moderate than Marianne's is in evidence throughout Jane Austen's work. The point is that, however foolish Marianne's enthusiastic address to leaves and hills may sound to the utilitarian ear, it is she who bestows aesthetic value on the natural environment by the quality of her response. What value dead leaves, or any other object, may have in the absence of a human eye to perceive them is a philosophical problem too large to admit here; but the very fact that Jane Austen can allow it to intrude into this early work shows that she would have well understood Coleridge's famous address to Nature:

> O Lady! we receive but what we give,
> And in our life alone does Nature live:
> Ours is her wedding garment, ours her shroud!
> ('Dejection: An Ode')

By the time Jane Austen was writing – which was the time of Coleridge and Wordsworth – there was a sharper awareness that the way an individual responded to nature was at the same time a revelation of the dispositions of his or her inner landscape, that nature is what we see her to be and name her to be. Marianne would at least bestow wedding-garments on nature, and, even if some of her responses are motivated by her literary enthusiasms, they do also indicate a generosity and warmth of spirit, a capacity for appreciation and sympathy, which Jane Austen unquestionably valued. (Marianne is said to have imagination, Elinor limits herself to fancy – an appropriately Coleridgean distinction.) Edward, one would have to admit, is more likely to put nature in a shroud. (This whole exchange reminds me of Ruskin's response to a lecturer who maintained that from the scientific point of view there is no such thing as a flower. Ruskin responds by having recourse to deliberately unscientific language. 'And when the leaves marry, they put on wedding-robes, and are more glorious than Solomon in all his glory, and they have feasts of honey, and we call them "Flowers". In a certain sense, therefore, you see the lecturer was quite right. There are no such things as Flowers – there are only – gladdened leaves.' That is, he counters the scientific vocabulary with the powerful biblical responses of his own style, and in the event one feels one would happily prefer to be 'wrong' with Ruskin than 'right' with the scientist, because of the superior power of his incomparable sensibility and language. There is no doubt that Marianne would.) Here, well this side of epistemology, we should stop; it is enough to realise that Jane Austen by no means intended an unqualified justification of the perspective and vocabulary of reason. As in behaviour, so in language, Marianne gives an added dimension of warmth and vitality to the world of the book and Jane Austen was well aware of it.

One final observation about the part played by language in the book. Aware of centrifugal and contrary tendencies in self, society and language, Jane Austen clearly saw balance as a prime virtue to be aimed at, and so when characters achieve equilibrium their speech also tends towards balance. For instance, when Marianne's illness brings her to a more 'balanced' awareness of things her speech reflects this change. 'Do not, my dearest Elinor, let your kĭndnĕss dĕfēnd whăt Ĭ knŏw yŏur jŭdgmĕnt mŭst censure.' By adding the scansion one can see her sentences starting to stabilise and balance themselves; the syntactical and metrical harmony of the speech are symptoms of a mind more in harmony with itself. It is the way Jane Austen herself often writes; thus, of Elinor: 'ĭmpātiĕnt tŏ sōothe, thŏugh tŏo hōnešt tŏ flāttĕr'. The prose, like the plot, tends towards, and even acts out, those steady symmetries which Jane Austen regarded as indispensable for a truly civilised existence.

Let us finally return to the two sisters, for the loving tension between them, the ongoing debate as to 'how to be' which is precipitated simply by their juxtaposition in any set of circumstances, provides the real subject of the novel. We might start by considering the telling differences in their response to the arrival of the unknown male, Willoughby, in the neighbourhood. Sir John, who has a tendency to assess a man by the canine company he keeps, tells them first that Willoughby has 'the nicest little black bitch of a pointer I ever saw'. Elinor, however, is not content with this somewhat marginal information. She wants to know who he is, where he is from, and 'has he a house at Allenham?' This in turn is of small importance to Marianne, who is much more interested in Willoughby's taste for excessive dancing and hunting; that is what she likes in a young man, that 'his eagerness in them should know no moderation'. Elinor wants to know about the social man – man the house-builder. Marianne is interested in the more primitive, even the more Dionysiac, man – man the dancer. The one activity is the transforming of energy into structure, the other the stylised releasing of energy as gesture. Both are, of course, essential to any sort of social life, but clearly a disposition to one or the other may preponderate. Just so, Elinor has an instinct for stillness and composure, while Marianne has a decided taste for rapid movement (it is when she falls while running that Willoughby finds her, and she takes to horse-riding as keenly as Mary Crawford in *Mansfield Park*), and what shows through her eyes is 'a life, a spirit, and eagerness'. We remember that Elinor's form was more 'correct', Marianne's more 'striking'. Clearly some combination of the two forms would most appeal to Jane Austen; yet, as clearly, she could see that they have an inherent tendency to separate. It is perhaps a weakness in the book, or a severity in the author, that no compromise between the two sisters seems countenanced, just as we miss in this book any notion of a man who might be something between the notably unexciting 'house-builders', Brandon and Ferrars, and the rather second-rate 'dancer' that Willoughby turns out to be (worthy neither of his predecessor, Lovelace, nor of his remote successor, Heathcliffe).

If the sisters differ in their attitude towards stability and energy, they also differ in a subtler way about the factors which should determine conduct. Here is a crucial exchange:

'I am afraid,' replied Elinor, 'that the pleasantness of an employment does not always evince its propriety.'

'On the contrary, nothing can be a stronger proof of it, Elinor; for if there had been any real impropriety in what I did, I should have been sensible of it at the time, for we always know when we are acting wrong, and with such a conviction I could have had no pleasure.'

Elinor belongs to that school of thought which considers that virtuous conduct can be an arduous business, involving painful adjustments to the controlling forms of society, and unpleasant frustration of personal proclivities. Such a school of thought we may identify as Christian, or Stoic, or even, vaguely, Classical. But another school of thought came out of the rationalism of the Enlightenment, a more optimistic view of man commonly associated with the French *Philosophes* but with many English adherents. John Stuart Mill characterised this school of thought with admirable clarity and brevity in his essay on Coleridge.

> The error of the philosophers was rather that they trusted too much to those feelings [of morality]; believed them to be more deeply rooted in human nature than they are; to be not so dependent, as in fact they are, upon collateral influences. They thought them the natural and spontaneous growth of the human heart; so firmly fixed in it, that they would subsist unimpaired, nay invigorated, when the whole system of opinions and observances with which they were habitually intertwined was violently torn away.

The Rousseauistic idea that innate human impulses are good and that it is society that obstructs or corrupts these has certainly reached Marianne, and she too would be happy to 'tear away' much of that 'system of opinions and observances' which more sober spirits such as Elinor (and indeed Mill himself) see as the necessary 'collateral influences' on good conduct. Marianne is a woman of whom it may be said, 'her motives are just her passions', as Henry James said of Hedda Gabler; the point is that she also believes that the feelings that well up spontaneously inside a person are inherently moral and therefore the best possible motives for action. Here again we can see Jane Austen bringing into focus an issue which materially determines the sort of society we live in – the virtues of 'freedom' opposing themselves to the necessities of 'control'. Elinor, with her unselfish tact, her instinct for arranging and keeping up appearances, and her modifying and reconciling powers, is clearly an indispensable member of society; indeed, in terms of the book she may be said to be one of the maintainers of it. Yet we surely respond very positively to Marianne's guileless sincerity, and we cannot fail to find attractive her generous capacity for feeling, nor fail to sympathise with her in her genuine suffering and sickness. We see quite plainly that much of the work of keeping society as truly civilised as possible falls on Elinor – and Jane Austen knows what a thankless task that can be. Yet this in no way serves to make less attractive the girl who, like Keats, believes in 'the holiness of the heart's affections'.

Two sisters then, though not a simple dualism. They are *not* simply ciphers for passion and reason, impulse and restraint, feeling and form, poetry and prose. Yet it is true that they do seem to project some basic division or rift in civilisation as Jane Austen knew it, perhaps as we know it. Throughout the nineteenth century you can find writers using brothers and sisters as ways of projecting different aspects of the single composite self. The most famous example is the Brothers Karamazov, who, with their differing emphases on body, mind and spirit, seem to be the three parts of one total individual – the collective son of their father, perhaps Man himself. Jane Austen is hardly attempting anything so ambitious as Dostoyevsky. Yet she makes it clear that Elinor and Marianne do embody slightly but crucially different notions about how to live and that society will only tolerate one of those notions (just as George Eliot does with Maggie and Tom Tulliver). It is abundantly clear that she put quite as much of herself into Marianne as into Elinor, so from one point of view we can imagine this to be a psychological parable written partly at least for her own benefit – the two sisters adding up to one divided self. And, if the ideal state of affairs would be that pointed to by E. M. Forster's phrase 'Only connect' – connect the Schlegels and the Wilcoxes, the poetry and the prose, the sensibility and the sense – the actual condition of social living as Jane Austen saw it was that they could not be fully connected but rather one was, and had to be, subordinated. This is why I introduced in passing the title of Freud's *Civilisation and its Discontents*, for Marianne does suffer from neurosis brought on by repression and her sickness is precisely the cost of her entry into the sedate stabilities of civilised life envisaged at the end. Before her illness her eyes are bright, eager, full of wayward spirit; after her illness – it is the very sign of her recovery – she looks up at Elinor with a 'rational though languid gaze'. 'My illness has made me think', she says, when apologising for her previous 'want of kindness to others'; it is as though social virtue and debility are closely connected. Freud could scarcely have hinted more succinctly at the price paid in sickness for the acquisition of 'reason'. Her vision is now clearer; but her energy is turned to languor. She is tamed and ready for 'citizenship'.

This points to what is certainly the weakest part of the book – the way Marianne is disposed of at the end. She is married off to Brandon to complete a pattern, to satisfy that instinct for harmonious arranging which is part of the structure both of that society and of the book itself. Her energy is sacrificed to the overriding geometry. Jane Austen even hints at coercion – albeit an affectionate pressure – involved in this resolution. Edward and Elinor want to see Marianne settled in Brandon's 'mansion-house' just as Jane Austen wants to see her firmly placed in the edifice of her novel. All the characters agree that Brandon has many virtues and has suffered sorrows, 'and Marianne, by general consent, was to be the reward of all'. 'With such a confederacy against her', Jane Austen continues with an appropriately ambiguous word, 'what could she do?' She capitulates; or one could say that the 'confederacy' of society *and* the author against her prove to be too much. And Jane Austen's summary of the change in Marianne is almost harshly curt. 'Marianne Dashwood was born to an extraordinary fate. She was born to discover the falsehood of her own opinions, and to counteract, by her conduct, her most favourite maxims.' And, one paragraph later, 'she found herself, at nineteen, submitting to new attachments, entering on new duties, placed in a new home, a wife, the mistress of a family, and the patroness of a village'. She is now safely 'placed' – in society, in the book. One can have at least two reactions to this. One can feel that there is something punitive in the taming of Marianne and all she embodies – indeed, one might think that something is being vengefully stamped out. It is as though Jane Austen had gone out of her way to show that romantic feelings are utterly non-viable in society. Looking back through the book one can see that very often the validity of Marianne's responses is subtly undermined by giving them an edge of caricature – as though Jane Austen was defending herself against her own creation. As her creator she is certainly fond of Marianne, but is she also a bit frightened of her? What is certainly true is that Jane Austen does not undertake a full exploration of 'sensibility' – as for instance George Eliot (a great admirer of Jane Austen) did with Maggie Tulliver, another figure irreconcilably at odds with society because of her passionate intensities. What George Eliot does have the courage to show is that Maggie can only die; constituted as she is there is literally no place for her in society. The same insight is to be found in the case of another of Marianne's descendants – Cathy in *Wuthering Heights*. Jane Austen stops well short of this kind of investigation. And yet Marianne does, in effect, die. Whatever the name of the automaton which submits to the plans of its relations and joins the social game, it is not the real Marianne, and in the devitalised symmetry of the conclusion something valuable has been lost. She 'dwindles' into marriage with a vengeance – to take up the phrase of another spirited lady, Congreve's Millimant. The novel has at least shown the existence and power of the inner subterranean life of the emotions, but it returns to the surface at the end and is resolved with such brusque manipulation of plot that one wonders if Jane Austen intended that as a last bitter irony. It is certainly hard to know how exactly to respond to the end. Among other things it reminds us that Jane Austen is also a beautiful screen-maker and it is hard not to feel that with this ending she is almost wilfully screening something off from herself. One is left with the lurking suspicion that one of the things hidden behind the screen is a potentially tragic ending.

On the other hand one might, at the end, applaud the hard-headed realism which recognises that the consolations of society are only achieved at the cost of a more or less rigorous curbing of the intensities of impulse and a disciplined diminishment in the indulgence of solitary emotional fantasies. Yet one may well wonder what consolations society will have for Marianne after her shattering experience – the real Marianne, like Ophelia, might well have opted for the blessed unconsciousness of the river. 'Had I died, it would have been self-destruction', she says, as though well aware of the capacity for suicide she carries inside her. Of course one must recognise here that for Jane Austen the structure of society was more powerful than the structure of feeling in any one individual and would always contain it – though, as this novel shows, she was well aware how painful that containment could be. But it would be for later novelists, such as Emily Brontë, to reveal how that state of affairs could be inverted and show social structure dissolving before the unanswerable force of individual passion. It is not that Jane Austen necessarily valued society more than the fate of individuals: on the contrary, no one before her showed so piercingly the possible miseries of a compulsory social existence. But for her it was the unalterable given, and whatever life sense and sensibility were going to have, whatever space and satisfaction intelligence and sensitivity were going to secure for themselves, would have to be within society.

There is perhaps more wisdom in the way the novel concludes than a post-Romantic generation – and we are all post-Romantics – can immediately recognise. But it would certainly not go against the spirit of the book if, while deferring to that wisdom, we remember the scream behind the screen, the scissors straining against the sheath. There is every evidence that Jane Austen intended a complex and not a complacent response.

For in a book which, at root, is about to what extent 'nature' has to be reshaped and 'pruned' to make 'society' possible, the resolution can only be a temporary pause in an endless dialectic. At one point we hear that John Dashwood, a fair example of the fatuous, selfish and stupid people who can thrive in society, is cutting down trees so that he can erect a greenhouse. 'The old walnut trees are all come down to make room for it.' It is just another minor example of his general insensitivity, and Elinor allows it to pass with an inward wince. Yet in a tiny way even this episode points to the abiding paradox of civilization. Man does continually devastate the magnificent wildness of nature in order to put up his little social hot-houses in the clearings; just how stifling and false life can be in that hot-house we have been shown in the scene at the party where Willoughby snubs Marianne. And Jane Austen would not be the first person to feel that there are some trees better left standing, and some greenhouses better left unbuilt. But she was not sentimental about wildness and she recognised that society is necessarily a more or less continuous depredation of unchecked nature. What is implied in all her work is that human society ought to be very good indeed to justify the inroads made on 'nature' – the feelings within us as well as the trees around us – to erect and secure it. To this end sense and sensibility should work together as closely as possible. But – it is another lesson of her novels – the work is not easy and there is the chance of pain at every step of the way. For a perfect balance between the two must remain an artist's dream, and meanwhile many houses serve merely as prisons for once-brilliant dancers, and the greenhouses continue to go up where once the great trees swayed in the more liberal air.

# 4

# Knowledge and Opinion:
## *Pride and Prejudice*

> Why do you like Miss Austen so very much? I am puzzled on
> that point. . . . I had not seen *Pride and Prejudice* till I read that
> sentence of yours, and then I got the book. And what did I
> find? An accurate daguerreotyped portrait of a commonplace
> face; a carefully fenced, highly cultivated garden, with neat
> borders and delicate flowers; but no glance of a bright, vivid
> physiognomy, no open country, no fresh air, no blue hill, no
> bonny beck. I should hardly like to live with her ladies and
> gentlemen, in their elegant but confined houses.

Thus Charlotte Brontë expressed her dissatisfaction with one of
the most enduringly popular of all English novels, in a letter to
G. H. Lewes written in 1848. I shall return to the terms of her
criticism later, and the significance of their connotations, but the
directness of her negative response prompts us to reconsider the
reasons for the lasting appeal of the novel and what relevance, if
any, it can still have for people living in very different social
conditions. I want to suggest various approaches to the novel,
which may help to clarify its achievement in terms of its own time
and also suggest why the form of that achievement could become
distasteful to a Romantic such as Charlotte Brontë. I also hope
that by showing the different ways we may look at the novel, its
abiding relevance for all of us may become more readily
apprehensible.

It is indeed possible to call its relevance to the society of the
time into question, for, during a decade in which Napoleon was
effectively engaging, if not transforming, Europe, Jane Austen
composed a novel in which the most important events are the fact
that a man changes his manners and a young lady changes her
mind. Soldiers do appear, but in the marginal role of offering
distractions to young girls, which in one case goes as far as to

produce an elopement. However, we should be careful here in case we adduce this fact to demonstrate Jane Austen's ignorance of – or indifference to – contemporary history. She makes it clear that the soldiers are the militia – and her readers would have recognised them as part of the body of men specifically raised for the defence of England in the event of an invasion from France (which was distinctly feared at the time). However, since the invasion never came, the men in the militia had plenty of leisure and could be a disruptive presence in the community – as Mr Wickham (a militia officer) is. It is Darcy who pays his debts and buys him a commission in the socially more prestigious regular army. Here again, as Christopher Kent has noted in ' "Real Solemn History" and Social History' (in *Jane Austen in a Social Context*), Jane Austen makes another telling contemporary point – for those who can read 'acutely' enough:

> Even as a regular soldier, Wickham is not sent abroad, but to Newcastle in the turbulently industrial North. This recalls another point: that the army was not simply for use against foreign enemies. In the almost complete absence of effective police forces in England the army was central to the maintenance of order at home.

Jane Austen must have known about the troubles in the industrial North just as she would surely have known about the naval mutinies of 1797 (thought to be Jacobin-inspired), given that she had brothers in the navy. So contemporary history *does* touch the periphery of this novel (it is more in evidence in her subsequent work). Nevertheless it is true to say that, although history is discernible out of the corner of the eye (it is contemporary history which brings about the arrival of the disrupter figure, Wickham – who is more of a danger to the community than the French, or mutinous sailors, or agitating workers), the overall impression given by the book is of a small section of society locked in an almost – *almost* – timeless, ahistorical present in which very little will or can, or even should, change. (It will be very different by the time we get to *Persuasion*.)

For the most part the people are as fixed and repetitive as the linked routines and established social rituals which dominate their lives. Money is a potential (never an actual) problem, and courtship has its own personal dramas; but everything tends towards the achieving of satisfactory marriages – which is exactly how such a society secures its own continuity and minimises the possibility of anything approaching violent change. In such a world a change of mind – an act by which consciousness demonstrates some independence from the patterns of thought which have predetermined its readings of things – can indeed come to seem a fairly momentous event, an internal modification matched in this novel by an external modification in an individual's behaviour. Let me put it this way. For the first two parts of the book Mr Darcy and Elizabeth Bennet believe that they are taking part in an action which, if turned into a fiction, should be called *Dignity and Perception*. They have to learn to see that their novel is more properly called *Pride and Prejudice*. For Jane Austen's book is, most importantly, about prejudging and rejudging. It is a drama of recognition – re-cognition, that act by which the mind can look again at a thing and if necessary make revisions and amendments until it sees the thing as it really is. As such it is thematically related to the dramas of recognition which constitute the great tradition of Western tragedy – *Oedipus Rex*, *King Lear*, *Phèdre* – albeit the drama has now shifted to the comic mode, as is fitting in a book which is not about the finality of the individual death but the ongoingness of social life.

I am not forgetting the immense charm of Elizabeth Bennet which has so much to do with the appeal of the book: 'I must confess that I think her as delightful a creature as ever appeared in print, and how I shall be able to tolerate those who do not like *her* at least I do not know . . .', wrote Jane Austen in a letter; and indeed her combination of energy and intelligence, her gay resilience in a society tending always towards dull conformity, would make her a worthy heroine in a Stendhal novel, which cannot be said for many English heroines. But at this point I want to suggest that a very important part of the book is how it touches on, indeed dramatises, some aspects of the whole problem of knowledge. Eighteenth-century philosophers had, of course, addressed themselves to what Locke called 'the discerning faculties of a man' with unusual analytic rigour, considering not only the question of what we know, but also the more reflexive matter of *how* we know what we know, and the limits set on knowledge by the very processes and instruments of cognition.

John Locke asserted at the start of his *Essay Concerning Human Understanding* that it was 'worth while to search out the bounds between opinion and knowledge; and examine by what measures, in things whereof we have no certain knowledge, we ought to regulate our assent and moderate our persuasion'. And he added, in a *caveat* which is important for understanding much eighteenth-century literature, 'Our business here is not to know all things, but those which concern our conduct.' Locke pointed out how, because of 'settled habit', often 'we take that for the perception of our sensation which is an idea formed by our judgement'. This fairly accurately sums up Elizabeth's earlier reactions to Darcy. She identifies her sensory perceptions as judgements, or treats impressions as insights. In her violent condemnation of Darcy and the instant credence she gives to Wickham, no matter how understandable the former and excusable the latter, Elizabeth is guilty of 'Wrong Assent, or Error', as Locke entitled one of his chapters. In it he gives some of the causes of man's falling into error, and they include 'Received hypotheses', 'Predominant passions or inclinations' and 'Authority'. These are forces and influences with which every individual consciousness has to contend if it is to make the lonely struggle towards true vision, as Elizabeth's consciousness does; and the fact that whole groups and societies can live in the grip of 'Wrong Assent, or Error', often with intolerably unjust and cruel results, only helps to ensure the continuing relevance of this happy tale of a girl who learned to change her mind.

The first title Jane Austen chose for the work which was finally called *Pride and Prejudice* was *First Impressions*, and I think this provides an important clue to a central concern of the final version. We cannot know how prominently 'first impressions' figured in the first version, since it is lost. There has, needless to say, been a great deal of scholarship devoted to the putative evolution of the novel, and I shall here quote from Brian Southam's *Jane Austen's Literary Manuscripts*, since his research in this area is well in advance of my own. He suggests that the book may have started out as another of Jane Austen's early burlesques, though adding that little remains in the final form to indicate such an origin.

The object of the burlesque is hinted at in the title, for the phrase 'first impressions' comes directly from the terminology of sentimental literature, and Jane Austen would certainly have met it in *Sir Charles Grandison*, where its connotations are briefly defined. She would have known a more recent usage in *The Mysteries of Udolpho* (1794), where the heroine is told that by resisting first impressions she will 'acquire that steady dignity of mind, that can alone counter-balance the passions'. Here, as commonly in popular fiction, 'first impressions' exhibit the strength and truth of the heart's immediate and intuitive response, usually love at first sight. Jane Austen had already attacked this concept of feeling in 'Love and Friendship', and in *Sense and Sensibility* it is a deeply-founded trait of Marianne's temperament. . . . There is a striking reversal of this concept in *Pride and Prejudice*, yet in circumstances altogether unsentimental.

He is referring to Elizabeth's 'first impressions' of Darcy's house, Pemberley, which are, as it were, accurate and authenticated by the book. She is also right, we might add, in her first impressions of such figures as Mr Collins and Lady Catherine de Bourgh. But she is wrong in her first impressions of Wickham; and her first impressions of Darcy, though to a large extent warranted by the evidence of his deportment and tone, are an inadequate basis for the rigid judgement which she then erects upon them.

Mr Southam suggests that 'the original title may have been discarded following the publication of a *First Impressions* by Mrs Holford in 1801', and he repeats R. W. Chapman's original observation that the new title almost certainly came from the closing pages of Fanny Burney's *Cecilia*. This book also concerns a very proud young man, Mortimer Delvile, who cannot bring himself to give up his family name, which is the rather perverse condition on which alone Cecilia may inherit a fortune from her uncle. The relationship between this book and Jane Austen's novel has also been explored by other critics and it will suffice here to quote from the wise Dr Lyster's speech near the end of the book:

'The whole of his unfortunate business', said Dr Lyster, 'has been the result of PRIDE AND PREJUDICE. Your uncle, the Dean, began it, by his arbitrary will, as if an ordinance of his own could arrest the course of nature! . . . Your father, Mr Mortimer, continued it with the same self-partiality, preferring the wretched gratification of tickling his ear with a favourite sound, to the solid happiness of his son with a rich and deserving wife. Yet this, however, remember: if to PRIDE AND PREJUDICE you owe your miseries, so wonderfully is good and evil balanced, that to PRIDE AND PREJUDICE you will also owe their termination.'

But, while conceding that the phrase 'first impressions' may be more than a glancing blow aimed at the conventions of the sentimental novel, I want to suggest a further possible implication in Jane Austen's original title. Without for a moment suggesting that she read as much contemporary philosophy as she did fiction (though with so intelligent a woman it is scarcely impossible), I think it is worth pointing out that 'impressions' is one of the key words in David Hume's philosophy, and the one to which he gives pre-eminence as the source of our knowledge. Thus from the beginning of the *Treatise of Human Nature*:

All the perceptions of the human mind resolve themselves into two distinct kinds, which I shall call IMPRESSIONS and IDEAS. The difference betwixt these consists in the degrees of force and liveliness, with which they strike upon the mind, and make their way into our thought or consciousness. Those perceptions, which enter with most force and violence, we may name *impressions*; and under this name I comprehend all our sensations, passions and emotions, as they make their first appearance in the soul. By *ideas* I mean the faint image of these in thinking and reasoning. . . . There is another division of our perceptions, which it will be convenient to observe, and which extends itself both to our impressions and ideas. This division is into SIMPLE and COMPLEX. . . . I observe that many of our complex ideas never had impressions, that corresponded to them, and that many of our complex impressions never are exactly copied in ideas. I can imagine to myself such a city as the *New Jerusalem*, whose pavement is gold and walls are rubies, tho' I never saw any such. I have seen *Paris*; but shall I affirm that I can form such an idea of that city, as will perfectly represent all its streets and houses in their real and just proportions?

Elizabeth has a lively mind – her liveliness is indeed one of the qualities which wins Darcy to her – and her impressions are comparably lively, since the quality of the registering consciousness necessarily affects the intensity of the registered impressions. Similarly she is capable both of complex impressions and of complex ideas – more of this later. Her problem, in Hume's terms, is that her complex ideas are not always firmly based on her complex impressions obtained from the scenes before her. Here we notice that eighteenth-century suspicion of imagination to which Jane Austen partially subscribed, since it was likely to make you believe ideas not based on impressions – to confuse the New Jerusalem and Paris. (In rebelling against eighteenth-century philosophy and psychology, Blake was to assert the primacy of the faculty which could envision the New Jerusalem and elevate it over the mere perception of Paris.)

If, says Hume, we wish to understand our ideas, we must go back to our impressions: 'By what invention can we throw light upon these ideas, and render them altogether precise and determinate to our intellectual view? Produce the impressions or original sentiments, from which the ideas are copied.' That is from *An Enquiry Concerning Human Understanding*. In the *Enquiry Concerning the Principles of Morals* he also stresses that

the senses alone are not implicitly to be depended on; but that we must correct their evidence by reason, and by considerations, derived from the nature of the medium, the distance of the object, and the disposition of the organ, in order to render them, within their sphere, the proper *criteria* of truth and falsehood.

And 'a false relish may frequently be corrected by argument and reflection'. Impressions beget inclinations, and those inclinations may then come under the consideration of reason. But reason, being cool and disengaged, is not a motive to action, and directs only the impulse received from appetite or inclination, by showing us the means of attaining happiness or avoiding misery. One further quotation:

> In every situation or incident, there are many particular and seemingly minute circumstances, which the man of greatest talent is, at first, apt to overlook, though on them the justness of his conclusions, and consequently the prudence of his conduct, entirely depend. . . . The truth is, an unexperienced reasoner could be no reasoner at all, were he absolutely unexperienced.

Without experience, no reason; without impressions, no experience. This suggests the particular importance of 'first impressions', because, although they may well need subsequent correction, amplification, supplementation, and so on, they constitute the beginning of experience. All the above quotations from Hume seem to me to apply very aptly to *Pride and Prejudice* and I do not think this aptness needs spelling out. For Jane Austen, as for Hume, the individual needs to be *both* an experiencer *and* a reasoner: the former without the latter is error-prone, the latter without the former is useless if not impossible (as exemplified by Mary Bennet's sententious comments; she is *all* 'cool and disengaged' reason, and thus no reasoner at all). Both experience and reason depend upon impressions, and first impressions thus become our first steps into full human life. To overstress this may become a matter suitable for burlesque, but as a general proposition it is not inherently so.

To add to this proposition the reminder that first impressions, indeed all impressions, may need subsequent revision is only to say that full human life is a complex affair, and Jane Austen makes us well aware of this complexity. From the problematical irony of the opening assertion – 'It is a truth universally acknowledged' – there are constant reminders of the shiftingness of what people take to be 'truth'; for what is 'universally acknowledged' can change not only from society to society but from person to person, and indeed within the same person over a period of time. There is in the book a whole vocabulary connected with the process of decisions, opinion, conviction, stressing or suggesting how various and unstable are people's ideas, judgements, accounts and versions of situations and people. After one evening of seeing Darcy 'His character was decided. He was the proudest, most disagreeable man in the world'; Elizabeth asks Wickham about Lady Catherine and 'allowed that he had given a very rational account'; she also believes his account of his treatment by Darcy and it is left to Jane to suggest that 'interested people have perhaps misrepresented each to the other'. Jane, however, has her own myopia, for, in her desire to think well of the whole world, she sees Miss Bingley's treatment of her as agreeable while Elizabeth more accurately discerns it as supercilious. However, Elizabeth is too confident, as when she asserts to her more tentative sister, 'I beg your pardon; one knows exactly what to think.' She is 'resolved' against Darcy and for a while takes pleasure in Wickham, who is, temporarily, 'universally liked'. She questions Darcy whether he has never allowed himself 'to be blinded by prejudice', without thinking that she may at that very moment be guilty of prejudging, with its resulting screening of vision. Opinions are constantly changing as people's behaviour appears in a different light. Elizabeth 'represents' a person or a situation in one way, while Jane adheres to her own 'idea' of things. It is Jane who, when Darcy is condemned by everybody else as 'the worst of men', 'pleaded for allowances and urged the possibility of mistakes'. Of course it is not long before opinion shifts against Wickham. 'Everybody declared that he was the wickedest young man in the world', just as everybody's opinion quickly reverses itself towards the Bennet family. 'The Bennets were *speedily pronounced* to be the luckiest family in the world, though only a few weeks before, when Lydia had first run away, they had been *generally proved* to be marked out for misfortune' (emphasis added). The fallibility of our 'proofs' and the prematurity of all too many of our 'pronouncements' are amply demonstrated in this novel. The 'anxious interpretation' which is made necessary on social occasions is examined, and the 'interest' which lies behind this or that reading of things is alluded to. When Mrs Gardiner *'recollected having heard* Mr Fitzwilliam Darcy *formerly spoken of* as a very proud, ill-natured boy' she takes it, temporarily, as knowledge (emphasis added).

It is of course Elizabeth who most importantly comes to 'wish that her former opinions had been more reasonable, her expressions more moderate'. As opposed to Jane, whom she calls 'honestly blind', Elizabeth has more 'quickness of observation'. But in Darcy's case her observation proves to be too quick. Not that we can or wish to count her wrong in her 'first impressions' of Darcy, for his manner *is* proud, patronising and, in his famous proposal, insulting and unworthy of a gentleman – as Elizabeth very properly points out to our great delight. But she had formed a fixed 'idea' of the whole Darcy on insufficient data, and in believing Wickham's account of the man – a purely verbal fabrication – she is putting too much confidence in unverified and, as it turns out, completely false, evidence.

However, it is important to note that her *éclaircissement* first comes through language as well – in the form of Darcy's letter. The passages describing her changing reaction to that letter are among the most important in the book. In effect she is having to choose between two opposed and mutually exclusive versions – Wickham's and Darcy's. 'On both sides it was only assertion.' She had at first been taken in by Wickham's plausible physical manner, but she gradually comes to put more trust in Darcy's authoritative writing-manner – she is discriminating between styles at this point. (Note that she immediately judges that Mr Collins is not a sensible man from the pompous style of his letter-writing – in this case, first impressions are validated.) She realises that 'the affair . . . was capable of a turn which must make him [Darcy] entirely blameless throughout the whole'. *The affair was capable of a turn* – there in essence is the whole problem which for ever confronts the interpreting human consciousness, which can turn things now this way, now that way, as it plays, seriously or sportively, with the varying versions of reality which it is capable of proliferating: one concrete world – many partial mental pictures of it. But if it is the problem of consciousness, it can also be its salvation, for it enables a person to change his version or interpretation of things. Just how tenacious a man can be of a fixed version, and how disastrous that tenacity can be when it is a wrong version, is indeed the very subject of *King Lear*. Elizabeth thinks for a time that her wrong version has cost her a perfect mate and a great house, crucial things for a young lady in that society:

She began now to comprehend that he was exactly the man

> who, in disposition and talents, would most suit her. . . . It
> was an union that must have been to the advantage of
> both. . . . But no such happy marriage could now teach the
> admiring multitude what connubial felicity really was.

But of course she does not have to undergo Lear's tribulations. By
an intelligent and just reading of Darcy's letter she not only
changes her mind about him: she comes to a moment of intense
realisation about herself.

> How differently did everything now appear in which he was
> concerned! . . . She grew absolutely ashamed of herself. Of
> neither Darcy nor Wickham could she think without feeling
> that she had been blind, partial, prejudiced, absurd. 'How
> despicably have I acted!' she cried; 'I, who have prided myself
> on my discernment! . . . Till this moment I never knew
> myself.'

This may seem somewhat excessive – it is part of Darcy's
improvement that he comes to acknowledge the justness of much
of what she has said about his behaviour and manner. The
important thing is that in perceiving her own pride and prejudice
– notice she uses both words of herself – Elizabeth can now begin
to be free of them. There can be few more important moments in
the evolution of a human consciousness than such an act of
recognition. There is much in our literature as well as our
experience to suggest that the person who never comes to the
point of saying, 'I never knew myself', will indeed remain for
ever cut off from any self-knowledge – what possible effect there
is on his or her vision and conduct need not here be spelt out. If
we don't know ourselves, we don't know our world.

It is not surprising that after wandering alone for two hours
'giving way to every variety of thought – re-considering events,
determining probabilities', as Elizabeth does after receiving
Darcy's letter, she experiences 'fatigue'. For she has indeed been
through an ordeal and engaged in a critical effort of rearranging
her mental furniture. As F. Scott Fitzgerald once wrote, 'I was
impelled to think. God, was it difficult! The moving about of great
secret trunks.' That there are internal expenditures of energy
quite as exhausting as any bout of external action is a truth which

Jane Austen, with her restricted position in a fairly immobile society, was peculiarly able to appreciate. Elizabeth's particular ordeal is indeed a very ancient one, for she has been confronting for the first time the problematical discrepancies between appearances and reality, and the unsuspected limits of cognition. It is a theme as old as *Oedipus Rex*, and, even if all that is involved is recognising a rake and a gentleman respectively for what they really are, in Elizabeth's society, no less than in ancient Greece, such acts of recognition are decisive in the procuring of happiness or misery.

The constant need to be alert to the difference between appearance and reality is made clear from the start. Compared with Bingley and Darcy, Mr Hurst 'merely looked the gentleman'. Since Mr Hurst alternates between playing cards and sleeping, he is hardly a problematical character. Wickham of course is more so. 'His appearance was greatly in his favour' and he has a 'very pleasing address'. He is 'beyond' all the officers of his regiment 'in person, countenance, air, and walk'. Elizabeth does not have it 'in her nature to question the veracity of a young man of such amiable appearance as Wickham'. He 'must always be her model of the amiable and the pleasing'. It is only after reading Darcy's letter that she has to start changing that model. As the above-quoted words make clear (none of them has pronounced ethical connotations), Elizabeth has hitherto responded to Wickham's manner, or that part of the self which is visible on social occasions. After the letter she thinks back:

> As to his real character had information been in her power, she had never felt a wish of inquiring. His countenance, voice, and manner had established him at once in the possession of every virtue. She tried to recollect some instance of goodness, some distinguished trait of integrity or benevolence . . . but she could remember no more substantial good than the general approbation of the neighbourhood.

She has now started to think about 'substance' as being distinct from 'appearance', and from this point on Darcy's character will continue to rise in her estimation as Wickham's falls, until she can complain to Jane, 'There certainly was some great mis-management in the education of these two young men. One has got all the goodness, and the other all the appearance of it.' Poor Jane, so reluctant to believe in the existence of human duplicity and evil scheming, would like to believe in the goodness of both men, but Elizabeth, with her more rigorous mind, points out that there is 'but such a quantity of merit between them; just enough to make one good sort of man; and of late it has been shifting about pretty much. For my part, I am inclined to believe it all Mr Darcy's.' Even here, as we can see, Elizabeth's sense of humour has not deserted her; and it enables her to disconcert Wickham with a nice irony. On her return from Rosings, Wickham asks if Darcy's 'ordinary style' has improved, adding, 'For I dare not hope that he is improved in essentials.' Elizabeth, by now convinced of the essential goodness of Darcy, can thus reply meaningfully, 'Oh, no! . . . In essentials, I believe, he is very much what he ever was.' Wickham makes a rather agitated retreat, adding with weak insolence, 'I must rejoice that he is wise enough to assume even the *appearance* of what is right.' The emphasis is Jane Austen's and the word occurs again later in the chapter, again italicised, as if to stress that Elizabeth is now fully awakened to the possible disparities between appearance and substance.

Just what constitutes a person's 'real character' is one of the concerns of the book: the phrase occurs more than once, usually with the added idea that it is something that can be 'exposed' (and thus, by the same token, concealed). In particular, Darcy in his letter writes that, whatever Elizabeth may feel about Wickham, it 'shall not prevent me from unfolding his real character', just as later in the letter he narrates Wickham's attempt to seduce Georgiana, 'a circumstance . . . which no obligation less than the present should induce me to unfold to any human being'. Cordelia's last words before being banished are

> Time shall unfold what plighted cunning hides
> Who covers faults, at last shame them derides.

'Unfolding' a hidden reality is of course replacing mere appearance with substance. The fact that reality can get folded up and hidden away – because we are so built that we are forced to work from first impressions which can be cynically manipulated –

means that it is very important to be careful about what we regard as convincing evidence. It is the mistake of both Lear and Othello that they ask for the wrong kind of evidence, thus making themselves vulnerable to those who are willing to fabricate a set of false appearances. But in Shakespearean tragedy, as also in *Pride and Prejudice*, the 'real character' of both the good and the bad – of Cordelia and Iago, of Darcy and Wickham – is 'unfolded'. The cost and process of the unfolding are of course very different in each case. But the perennial theme is common to both.

At this point we may ask if Elizabeth has any more than calligraphic evidence for her new belief as to the relative merits of Darcy and Wickham. Obviously something more is required to give 'substance' to what could be mere 'assertion'. There is of course the magnanimous part he plays in the crisis precipitated by the elopement of Lydia and Wickham, but Elizabeth's improved vision has already by then 'learned to detect' the boring affectation in Wickham's manner, and appreciate the solid merit of Darcy. The education of her vision, if we may call it so, starts with Darcy's letter, but it is not complete until she has penetrated his house and confronted his portrait. This occurs on her visit to Derbyshire when the Gardiners persuade her to join them in looking round Pemberley, Darcy's fine house, and its beautiful grounds. This physical penetration of the interior of Pemberley, which is both an analogue and an aid for her perceptual penetration of the interior quality of its owner, occurs at the beginning of Book III, and after the proposal-letter episode I regard it as the most important scene in the book and wish to consider it in some detail.

The word 'picture' occurs frequently in the novel, often in the sense of people 'picturing' something – a ball, a married couple, a desired situation – to themselves. One important example of this is the following: 'Had Elizabeth's opinion been all drawn from her own family, she could not have formed a very pleasing picture of conjugal felicity or domestic comfort.' These pictures, then, are mental images, either derived from impressions or conjured up by imagination. (It is of course a particular quality of Elizabeth's that she is able to think outside the reality picture offered to her by her own family.) There are also more literal references to pictures – as when Miss Bingley suggests to Darcy, by way of a spiteful joke, that he should hang portraits of some of

Elizabeth's socially inferior (to Darcy) relatives at Pemberley, adding, 'As for your Elizabeth's picture, you must not attempt to have it taken, for what painter could do justice to those beautiful eyes?' The relation between actual portraits and mental pictures is suggested when Darcy is dancing with Elizabeth. She has teased him with a witty description of their common characteristics. ' "This is not a very striking resemblance of your own character, I am sure," said he. "How near it may be to *mine*, I cannot pretend to say. *You* think it a faithful portrait undoubtedly." ' Later in the same dance he says, 'I could wish, Miss Bennet, that you were not to sketch my character at the present moment, as there is reason to fear that the performance would reflect no credit on either.' Her answer is, 'But if I do not take your likeness now, I may never have another opportunity.' This is more than mere banter because, since we cannot literally internalise another person, it is at all times extremely important what particular picture or portrait of that person we carry with us. The portrait metaphor allows one to suggest that the picture should be done with some care in order that the gallery of the mind should not be hung with a series of unjust unlikenesses.

We know that Jane Austen herself went to art galleries when she could. Thus in a letter to Cassandra in 1811: 'May and I, after disposing of her Father and Mother, went to the Liverpool Museum, & the British Gallery, & I had some amusement at each, tho' my preference for Men & Women, always inclines me to attend more to the company than the sight.' And in 1813 it is clear that when she went to a portrait gallery she had her own fictional portraits in mind. Again the letter is to Cassandra:

Henry and I went to the Exhibition in Spring Gardens. It is not thought a good collection, but I was very well pleased – particularly (pray tell Fanny) with a small portrait of Mrs Bingley, excessively like her. I went in hopes of finding one of her Sister, but there was no Mrs Darcy; – perhaps, however, I may find her in the Great Exhibition which we shall go to, if we have time; – I have no chance of her in the collection of Sir Joshua Reynolds Paintings which is now shewing in Pall Mall & which we are also to visit. – Mrs Bingley's is exactly herself, size, shaped face, features and sweetness; there never was a greater likeness. She is dressed in a white gown, with green ornaments, which convinces me of what I had always supposed, that green was a favourite colour with her. I dare say Mrs D. will be in Yellow.

Later in the letter she adds,

We have been both to the Exhibition & Sir J. Reynolds', – and I am disappointed, for there was nothing likes Mrs D at either. I can only imagine that Mr D. prizes any Picture of her too much to like it should be exposed to the public eye. – I can imagine he wd have that sort of feeling – that mixture of Love, Pride & Delicacy. – Setting aside this disappointment, I had great amusement among the Pictures. . . .

It is worth noting that she does not expect to find a recognizable portrait of Elizabeth in Sir Joshua Reynolds's collection. For Reynolds, the artist, including the portraitist, 'acquires a just idea of beautiful forms; he corrects nature by her self, her imperfect state by her more perfect'. In his *Discourses* Reynolds laid typical neoclassical stress on 'central forms', and generalised figures which are not 'the representation of an individual, but of a class'. This neoclassic approach tended to minimise the individuating qualities of a person or thing in favour of more generic attributes or in deference to classical models. But for Jane Austen, the novelist and admirer of Richardson, it was precisely the individuating qualities, which sharply differentiated even the sisters in the same family, which held most interest. Elizabeth is not a type; indeed she has that kind of independent energy which is most calculated to disturb a typological attitude to people. She wants recognising for what she *is* and not what she might represent (Mr Collins's regard for her, as for Charlotte, is, she knows, wholly 'imaginary' – he sees her only as a suitable wife figure, and is dismissed according to his deserts). She is fortunate in attracting the discerning eye of Darcy – he is always staring at her, as if trying to read her fully, or capture the most complete likeness for his memory – for he alone of the men in the book is equipped to do justice to all her real qualities. It is thus only right that she should be brought to a full recognition of *his* real qualities. And this finally happens at Pemberley.

As they drive through the grounds Elizabeth admires the

unobtrusive good taste in evidence – 'neither formal nor falsely adorned' – and 'at that moment she felt that to be mistress of Pemberley might be something!' Then they are led through the house, where again the elegance and genuine taste – 'neither gaudy nor uselessly fine' – awakens her admiration, and she again reverts to what she regards as her lost opportunity: ' "And of this place," thought she, "I might have been mistress!" ' Showing them round the house is Mrs Reynolds, a sort of cicerone who may be guilty of 'family prejudice' but whose testimony concerning the youthful qualities of Darcy and Wickham has authority for Elizabeth. She is a voice from *within* the house and thus acquainted with Darcy from his origins, and is not, as Elizabeth necessarily is, a purely social acquaintance. She shows them some miniatures, including one of Darcy ('the best landlord, and the best master') and invites Elizabeth to go and look at a larger portrait of Darcy upstairs in the picture gallery. Elizabeth walks among the portraits

> in quest of the only face whose features would be known to her. At last it arrested her – and she beheld a striking resemblance of Mr Darcy, with such a smile over the face as she remembered to have sometimes seen when he looked at her. She stood several minutes before the picture, in earnest contemplation. . . . There was certainly at this moment, in Elizabeth's mind, a more gentle sensation towards the original than she had ever felt in the height of their acquaintance. . . . Every idea that had been brought forward by the housekeeper was favourable to his character, and as she stood before the canvas on which he was represented, she fixed his eyes upon herself, she thought of his regard with a deeper sentiment of gratitude than it had ever raised before; she remembered its warmth, and softened its impropriety of expression.

One can almost detect the unformulated thought: 'and of this man I might have been the wife'. It is a thought which explicitly occurs to her in due course.

Standing in the middle of the house, contemplating the qualities in the face in the portrait (qualities imparted and corroborated to some extent by the housekeeper), Elizabeth completes the act of recognition which started with the reading of

Darcy's letter. Notice the fact that the truest portrait is the large one in the more private part of the house upstairs; downstairs Darcy is only visible in 'miniature'. We can imagine that, the further a man goes from the house in which he is truly known, the more liable he is both to misrepresentation and to non-recognition. Standing before the large and true image of the real Darcy, Elizabeth has in effect completed her journey. When she next meets the original, outside in the grounds, she is no longer in any doubt as to his true worth. The rest of the book is, indeed, for the most part concerned with externalities – the mere melodrama of Wickham's elopement with Lydia, which gives Darcy a chance to reveal his qualities in action. But all this is only delay, not advance, in terms of the novel. For the most important action is complete when Elizabeth has finished the contemplation of the portrait. In answer to Jane's questions concerning when Elizabeth first realised she was in love with Darcy, Elizabeth replies, 'I believe it must date from my first seeing his beautiful grounds at Pemberley.' This is not wholly a joke, nor should it be taken to indicate that at heart Elizabeth is just another materialist in what is shown to be a distinctly materialistic society. In this case the grounds, the house, the portait all bespeak the real man – they represent a visible extension of his inner qualities, his true style. And, if Pemberley represents an ordering of natural, social and domestic space which is everything that the Bennet household is not, who shall blame Elizabeth for recognising that she would be more truly at home there? However, it is true that such a remark could only be made in the context of a society which shared certain basic agreements about the importance and significance of objects, domiciles and possessions. One can well imagine Charlotte Brontë's response to a remark of this kind. But these are matters to which we shall return.

Having mentioned the central importance of Darcy's letter, which contains an 'account of my actions and their motives' for Elizabeth to peruse and reperuse in private, we might at this point consider the overall importance of letters in this novel. So much of the main information in the novel is conveyed by letter – whether it be Mr Collins's vapid but acquisitive pomposity, or Miss Bingley's competitive coldness, or Mr Gardiner's account of Darcy's role in securing the marriage of Lydia and Wickham –

that there has been some speculation that the novel was initially conceived in epistolary form. Thus Brian Southam:

> In *Sense and Sensibility*, twenty-one letters are mentioned, quoted, or given verbatim, and in *Pride and Prejudice* no fewer than forty-four, including references to a 'regular and frequent' correspondence between Elizabeth and Charlotte Lucas, and the further regular communications of Elizabeth and Jane with Mrs Gardiner, a very credible system of letters to carry much of the story in epistolary form. If this reconstruction is feasible it supports my theory that, like *Sense and Sensibility*, *Pride and Prejudice* was originally a novel-in-letters.

On the other hand critics have been drawn to note the brilliance of much of the dialogue and have suggested that the novel has close affinities with the drama. In an excellent essay entitled 'Light and Bright and Sparkling' Reuben Brower writes, 'In analysing the ironies and the assumptions, we shall see how intensely dramatic the dialogue is, dramatic in the sense of defining characters through the way they speak and are spoken about', and he proceeds to show just how much, and how subtly, is revealed in various passages of dialogue. Walton Litz in his book on Jane Austen says that the tripartite structure of the novel is similar to the structure of a three-act play, and adds that in many of the passages 'we are reminded of the novel's affinities with the best in eighteenth-century drama'. But he also notes that the early part of the novel is more dramatic than the latter.

Howard S. Babb has shown how Jane Austen plays on the word 'performance' in the early dialogues, bringing all the implications of the word together in the great scene at Rosings, where Elizabeth's actual performance at the piano becomes the centre of a dramatic confrontation. 'But after the scene at Rosings, when Darcy's letter begins Elizabeth's movement toward self-recognition, the term "performance" quietly disappears from the novel. The first half of *Pride and Prejudice* has indeed been a dramatic performance, but in the second half a mixture of narrative, summary, and scene carries the plot towards the conclusion.' As he rightly says, this reveals that Jane Austen felt able to take advantage both of scenic representation and of authorial omniscience using third-person narrative, but I think there is another interesting aspect of the combination of the dramatic and the epistolary – particularly bearing in mind that, as Babb has noted, the word 'performance' fades after Elizabeth receives Darcy's letter.

In essence a letter is written and read in retirement from the social scene; this is certainly true of Darcy's major epistolary clarification. The letter enables him to formulate things and convey information in a way which would not be possible on a social occasion, where public modes of utterance necessarily restrict the more private ones. A letter is also a transforming of action into words, which may then be reflected on in a way which is impossible while one is actually involved in the action. 'Introspection is retrospection', said Sartre, and so is letter-writing, even if the letter seems to be written in the midst of some anxious situation. By combining the dramatic and the epistolary modes, Jane Austen has deftly set before us a basic truth – that we are both performing selves and reflective selves. It is in social performance that Elizabeth reveals all her vitality, vivacity and wit, as well as her actual physical magnetism; it is in private reflection ('reflection must be reserved for solitary hours') that she matures in judgement, reconsiders first impressions, and is able to make substantial changes to her mental reality picture. How suitable, then, that after giving us some of the most brilliant 'performances' in English fiction, Jane Austen should allow her novel to move away from performance towards reflection after Darcy's letter. She thus subtly offers an analogue of how – in her view – the individual should develop. For, if the human being is to be fully human, then to the energy of performance must be added the wisdom of reflection.

The idea of the self as a performer has taken hold of much recent thought, and most people recognise that society is effectively held together by a series of tacitly acknowledged rituals in which we all play a number of different parts. Jane Austen certainly believed in the value of the social rituals of her time – be they only balls, dinners, evening entertainments – and would have seen them, at their best, as ceremonies and celebrations of the values of the community. What she was also clearly aware of was how the failings of some of the performers – insensitivity, malice, arrogance, foolishness and so on – could spoil the ritual, and transform a ceremony to be enjoyed into a nightmare to be endured, as Elizabeth has so often to endure her mother's agonising ceremonial violations. But, although we are all role-players for much of the time we spend with other people, there will obviously be a difference between those people who are unaware of the fact – who disappear into their roles, as it were – and those who are at all times quite aware that the particular role they are performing in any one particular situation is not to be identified as their self, that they have facets and dimensions of character which cannot always be revealed on every occasion. The former type of person may sometimes appear to be something of an automaton, incapable of reflection and detachment, while the latter type of person may often wish to make a gesture of disengagement from the roles he is called on to play, to indicate that he has not become mindlessly imprisoned in those roles. Such gestures are expressive of what Erving Goffman calls 'role distance'.

Considering the characters in Jane Austen's novel in this light, we can see that Mr Bennet has become completely cynical about the social roles he is called on to play. He extracts a somewhat bitter pleasure from making gestures of disengagement from these roles, to compensate for the familial miseries brought about by his having married a sexually attractive but unintelligent woman (another example of the dangers of unreflective action based on first impressions – Lydia is her father's daughter as well as her mother's). It is Lydia's precipitous elopement, in addition to the more remote but not dissimilar marriage of her father, that provokes Jane Austen to her most direct attack on first impressions. She is justifying Elizabeth's change of mind about Darcy.

If gratitude and esteem are good foundations of affection, Elizabeth's change of sentiment will be neither improbable nor faulty. But if otherwise – if the regard springing from such sources is unreasonable or unnatural, in comparison of what is so often described as arising on a first interview with its object, and even before two words have been exchanged – nothing can be said in her defense, except that she had given somewhat of a trial of the latter method in her partiality for Wickham, and that its ill success might, perhaps, authorize her to seek the other less interesting mode of attachment.

It is fairly clear here that Jane Austen is showing her particular suspicion of the pre-verbal immediacy of sexual attraction. In this area in particular, she obviously thought that to act on first impressions could only be disastrous.

Mr Bennet effectively abdicates from the one role it is most incumbent on him to perform: that is, the role of father. He has taken refuge in mockery just as he takes refuge in his library – both are gestures of disengagement from the necessary rituals of family and society. Mrs Bennet, incapable of reflection, loses herself in her performance. Unfortunately she has a very limited view of the requirements of that performance; lacking any introspective tendencies she is incapable of appreciating the feelings of others and is *only* aware of material objects – hats, dresses, uniforms – and marriage, not as a meeting of true minds but as a disposing of redundant daughters. On another level Lady Catherine de Bourgh has none of what Jane Austen elsewhere approvingly calls 'the Dignity of Rank' but only the mindlessness of rank. She thinks her position entitles her to dictate to other people and impose her 'schemes' on them (a recurrent word in the book). She has never thought out, or thought round, the full implications of her performance. Being incapable of reflection she makes people suffer. At the other extreme Mary Bennet sees herself as a sage reflector before she has had any experience; when reflection portentously precedes performance in this way it is shown to be comical and useless. Darcy of course *has* thought about all the implications of his role in society, at least by the end of the book. His hauteur makes him go in for a certain amount of 'role distance', as at the first ball, when he slights Elizabeth to show his contemptuous detachment from the social ritual of the moment; but, unlike Wickham, he is not cynical about role-playing, and by the end his performing self is shown to be in harmony with his reflecting self.

Jane Bennet is incapable of role distance, but she has such a generous and high-minded conception of the roles she has to perform – daughter, sister, lover, wife – that she strikes us at all times as being both sensitive and sincere. Much the same could be said of Bingley, whose rather spineless plasticity in the hands of Darcy's more decisive will indicates nevertheless that his basic good nature extends to a willingness to perform roles which are thrust upon him – obviously a potential source of vulnerability.

Elizabeth is of course special. She can indeed perform all the roles that her familial and social situations require of her; moreover, she performs many of them with an *esprit* or an irony which reveal, as it were, a potential overspill of personality, as if there is more of her than can ever be expressed in any one role. She is also capable of role distance, not in her father's spirit of cynicism but in her own spirit of determined independence. She will put truth to self above truth to role. Thus in two of the scenes which give us the most pleasure to read we see her refusing to take on the roles which people in socially superior positions attempt to impose on her. To Darcy's first, lordly proposal she refuses to respond in the role of passive grateful female, as he obviously expects she will; while in the face of Lady Catherine's imperious insistence that she promise not to marry Darcy she refuses to act the compliant social inferior to which role Lady Catherine is relegating her. The assertion of the free-choosing self and its resistance to the would-be tyranny of roles imposed on it from socially superior powers is a spectacle which delights us now quite as much as it can have done Jane Austen's contemporaries.

All that has been said makes it clear that there are at least two different kinds of characters in the book: those who are fully defined by their roles, even lost in them, and those who can see round their roles and do not lose awareness of what they are doing. D. W. Harding uses the terms character and caricature to point to this difference, and, commenting that 'in painting it must be rather rare for caricature and full portraiture to be brought together in one group', he goes on to show what Jane Austen achieves by her carefully handled interaction of character and caricature, and what she is implying about a society in which such interactions are possible. (Examples are the meetings between Elizabeth and Mr Collins, and Elizabeth and Lady Catherine. See 'Character and Caricature in Jane Austen' in *Critical Essays on Jane Austen*, ed. B. C. Southam.) There is an important conversation in which Elizabeth announces that she comprehends Bingley's character completely. He replies that it is pitiful to be so transparent. 'That is as it happens. It does not necessarily follow that a deep, intricate character is more or less estimable than such a one as yours.' Bingley replies that he did not know she was a 'studier of character'.

'It must be an amusing study.'

'Yes, but intricate characters are the *most* amusing. They have at least that advantage.'

'The country', said Darcy, 'can in general supply but few subjects for such a study. In a country neighbourhood you move in a very confined and unvarying society.'

'But people themselves alter so much, that there is something new to be observed in them forever.'

Elizabeth's last remark is not wholly borne out by the book, for the Collinses and the Mrs Bennets and Lady Catherines of this world do not change. But 'intricate' characters are capable of change, as both she and Darcy change. Marvin Mudrick has examined this separation of Jane Austen's characters into the simple and the intricate, and shown how central it is to *Pride and Prejudice*, and there is no point in recapitulating his admirable observations here. Very generally we can say that obviously it is always likely to be in some ways oppressive for an intricate person to find himself or herself forced to live among simple people. Elizabeth has a dimension of complexity, a questing awareness, a mental range and depth which almost make her an isolated figure trapped in a constricting web of a small number of simple people. Darcy is posited as intricate to make her a match, but in truth he appears more to be honourable and reserved. He is not Benedick to Elizabeth's Beatrice. He is, however, capable of appreciating the intricacy of Elizabeth, so that in effect he can rescue her from the incipient claustrophobia of her life among simple people, and offer her more social and psychological space to move around in. (The good simple people, Jane and Bingley, join them in Derbyshire – the rest are left behind.)

This matter of social space is an important one, but another word may be said about what we may refer to as mental space or range, and its effect on language. We can recognise at least two very different ways in which people use language in this book. Some people employ it unreflectively as an almost automatic extension of their other behaviour; they are unable to speak, as they are unable to think, outside their particular social situation. (Consider, for example, the extremely limited range of Mrs Bennet's conversation, its obsessive repetitions, its predictable progressions.) Others, by contrast, are capable of using language reflectively and not just as an almost conditioned response to a social situation. Such people seem to have more freedom of manoeuvre within language, more conceptual space to move around in, and as a result they can say unpredictable things that surprise both us and the other characters in the book, and they seem capable of arriving at independent and thought-out conclusions of their own. Obviously such people are capable of thinking outside their particular social context – thus Elizabeth's mind and conversation are not limited to what she has seen and heard within her own family. (Compare Basil Bernstein's work in socio-linguistics, in which he differentiates between a restricted speech code and an elaborated speech code, the former determined by a person's particular position in the social structure, while the latter is not thus restricted.) It is not surprising that a person who has achieved a certain amount of mental independence will wish to exercise as much free personal control over his or her own life as is possible. He, or she, will not readily submit to the situations and alliances which society seems to be urging them into – hence Elizabeth's incredulity when Charlotte unhesitatingly accepts the role of Mr Collins's wife, to Elizabeth an inconceivable capitulation to the solicitations of social convenience. By contrast she will strive for a maximum of personal control (in defiance of real economic and family pressures), as is consistent with her having the quickest and furthest-ranging mind, and the most richly developed linguistic capacities.

Because the same space is occupied by people using language both reflectively and unreflectively, the claustrophobia for someone highly sensitive to speech can become very great, as witness the agonies of embarrassment which Elizabeth goes through while her mother rattles unreflectively on. This can obviously lead to a desire to escape, and, although Jane Austen does not seem to envisage how someone might renounce society altogether, she does show the relief with which an intricate person seeks out some solitude away from the miseries which can be caused by the constant company of more limited minds. Thus in the fragment *The Watsons*, which Jane Austen wrote some time between *First Impressions* and *Pride and Prejudice*, the isolated, because more complex, consciousness of the heroine, Emma, is glad to seek out the refuge of her father's quiet sick-room away from the family downstairs:

> In *his* chamber, Emma was at peace from the dreadful mortifications of unequal Society, & family Discord – from the immediate endurance of Hard-hearted prosperity, low-minded Conceit, & wrong-headed folly, engrafted on an ontoward Disposition. She still suffered from them in the Contemplation of their existence; in memory & in prospect, but for the moment, she ceased to be tortured by their effects.

(Compare Elizabeth, who 'sick of this folly, took refuge in her own room, that she might think with freedom'.) Elizabeth is fortunate to make a more permanent escape through marriage to Darcy; 'she looked forward with delight to the time when they should be removed from society so little pleasing to either, to all the comfort and elegance of their family party at Pemberley'. Pemberley is an all but impossible dream of a space – both social and psychic – large enough to permit a maximum of reflecting speech and personal control.

There is another aspect to the problems which can be posed by lack of social space. In a clearly stratified class society, such as Jane Austen depicts, there are invisible restrictions, boundaries and chasms, which the properly deferential person will not dare to traverse. There are quite a number of malicious remarks about people in trade made by some of the members of the landed aristocracy; one of the things Darcy has to do is to learn to appreciate the merits of people such as the Gardiners. The absurd and cringing servility of Mr Collins is an extreme example of the kind of mind, or rather mindlessness, which such a society can exact as a condition of belonging. It is a point, indeed, whether Elizabeth can be contained within such a society. One of the trials which Darcy has to pass is to confront the fact that he will become related not only to Mrs Bennet, but also to Wickham, if he marries Elizabeth. Elizabeth is sure that there is 'a gulf impassable between them' after the marriage of Lydia and Wickham. 'From such a connection she could not wonder that he should shrink.' Lady Catherine insists to her that 'connection with you must disgrace him in the eyes of everybody'. In this society, as in any highly structured society, it is a matter of some moment just who may be 'connected' to whom. Darcy has already dissuaded Bingley from a defiling connection with the Bennets, and the connection – from an external point of view – had indeed become more disgraceful by the end. The question is, can Darcy cross the social space which, in the eyes of society (and in his own up to a certain stage) exists between himself and Elizabeth?

There is a curious little scene between Elizabeth and Darcy shortly before he proposes to her for the first time. They are discussing, of all apparently trivial things, whether it could be said that Charlotte Lucas is living near to her family, or far from them, now that she has moved fifty miles and become Mrs Collins. Darcy says it is near, Elizabeth that it is far; it is possible that he is wondering whether he will be able to move Elizabeth a sufficient distance away from the rest of her socially undesirable family. Elizabeth makes the politic remark, 'The far and the near must be relative, and depend on varying circumstances.' At this point Darcy 'drew his chair a little towards her', then a little later in the conversation he 'experienced some change of feeling; he drew back his chair, took a newspaper from the table', and coldly changes the drift of the conversation. In that small advance and retreat of his chair, Darcy is miming out, albeit unconsciously, his uncertainty as to whether he can bring himself to cross the great social space which, as he sees it (he is still proud), separates Elizabeth from himself. They live in a society which all but dictates certain 'connections' and works strongly to prevent others. Part of the drama is in seeing whether two people can resist the connections which society seems to be prescribing for them (as Lady Catherine has the 'rational scheme' of marrying her daughter to Darcy,* and Mrs Bennet wishes to thrust

* 'It was the favourite wish of *his* mother, as well as of hers. While in their cradles, we planned the union: and now, at the moment when the wishes of both sisters would be accomplished in their marriage, to be prevented by a young woman of inferior birth, of no importance in the world, and wholly unallied to the family!'

The spectacle of Elizabeth holding out against the wishes, plans, schemes of society – positional control – is one which helps to sustain our belief in the possibility of some degree of individual autonomy. (It is tolerably savage comment on this society's power to enforce connections based on respectability that it is felt to be a blessing by the Bennets when it is announced that Wickham is

Elizabeth at Mr Collins), and make a new connection of their own, one which is not made in response to society's controlling power but freely made according to the dictates of their judgement, their reason and their emotions. One of the gratifications of the book is that Elizabeth and Darcy seem to demonstrate that it is still possible for individuals to make new connections in defiance of society. That there is perhaps a fairy-tale touch to their total felicity at the conclusion in the dream world of Pemberley should not discourage us from recognising the importance of holding on to this possibility as one which is essential to a healthy society. That is to say, a society in which the individual can experience freedom as well as commitment.

At this point it is perhaps worth considering in a little more detail just what kind of society Jane Austen does portray in this novel. It is a society which stresses social control over individual ecstasy, formality over informality, sartorial neatness over bodily abandon, and alert consciousness over the more Romantic states of reverie and trance. The schemes and structures of the group – family, community, society – tend to coerce and even predetermine the volition and aspirations of the self. No novelist could have valued consciousness more than Jane Austen, and some of the dialogue between Elizabeth (in particular) and Darcy requires a very high degree of alertness of consciousness. Indeed, this is just the point, that in this society linguistic experience is stressed almost to the exclusion of bodily experience. True, the men hunt, the women go for walks, and the sexes may come together at a ball. But all the important transactions (and most of the unimportant or vexatious ones) take place through language. When Darcy makes his second, and now welcome, proposal, we read of Elizabeth, 'though she could not look, she could listen, and he told of feelings which . . . made his affection every moment more valuable'. At this crucial moment 'love' has been

---

to marry Lydia after the elopement. 'And they *must* marry! Yet he is such a man! . . . How strange this is! And for *this* we are to be thankful.' Elizabeth's characteristically penetrating sense of the ironies in her society sees at once the strangeness of a marriage which is at once undesirable, in view of the character of the bridegroom, and absolutely essential in view of society's rigid rules. Public propriety entirely pre-empts private felicity. The fact of the connection has become more important than the individuals who will compose it.)

transformed into a completely linguistic experience. This is quite appropriate in a society setting a high value on consciousness.

Intimate physical contacts and experiences, while not denied, are minimised. Hands may meet, though it is more likely to be the eyes which come together across a distinct social space. Faces may be turned towards, or away from, other faces, and Elizabeth is prone to a good deal of blushing (allowing that the body has its own language, it is perhaps not entirely irrelevant to note that Norman O. Brown, following Freud, suggests that blushing is a sort of mild erection of the head). In general we are more likely to be shown dresses than bodies, public greetings than private embraces. It is interesting to compare, for instance, Jane Austen's description of an important ball with Tolstoy's. In Jane Austen the dancing (which from her letters we know she thoroughly enjoyed) is almost exclusively an occasion for conversation; indeed, it is a social ritual which permits something approaching private conversation in public, and there are some important exchanges between Darcy and Elizabeth while dancing. There is movement, there is grouping; there are *longueurs* and excitements. (In *The Watsons*, interestingly, Jane Austen describes what it is like for a young girl to enter a ball – the sweeping of dresses on the floor, the cold and empty room in which conversation is stiffly started, the noise of approaching carriages, and so on – a rather unusual excursion into private sensations which is not, however, taken very far.) What we do not get is the *physicality* of a ball. The following passage from *Anna Karenina* is inconceivable in Jane Austen. Kitty is watching Anna and Vronsky at the moment when they are falling in love with each other:

> She saw that they felt as if they were alone in the crowded ballroom. And she was struck by the bewildered look of submission on Vronsky's face, usually so firm and self-possessed – an expression like that of an intelligent dog conscious of having done worng.
>
> If Anna smiled, he smiled in reply. If she grew thoughtful, he looked serious. Some supernatural force drew Kitty's eyes to Anna's face. She was charming in her simple black gown, her rounded arms were charming with their bracelets, charming the firm neck with the string of pearls, charming the unruly

curls, charming the graceful, easy movements of her little hands and feet, charming the lovely, animated face: but in that charm there was something terrible and cruel.

Kitty is 'sure that the blow had fallen'. At this decisive moment when the blow falls which will determine the rest of their lives, there is no language. It is Anna's body which is speaking to Vronsky, and speaking a language which Kitty can also read. Rational consciousness is drowned in an intensity of purely physical, sensory awareness and response. We have moved a long way from the sparkling dialogue maintained by Elizabeth with her partners, and are indeed approaching something like a state of trance, each dancer almost drugged just by the presence and proximity of the other. This is not intended as any indictment of Jane Austen's novel, for who would wish it other than it is? It is pointing to something characteristic of the society she wrote out of and in turn portrays: namely, the minimising of a whole range of physical experiences which can often change lives more forcibly than rational reflection.

As we have mentioned, Jane Austen is particularly suspicious of the immediacy of sexual attraction. It is worth asking, then, what is 'love' as it emerges from the book? And we should notice first that, if Jane Austen's society minimises the bodily dimension, so it does the possibility of a transcendental one. Her concern is with conduct, almost never with religious experience. (Gilbert Ryle points out in his interesting essay 'Jane Austen and the Moralists' (which appears in *Critical Essays on Jane Austen*, ed. B. C. Southam) in which he argues that Shaftesbury's ideas influenced Jane Austen's ethics–aesthetics, that, while she often uses the word 'Mind', she almost never uses the word 'soul'.) Her society is secular and materialistic, and the terms need not be pejorative. It was a society which valued objects and the actual edifices which made up its structure; it was quite capable of sustaining a fairly nominal or unexamined piety towards the Unknown, but at its best it concentrated on how man and woman may best live in harmony with each other. (What may happen in such a society when it is not at its best, Jane Austen unsparingly reveals.) All of this obviously influenced the notion of 'love' and its relationship to marriage. Mrs Gardiner complains to Elizabeth that 'that expression of "violently in love" is so hackneyed, so doubtful, so indefinite, that it gives me very little idea', and Elizabeth duly rephrases her reading of Bingley's attitude towards Jane as a 'promising inclination'. Early in the book Charlotte and Elizabeth discuss the conscious strategies that a woman must deploy to secure the attachment of a man, and Charlotte of course demonstrates the complete triumph of conscious calculation over spontaneous emotion by her decision to marry Mr Collins. She admits that she is 'not romantic' and asks only for 'a comfortable home'. Of course Mr Collins's company is 'irksome', but in her eyes the state of marriage, as a 'preservative from want', is much more important than the actual man who makes up the marriage. As Elizabeth realises when she sees them married, Charlotte will survive by having recourse to selective inattention, deriving satisfaction from the house and screening out as far as possible the man who provided it. Elizabeth's spontaneous reaction when told of their coming marriage is, 'Impossible', but her remark is not only indecorous: it is excessive. In such a society, the need for an 'establishment' is a very real one, and in putting prudence before passion Charlotte is only doing what the economic realities of her society – as Jane Austen makes abundantly clear – all but force her to do.

Indeed passion, as such, is hardly differentiated from folly in the terms of the book. Lydia's elopement is seen as thoughtless and foolish and selfish, rather than a *grande passion*; while Mr Bennet's premature captivation by Mrs Bennet's youth and beauty is 'imprudence'. This is a key word. Mrs Gardiner warns Elizabeth against becoming involved with the impoverished Wickham, yet when it seems he will marry a Miss King for her money she describes him as 'mercenary'. As Elizabeth asks, 'what is the difference in matrimonial affairs, between the mercenary motive and the prudent motive?' Elizabeth will simply not accept Charlotte's solution as a model of true 'prudence', nor will we. There must be something between that kind of prudence and her father's imprudence. And one of the things the book sets out to do is to define a rationally based 'mode of attachment' – something between the exclusively sexual and the entirely mercenary. Thus words such as 'gratitude' and 'esteem' are used to describe Elizabeth's growing feeling for Darcy. She comes to feel that their union would have been 'to the advantage of both: by her ease and liveliness, his mind might have softened, his manners improved; and from his judgement, information, and knowledge of the world, she must have received benefit of greater importance'. A word to note there is 'advantage': consciousness has penetrated so far into emotions that love *follows* calculations and reflections. What differentiates Elizabeth's choice from Charlotte's is not its greater impetuosity – indeed, it is Charlotte who is the more precipitate. It is the fact that it is a free choice which is not dictated by economic pressure (though Pemberley is a great attraction, as she readily admits); and it is a choice which is based on more awareness, knowledge, and intelligence than Charlotte brings to her cool but instant capitulation. Elizabeth loves for the best reasons, and there are always reasons for loving in Jane Austen's world. Consider this sentence from Tolstoy's *Resurrection*: 'Nekhludov's offer of marriage was based on generosity and knowledge of what had happened in the past, but Simonson loved her as he found her; *he loved her simply because he loved her*' (emphasis added). Tolstoy takes in a far wider world than Jane Austen, both socially and emotionally. He knew that there are feelings of such intensity, directness and tenacity that they reduce language to tautology when it attempts to evoke them. The kind of emotion pointed to in the remarkable clause I have emphasised – not to be confused with lust, for this is far from being a purely sexual attraction – is a kind of emotion which is not conceived of, or taken into account, in Jane Austen's world. This is not to censure Jane Austen for blinkered vision. It is, rather, to point out that in her books, and thus in the society they reflect, emotion is either rational – capable of being both conceptualised and verbalised – or it is folly.

And yet we sense that there is a capacity for depths and animations of feeling in Elizabeth which is not allowed for in the above description of the 'rationally founded' emotions preferred by Jane Austen. It is that extra something which dances through her words conveying an emotional as well as a semantic energy; it is what glows from her eyes and brings the blood to her cheeks so often; it is what sends her running across the fields and jumping over stiles when she hears that Jane is ill at Netherfield. After this last piece of anxious exertion she is said to look 'almost wild', and there in fact we have the beginning of a problem. The word 'wild' is applied to Elizabeth – and to Lydia, and to Wickham. In the case of the last two named, 'wildness' obviously has nothing to recommend it and is seen as totally and reprehensibly anti-social. Elizabeth's special quality is more often referred to as 'liveliness'; this is what Darcy is said to lack (his understanding – i.e. rational consciousness – is apparently impeccable), and it is the main quality that Elizabeth will bring to the marriage. It is a fine point, and not perhaps a fixed one, at which liveliness becomes wildness, yet the latter is a menace to society, while without the former society is merely dull. Elizabeth is also often described as laughing (she differentiates her state from Jane's by saying, 'she only smiles, I laugh') and laughter is also potentially anarchic, as it can act as a negation of the principles and presuppositions, the rules and rituals, which sustain society. (Her famous declaration, 'I hope I never ridicule what is wise and good. Follies and nonsense, whims and inconsistences, *do* divert me, I own, and I laugh at them whenever I can', puts her in the line of eighteenth-century satirists who worked to uphold certain values and principles by drawing comic attention to deviations from them. But Elizabeth's love of laughter goes beyond the satisfactions of a satirical wit, and she admits to a love of 'absurdities'. A sense of the absurd in life can be very undermining of a belief in society's self-estimation.)

With her liveliness and laughter it is not at first clear that Elizabeth will consent to be contained within the highly structured social space available to her. There is a suggestive episode when Mrs Hurst leaves Elizabeth and joins Darcy and Miss Bingley on a walk. The path only allows three to walk abreast and Darcy is aware of the rudeness of leaving Elizabeth out in this way. He suggests they go to a wider avenue, but Elizabeth 'laughingly answered – "No, no; stay where you are. – You are charmingly group'd, and appear to uncommon advantage. The picturesque would be spoilt by admitting a fourth. Good-bye." She then ran gaily off, rejoicing as she rambled about. . . .' Social rules, like aesthetic prescriptions, tend to fix people in groups. Elizabeth is happy to leave the group, laughing, rambling, rejoicing. It is only a passing incident, but it aptly suggests an independence and liveliness of temperament which will not readily submit to any grouping found to be unacceptably restricting. Marriage is part of the social grouping and is also a restriction. The dream aspect of Pemberley is that it presumably offers an amplitude which, while still social, is large enough to offer a maximum field for expansion of both liveliness and understanding in which they can complement rather than constrain each other, and in which liveliness need never seek to express itself as anti-social wildness.

At one point Elizabeth is said to pass beyond the 'bounds of decorum' and it is part of her attraction that her energy and vitality seem to keep her right on that boundary where the constrained threatens to give way to something less willingly controlled. It is, indeed, just this that attracts Darcy to her, for, while the cold 'critical eye' which he casts on society immediately detects failures of 'perfect symmetry in her form', he is 'caught' by the 'easy playfulness' of her manners, and he stays caught by it. Where there is what Darcy calls 'real superiority of mind' he maintains that 'pride will always be under good regulation', and throughout his behaviour is a model of regulation. But 'good regulation' is not sufficient for a good society; it is what we expect from an efficient machine, and the danger in the sort of society portrayed by Jane Austen is a tendency away from the organic towards the mechanical. (Thus Elizabeth finds out that the 'civilities' of Sir William Lucas are 'worn out, like his information'. With his empty repetitions Sir William is a dim adumbration of some of Dickens's more memorable automata.) In a society that is still alive there will always be some awareness of, and pull towards, those qualities which that society has had to exclude in order to maintain itself. Ralph Ellison puts the idea in its sharpest form when the narrator of *The Invisible Man* asserts that 'the mind that has conceived a plan of living must never lose sight of the chaos against which that pattern was conceived'. It would be foolish indeed to pronounce Elizabeth as a spirit of chaos with Darcy as the incarnation of pattern. (Indeed, in many ways Elizabeth is the best citizen, for she brings real life to the values and principles to which too many of the others only pay lip service, or which they mechanically observe in a spirit of torpid conformity.) But in their gradual coming together and Darcy's persistent desire for Elizabeth we do witness the perennial yearning of perfect symmetry for the asymmetrical, the appeal which 'playfulness' has for 'regulation', the irresistible attraction of the freely rambling individual for the rigidified upholder of the group. Indeed, it could be said that it is on the tension between playfulness and regulation that society depends, and it is the fact that Elizabeth and Darcy are so happily 'united' by the end of the book which generates the satisfaction produced by the match.

'Uniting them' are the last two words of the book, and we do, I suggest, witness apparently mutually exclusive qualities coming into unity during the course of the book. Elizabeth at one point, in the presence of the insupportable Mr Collins, is said to try to 'unite truth and civility in a few short sentences'. The casual phrase is a passing reminder that civility is so often a matter of considerate lying, and another part of Elizabeth's appeal is her determination to hold on to what she refers to as 'the meaning of principle and integrity'. As Jane Austen shows, it is not always possible to unite civility and truth in this society, and the fact that there is often a dichotomy between the two produces that mixture of outward conformity and inner anguish experienced by her more sensitive characters. Pemberley is, once again, that dream place where such unities are possible. Given the importance of Elizabeth's 'playfulness' – for Darcy, for society, for the book – there is perhaps something too abject in her self-accusing retraction and apology to Darcy near the end. Although Darcy concedes to Elizabeth that 'By you I was properly humbled', we may feel that she is somewhat too willing to abandon her 'playfulness'. (For example, she redefines her 'liveliness' of mind as 'impertinence'.) There is the famous moment near the end when Elizabeth is about to make an ironical remark at Darcy's expense, 'but she checked herself. She remembered that he had yet to learn to be laughed at, and it was rather too early to begin.' One might be prompted to speculate whether Darcy will learn to laugh at himself (as the sentence half promises) or whether this is just the first of many and more serious checks and repressions which Elizabeth will be obliged to impose on herself as she takes her place in the social group.

But this is a happy book and we are not shown the wilting of playfulness under the force of regulation, but rather a felicitous 'uniting' of both. In 1813 Jane Austen wrote to Cassandra about *Pride and Prejudice*,

> I had had some fits of disgust. . . . The work is rather too light, and bright, and sparkling; it wants shade, it wants to be stretched out here and there with a long chapter of sense, if it could be had; if not, of solemn specious nonsense, about

something unconnected with the story; an essay on writing, a critique on Walter Scott, or the history of Buonaparte or anything that would form a contrast, and bring the reader with increased delight to the playfulness and epigrammatism of the general style. I doubt your quite agreeing with me here. I know your starched notions.

Some critics have taken this as indicating Jane Austen's repudiation of her own light, bright, sparkling qualities; and it is true that, in going on to write about Fanny Price in *Mansfield Park*, Jane Austen turned to a heroine not only in a different plight, but of a very different disposition, while giving all the 'playfulness' to the socially unreliable and ultimately undesirable Mary Crawford. And there is no doubt that there is a diminishing of playfulness, a growing suspicion of unsocialised energy, in Jane Austen's subsequent work. Nevertheless I do not think this letter should be taken too seriously as an omen of repression to come. It is in fact ironical at the expense of books stuffed with the sort of sententiousness which Mary Bennet delights to quote, or the meandering digressions which could be found in many of the less well-formed works of the day. Jane Austen's disparagement of playfulness is here, surely mock-disparagement. She is herself still being 'sparkling', and if her later works grow more sombre in tone we may yet be glad that she gave us this one novel in which the brightness and the sparkle of the heroine's individuality are not sacrificed to the exacting decorums or the manipulative persuasions of the social group. Elizabeth Bennet says she is 'checked', but we shall always remember her as laughing.

As it can be seen, we are in the proximity of a major problem here: namely, that of the relationship and adjustment between individual energy and social forms. If one were to make a single binary reduction about literature, one could say that there are works which stress the existence of, and need for, boundaries; and works which concentrate on everything within the individual – from the sexual to the imaginative and the religious – which conspires to negate or transcend boundaries. Looking back at the terms of Charlotte Brontë's criticisms of *Pride and Prejudice* quoted at the start of this chapter, we notice a preponderant vocabulary of boundaries – 'accurate', 'carefully fenced, highly cultivated gardens', 'neat borders', 'elegant but confined houses'. Her own impulse is towards the 'open country' and the boundless 'air', as the whole progress of her aptly named Jane Eyre reveals. In the eighteenth century, however, the stress was on the need for, or inevitability of, boundaries. Thus Locke in the first chapter of his *Essay Concerning Human Understanding*:

> I suspected we began at the wrong end, and in vain sought for satisfaction in a quiet and sure possession of truths that most concerned us, while we let loose our thoughts into the vast ocean of Being; as if all that boundless extent were the natural and undoubted possession of our understandings, wherein there was nothing exempt from its decisions, or that escaped its comprehension. . . . Whereas, were the capacities of our understandings well considered, the extent of our knowledge once discovered, and the horizon found which sets the bounds between the enlightened and dark parts of things – between what is and what is not comprehensible by us – men would perhaps with less scruple acquiesce in the avowed ignorance of the one, and employ their thoughts and discourse with more advantage and satisfaction in the other.

And thus Hume:

> Nothing, at first view, may seem more unbounded than the thought of man, which not only escapes all human power and authority, but is not even restrained within the limits of nature and reality. . . . And while the body is confined to one planet, along which it creeps with pain and difficulty; the thought can in an instant transport us into the most distant regions of the universe; or even beyond the universe, into the unbounded chaos, where nature is supposed to lie in total confusion. . . . But though our thought seems to possess this unbounded liberty, we shall find, upon a nearer examination, that it is really confined within very narrow limits, and that all this creative power of the mind amounts to no more than the faculty of compounding, transposing, augmenting, or diminishing the materials afforded us by the senses and experience.

By turning the negative words in these passages into positive ones, and vice versa, one could begin to establish a basic vocabulary to describe the very different kind of epistemology posited by the whole movement we know as Romantic. 'The vast ocean of Being', 'the most distant regions of the universe', even 'the unbounded chaos, where nature is supposed to lie in total confusion' – these were the very realms the Romantic imagination set out to explore; for it *did* claim for itself 'unbounded liberty' and refused to accept the notion that man and his mind are 'really confined within very narrow limits'. Locke invites us, in the interests of sanity, to recognise and accept the 'horizon' which 'sets the bounds between the enlightened and dark parts of things'. Blake took the word 'horizon', transformed it into 'Urizen' and made that figure the evil symbol of all that restricted and restrained man. He thus stood the Enlightenment on its head, and, if it was at the cost of his sanity, then, like other Romantics, he preferred to enjoy the visionary intensities of his 'madness' rather than subscribe to the accepted notions of mental health. Other Romantics too have preferred to cross that horizon and boundary and explore 'the dark parts of things', and often they have found this sphere to be full of dazzling illuminations.

This is not the place to embark on a summary of the Romantic movement. The point is that Jane Austen was brought up on eighteenth-century thought and was fundamentally loyal to the respect for limits, definition and clear ideas which it inculcated. Yet among writers who published work the same year as *Pride and Prejudice* were Byron, Coleridge, Scott and Shelley; the *Lyrical Ballads* were already over a decade old, and Keats would publish four years later. Jane Austen was writing at a time when a major shift of sensibility was taking place, as indeed major social changes were taking place or were imminent, and to some extent she was certainly aware of this. She had depicted at least one incipient Romantic in the figure of Marianne Dashwood in *Sense and Sensibility*, and her treatment is a rather ambiguous mixture of sympathy and satire. In the figure of Elizabeth Bennet she shows us energy attempting to find a valid mode of existence within society. One more quotation from Blake will enable me to conclude the point I am trying to make. In the *Marriage of Heaven and Hell* Blake writes, 'Energy is the only life, and is from the Body; and Reason is the bound or outward circumference of

Energy. Energy is eternal Delight.' As I have said, I think that Jane Austen's suspicion of energy increased in her later work. But in *Pride and Prejudice* she shows us energy and reason coming together, not so much as a reconciliation of opposites, but as a marriage of complementaries. She makes it seem as if it is possible for playfulness and regulation – energy and boundaries – to be united in fruitful harmony, without the one being sacrificed to the other. Since to stress one at the expense of the other can either way mean loss, both to the self and to society, the picture of achieved congruence between them offered in *Pride and Prejudice* is of unfading relevance. It is perhaps no wonder that it has also proved capable of giving eternal delight.

# 5

# The Quiet Thing:
## *Mansfield Park*

Many great novels concern themselves with characters whose place in society is not fixed or assured. Foundlings, orphans, outsiders, people moving from one country to another, people moving from one class to another, those who have to create the shape of their lives as they go along, or those who find themselves involved in movements or changes over which they have only partial control – such people are common frequenters of the novel. Whether you think of Tom Jones, or Julien Sorel (in *Le Rouge et le noir*), or Becky Sharp (in *Vanity Fair*), or Jude Fawley (in *Jude the Obscure*), or Isabel Archer (in *The Portrait of a Lady*), or Paul Morel (in *Sons and Lovers*), or even of Saul Bellow's Augie March, these are all characters who at the start of the novel are not defined or fulfilled by their status or locality or position. They cannot and do not take their place in society for granted, and they end up – whether happily or otherwise – with a different social identity. In the course of such novels there has been choice and change. The characters might have their virtue ultimately rewarded, like Tom Jones; or their ambitions thwarted, like Jude; or they may be imprisoned by the hateful consequences of their own errors, like Isabel Archer. In every case we can generally say that we are watching the initially undefined and uncommitted self having to take on definition through what happens to it in society. The self may be able to choose what happens, it may simply permit it, or it may have to suffer it: its quest for definition may entail true discovery of the self, and it may finally precipitate destruction of the self. But, whatever else happens to these characters, they have moved. They are not where they were; they are not what they were. And so it is with Fanny Price, the heroine of *Mansfield Park*.

Fanny starts her life in a very lower-middle-class family in Portsmouth: we last see her effectively accepted as the mistress of

Mansfield Park. Initially an object of charity, she ends up cherished as the indispensable mainstay of the Mansfield family. With her final marriage and full social and familial recognition, her self is successfully and rightfully defined. And yet Fanny Price exhibits few of the qualities we usually associate with the traditional hero or heroine. We expect them to have vigour and vitality: Fanny is weak and sickly. We look to them for a certain venturesomeness or audacity, a bravery, a resilience, even a recklessness; but Fanny is timid, silent, unassertive, shrinking and excessively vulnerable. Above all, perhaps, we expect heroes and heroines to be active, rising to opposition, resisting coercion, asserting their own energy; but Fanny is almost totally passive. Indeed, one of the strange aspects of this singular book is that, regarded externally, it is the story of a girl who triumphs by doing nothing. She sits, she waits, she endures; and, when she is finally promoted, through marriage, into an unexpectedly high social position, it seems to be a reward not so much for her vitality as for her extraordinary immobility. This is odd enough; yet there is another unusual and even less sympathetic aspect to this heroine. She is never, ever, wrong. Jane Austen, usually so ironic about her heroines, in this instance vindicates Fanny Price without qualification. We are used to seeing heroes and heroines confused, fallible, error-prone. But Fanny always thinks, feels, speaks and behaves exactly as she ought. Every other character in the book, without exception, falls into error – some fall irredeemably. But not Fanny. She does not put a foot wrong. Indeed, she hardly risks any steps at all: as we shall see, there is an intimate and significant connection between her virtue and her immobility. The result of these unusual traits has been to make her a very unpopular heroine. Even sympathetic readers have often found her something of a prig, and severer strictures have not been lacking. Kingsley Amis calls her 'a monster of complacency and pride'. It is not as though Jane Austen could not create attractive heroines: Elizabeth Bennet and Emma Woodhouse are among the most beloved figures in English fiction. But nobody falls in love with Fanny Price. What, then, was Jane Austen doing in this book? The question is worth asking because, if Fanny Price is her least popular heroine, it is arguable that *Mansfield Park* is her most profound novel (indeed, to my mind, it is one of the most profound novels of the nineteenth century). And what such a poor sort of heroine is doing in such a great book is a matter worth examining with some care.

To grasp the full meaning of the various characters and incidents, it is important to understand the world of the novel and be alert to the significant differences between life in Portsmouth, life in London, and life at Mansfield Park. And in connection with this it might be worth reminding ourselves what England was like in the years 1811–13, the very eve of Waterloo, when Jane Austen was writing the novel. In general we can see that it was a period of great stability just about to give way to a time of unimagined changes. At that time most of the population (some 13 million) were involved in rural and agricultural work; yet within another twenty years the majority of Englishmen became urban dwellers involved with industry, and the great railway age had begun. Throughout the early years of the century the cities were growing at a great rate; the network of canals was completed, the main roads were being remade. Regency London, in particular, boomed and became, among other things, a great centre of fashion. On the other hand, England in 1813 was still predominantly a land of country towns and villages, a land of rural routines which were scarcely touched by the seven campaigns of the Peninsular War against Napoleon. The Prime Minister was the unremarkable Lord Liverpool and politics were still dominated by the aristocracy and landed gentry, with only a few spokesmen for the new commercial and manufacturing interests. Their main general concern was the possibility of French 'Jacobinism' spreading among the discontented lower classes in England. There was not a lot of difference between the Tory and the Whig parties. The Tory party was more conservative, almost totally opposed to any sort of popular radicalism and political reform; it was the party of the Church of England and identified itself with tradition, continuity, order and an aristocratic attachment to the land. The Whigs were a little closer to the City and business interests, and they wanted some reforms in the system of government which would lessen the power of the landed interest. Since the question of attitude towards traditional rural life is important in Jane Austen, it is worth drawing on a quotation from William Cobbett which reveals the emergence of a new, and wrong, type of landowner. Cobbett often stressed the difference between a resident *native* gentry, attached to the soil, known to every farmer and labourer from their childhood, frequently mixing with them in those pursuits where all artificial distinctions are lost, practising hospitality without ceremony, from habit and not on calculation; and a gentry only now-and-then resident at all, having no relish for country delights, foreign in their manners, distant and haughty in their behaviour, looking to the soil only for its rents, viewing it as a mere object of speculation, unacquainted with its cultivators, despising them and their pursuits, and relying, for influence, not upon the good will of the vicinage, but upon the dread of their power.

The figure in Jane Austen's work who most nearly fits this description of Cobbett's is Sir Walter Elliot in *Persuasion*, who 'rents' his country house – Kellynch Hall. Jane Austen was clearly aware of the culpable dereliction of social (and familial) duties and responsibilities which this action entails. (See the chapter on *Persuasion*.) Jane Austen, the daughter of a Tory parson, valued the old rural way of life, and she too was well aware of a new attitude abroad in the land – speculative, acquisitive, calculating and irreverent. In Mansfield Park quite a lot can be told about people from their differing attitudes to rural life. If Jane Austen does seem to have lived a life of placid rural seclusion in north Hampshire, she was at the same time very aware of a whole range of new energies and impulses, new ideas and powers, which were changing or about to change England – and indeed the whole Western world – with a violence, a suddenness and a heedlessness which would soon make Jane Austen's world seem as remote as the Elizabethan Age. It is well to remember that a few years later, when Thomas Arnold saw his first train tearing through the countryside near Rugby, he said, 'Feudality is gone forever.' So close was it possible then to feel to the immemorial, static feudal way of life; so quickly was that way of life to vanish as the modern world laboured to be born. Jane Austen, then, was living in a diminishing enclave of traditional rural stability just prior to a period of convulsive, uncontrollable change. I think that is important to remember when we read *Mansfield Park*, which, among other things, is a novel about rest and restlessness, stability and change – the moving and the immovable.

Seen against this general background, what, then, is the larger significance of the three major areas or 'worlds' in the novel – Mansfield Park, London and Portsmouth? Mansfield Park (based on Cottesbrooke) is set in the county of Northampton and is effectively a stronghold of the old rural Tory values. Growing up inside this world and exposed to the shortcomings of its inhabitants, Fanny does not really comprehend the symbolic value of Mansfield Park until she returns to visit her birthplace in Portsmouth. The contrast throws the differing values of each world into clear relief. The house in Portsmouth is 'the abode of noise, disorder, and impropriety. Nobody was in their right place, nothing was done as it ought to be.' Her father is a dirty, boorish drinker; her mother, an incompetent, ill-judging slattern. The children are brought up wrongly in as much as they are brought up at all. Here there is no real affection, no true delicacy of feeling, no harmony or coherence of behaviour. As Fanny's brother William says so suggestively, 'The house is always in confusion.' It is not a place of vice, but a place of chaos. Nothing has been done to shape and restrain life into any decency or decorum. Human impulses here are not perverted; but they are unregulated.

It should be noted that the prose used to describe the Portsmouth household is – to my mind – the most violent Jane Austen ever used. People 'rush' and 'push'; children 'squabble' and 'kick'; it is all 'mismanagement and discomfort'. The 'smallness of the house' is constantly emphasised, and the 'thinness of the walls' is stressed. The noise is constant and all-pervasive; everybody is always in everybody else's way. 'Nobody sat still' – 'motion', of the most mindless sort, is perpetual. Fanny is 'shocked' and 'stunned'. Appropriately, for she is the veritable incarnation of the virtues of 'stillness', the profoundest instinctive critic of thoughtless 'motion'. In this she is a crucial representative of values which Jane Austen saw as essential to the proper preservation of society. The disintegrative dangers of thoughtless 'motion' loom larger – and darker – in her work, to culminate in the total social chaos of *Sanditon*. It is notable that Fanny 'was very anxious to be useful', but at Portsmouth she cannot fully exercise that influence for regularity and propriety which is effectively to save Mansfield. Significantly, she is at first almost invisible – 'it is so dark you do

not see her', says William to her father, who indeed never truly
'sees' her at all. And notice that it is the 'impropriety' not the
'poverty' of Portsmouth which is stressed. It serves as a model of
everything which society ought not to be and to emphasise the
profound social – and political – importance of 'propriety'. It is
the 'propriety' not the prosperity of Mansfield which now seems
doubly desirable to Fanny. In this house of confusion, Fanny

> could think of nothing by Mansfield, its beloved inmates, its
> happy ways. Every thing where she now was was in full
> contrast to it. The elegance, propriety, regularity, harmony –
> and perhaps, above all, the peace and tranquillity of Mansfield,
> were brought to her remembrance every hour of the day, by the
> prevalence of every thing opposite to them *here*.

Fanny is idealising Mansfield (Mrs Norris, for instance, is nastier
than anyone in the Portsmouth house); but that is only to say that
she is discovering the true symbolic value of all it stands for. It
becomes a house of order, in which there is very little noise and
no unnecessary movement – 'no sounds of contention, no raised
voice, no abrupt bursts, no tread of violence'.

It is important that it is while she is staying at Portsmouth that
the question of which is her true 'home' occurs to Fanny.

> When she had been coming to Portsmouth, she had loved to
> call it her home, had been fond of saying that she was going
> home; the word had been very dear to her; and so it still was,
> but it must be applied to Mansfield. *That* was now the home.
> Portsmouth was Portsmouth; Mansfield was home.

This is important, because, when the uncommitted self finally
chooses its 'home', it is in effect identifying itself with a certain
way of life and a role within it. Throughout *The Portrait of a Lady*,
for example, Isabel Archer is inspecting houses to see whether
she can find one she is willing to call 'home'. Her final choice of
Osmond's sterile little palace of art is a major error; Fanny's
transfer of her allegiances from her actual birthplace to her place
of upbringing is evidence of her capacity for true judgement. She
has found her real, spiritual, 'home'. Very early in the novel,
when there is some chance of Fanny going to live with Mrs

Norris, the insensitive Lady Bertram says to her, 'It can make very little difference to you, whether you are in one house or the other.' But, when houses come to represent edifices of values, as they do in this novel, it makes all the difference in the world. It is entirely right that, when Fanny finally returns to Mansfield Park, soon to become one of its most important guardians, Jane Austen invests the landscape with a verdant, symbolic promise:

> It was three months, full three months, since her quitting it; and the change was from winter to summer. Her eye fell every where on lawns and plantations of the freshest green; and the trees, though not fully clothed, were in that delightful state, when farther beauty is known to be at hand, and when, while much is actually given to the sight, more yet remains for the imagination.

The prospects in the landscape reflect the prospects in Fanny's life.

Mansfield, as a place, as an institution, can take raw material from Portsmouth and refine it – as it does with Fanny, as it effectively does with her brother William (by securing him a career in the navy), as it promises to do with her sister Susan. Indeed, these new recruitments are essential to the maintaining of the 'house' because so many of its actual blood descendants go to the bad and betray their trust. Jane Austen is conceivably making a class point here: without going outside to the unformed world of Portsmouth for fresh potential, the world of Mansfield Park may wither from within. But London, the world of liberty, amusement and fashion, has no redeeming virtues. It is there that Maria falls into the ways which will lead to her adulterous corruption and ultimate disgrace and banishment. It is there that Julia involves herself with the worthless Mr Yates. It is there that Tom wastes his substance and, as a result, nearly loses his life. Above all, it is London that has made and formed the attractive Crawfords, who very nearly bring total ruin to the world of Mansfield Park. For if Mansfield, at its best, perfects people, London, at its worst, perverts them.

It is, significantly, during the absence of Sir Thomas, the patriarchal guardian of Mansfield, that Mary and Henry Crawford arrive, thus suggesting that the absence of the responsible lawgiver of Mansfield Park makes its rural ethos vulnerable to the disruptive forces of a newer, urban, world. We are told that 'his business in Antigua had latterly been prosperously rapid'. This indicates not only that he was making his money from the West Indies sugar trade – rather than his own land – and exploited black labour, probably slaves; it also shows that Jane Austen was aware of the struggles between the English and the French in the West Indies – related to the war – and the crisis in Antigua precipitated by a slump in sugar prices caused by the Napoleonic blockade. It is this crisis which presumably takes Sir Thomas away from Mansfield. This indicates a dangerous split in his loyalties: he believes in the values associated with landed property in England; but also in the financial profits to be made from a trade involved in slavery. It is a reminder of how aware Jane Austen was of the larger pressing issues of her time – such as the war with France and the debates concerning the abolition of slavery – and how flawed and possibly unreliable in his commitments to true English property-class values even a man so apparently firm in his upholding of those values as Sir Thomas is could be. His absence – abdication – from Mansfield at a critical time has larger social and political implications. During his arguably culpable abandonment of his home, the symbolic values of Mansfield are effectively in Fanny's keeping.

From the start the Crawfords are identified with London. As soon as they arrive, Mrs Grant is worried lest they get bored, because they are 'mostly used to London'. They are, indeed, all for amusements, and translated into the rural world of Mansfield their irresponsible taste for distractions becomes a potentially dangerous force. Thus Henry Crawford distracts Julia, seduces Maria and tries to ensnare Fanny; while Mary toys with Tom and all but seduces Edmund from his high-mindedness and his clerical calling. Thus between them they tamper with all the young people who are responsible for the continuance of Mansfield Park; and, as we shall see, it is only Fanny's stubborn tenacity that prevents their complete usurpation and demolition of that world. The Crawfords are far from villains: indeed, Jane Austen had the insight to endow them with many of the most superficially attractive qualities in the book; but they have been spoilt and subtly corrupted by their prolonged immersion in the amoral fashionable London world. (It was, it is worth remembering, the age of Beau Brummell.) Fanny, we read, 'was disposed to think the influence of London very much at war with all respectable attachments'. And so it proves to be in the book. We infer – through the Crawfords – that London is a world of glamour, excitement, activity, amusement and all the attractions of worldly wit and casual relationships; but we also infer that it is a world of endlessly false appearances, a world in which manners substitute for morals, a world given over to cold deception, manipulation and exploitation.

A minor incident, prophetic of the disruptive threat which the Crawfords pose to the life connected with Mansfield, occurs shortly after their arrival. Mary reveals that she had surprising difficulty in trying to hire a cart for the transportation of her harp (fit accessory for the siren she is – Fanny, typically, cannot play a musical instrument). She expresses her rather contemptuous amazement that, because of the harvesting to be done, there was no cart to be had at any price – indeed, that she offended the farmers by expecting to be able to procure one. It is gently pointed out to her how important it is for the farmers to get the harvest in, how impossible it should be that they could spare any carts. Mary answers, 'I shall understand all your ways in time; but coming down with the true London maxim, that every thing is to be got with money, I was a little embarrassed at first by the sturdy independence of your country customs.' Much of the novel is implied here. Mary comes from a world governed only by considerations of money: she has no instinct for the traditional rural ways and values. (It is of course only a further irony – and a sign of grievously impaired social alliances – that her money in fact comes from the land.) She would interfere with the harvest to satisfy a whim. The point is, will those country customs be sturdy enough to resist her London manners and her London code? The issue is raised another way when Mary's sister, Mrs Grant, chides her for her worldly standards and her bantering manner: 'You are as bad as your brother, Mary; but we will cure you both. Mansfield shall cure you both – and without any taking in. Stay with us and we will cure you.' Can Mansfield cure what has been spoilt by London; or will the products of London finally undermine all that Mansfield strives to perpetuate? The novel thus reveals a battle between worlds as well as concentrating on the relationships of a few characters. Without any crude allegorising – indeed, with a minute attention to local detail – Jane Austen has produced a story which touches profoundly on the past and future of England itself. And, if, in the novel, she allowed the world of Mansfield to triumph, even though she sensed that the future belonged to London, then that is something we must consider later.

We can now consider the various characters from the point of view of their varying relationships with Mansfield Park. We may group them thus: the guardians, the inheritors and the interlopers. Fanny we shall consider separately. Sir Thomas is of course the chief guardian. He believes in 'duty' and is (up to a point) just, benevolent and responsible. In his absence Mansfield Park falls into confusion; after his return, order is reimposed. It is he who finally signals Fanny's real reception into the family by ordering a fire to be put in her cold room. But, nearly all his children go wrong and it is made clear that he is not blameless: 'though a truly anxious father, he was not outwardly affectionate, and the reserve of his manner repressed all the flow of their spirits before him'. Worse, he entrusts their upbringing to Mrs Norris, which must be accounted a major failure of judgement; hence his relief when she finally leaves Mansfield Park: 'she seemed a part of himself' – that is, she has been like a cancer he has permitted to grow in his own family, in his own mind. Clearing his mind involves cutting her away. It is a mark of his increased self-knowledge that he comes to see where he has been at fault in the education of his children. He has cared about their 'elegance and accomplishments' but has been negligent of any 'moral effect on the mind'. 'He had meant them to be good, but his cares had been directed to the understanding and manners, not the disposition; and of the necessity of self-denial and humility, he feared they had never heard from any lips that could profit them.' Not only is he cold and remote: his domestic instincts are corrupted by mercenary considerations. He allows Maria to marry Mr Rushworth, though he knows him to be a fool, because he is very rich. Worse, he tries to force Fanny to marry Henry Crawford against her will because it would be such a fine match. It is not that he is a cruel tyrant; but he is lacking in an important quality. As Fanny muses after he has exerted pressure on her to marry Crawford, 'He who had married a daughter to Mr Rushworth. Romantic delicacy was certainly not to be expected from him.' An adherence to duty is insufficient if it is not tempered by a sense of delicacy. With his repressive, indelicate inflexibility, Sir Thomas nearly brings about the ruin of Mansfield Park, and it is only at the end that he finds himself truly 'sick of ambitious and mercenary connections' and more and more appreciative of 'the sterling good of principle and temper'. Yet he does also represent the values of Mansfield, although it is only Fanny who can properly appreciate this. When the other children complain of the gloom Sir Thomas brings into the house, Fanny says, 'I think he values the very quietness you speak of, and that the repose of his family-circle is all he wants.' In standing for 'quietness' and 'repose', Sir Thomas is upholding two of the major values in the world of the book.

Lady Bertram is a travesty of those values. She is utterly inert, unaware, and entirely incapable of volition, effort or independent judgement. She is of course an immensely amusing character; but she also reveals the Mansfield values run to seed. In effect, she never thinks, moves, or cares: amiable enough in that she is not malicious, she is, in her insentient indolence, useless as a guardian of Mansfield Park and positively culpable as a parent. And it is her sofa-bound inertia which permits the ascendancy of Mrs Norris. Lady Bertram does not represent quietness and repose so much as indifference and collapse. Mrs Norris is one of Jane Austen's most impressive creations and indeed one of the most plausibly odious characters in fiction. Pretending, perhaps believing herself, to be one of the guardians of Mansfield, she most nearly contrives its destruction through her arid selfishness, and her stupid and vicious interferences and meddlings. In her combination of malice and menace she is the nearest thing to real evil in the world of the book. That such a figure should have attained such a position of influence in Mansfield is a damning comment on the current state of guardianship. It is she who arranges Maria's disastrous marriage; it is she who is responsible for the superficial and unprincipled education of the Bertram children. And above all it is she who persecutes Fanny with remorseless malevolence and unmotivated hatred – as though she had an instinctive loathing for all guileless sincerity. Mrs Norris is far too addicted to 'arranging' things – often cruelly, always wrongly; her mean, officious ways are so devoid of delicacy and affection that they usually promote discomfort or disaster. If Lady Bertram represents the wrong kind of quietness, Mrs Norris reveals very much the wrong sort of administration. It is a comment on the internal deterioration of Mansfield Park that it takes so long to expel Mrs Norris; and she only goes when the healing presence of Fanny finally becomes dominant in the house.

Under such guardians it is hardly surprising that the legitimate inheritors go wrong, since they have not been brought up to respect and maintain their heritage. Tom, the eldest son, dissipates his energy in racing and generally gadding about. His life is not at all 'self-denying' and it takes a nearly fatal illness to bring him to some consciousness of true Mansfield values: 'He had suffered, and he had learnt to think, two advantages that he had never known before. . . . He became what he ought to be, useful to his father, steady and quiet, and not living merely for himself.' Maria and Julia suffer from the bad influence of Mrs Norris: they are 'entirely deficient in the less common acquirements of self-knowledge, generosity, and humility'. With Maria, Mrs Norris's favourite, the rot goes deepest. Mansfield Park merely signifies repression to her flighty mind, while she makes her foolish marriage for entirely base reasons. As Jane Austen makes clear in one of her most bitterly ironic passages,

In all the important preparations of the mind she was complete; being prepared for matrimony by an hatred of home, restraint, and tranquillity; by the misery of disappointed affection, and contempt of the man she was to marry. The rest might wait.

It is worth noting that all the characters who go wrong share a distaste for 'tranquillity'. It is harsh but fitting that Maria should end up in a little hell with Mrs Norris. Julia elopes with a trivial man but she is perhaps redeemable, since 'education had not given her so very hurtful a degree of self-consequence'. Edmund is the most nearly perfect inheritor. He is quite sincere in his desire to be ordained and wishes to devote himself to true Christian activities. He it is, alone in the family, who takes pity on Fanny and helps to educate her properly. He is indeed quite as solemn and committed to piety as Fanny – yet he too is flawed. He is deceived by the surface attractiveness of the Crawfords; he finally succumbs to the theatricals and agrees to take a part; he is blind enough to Mary's faults to imagine himself in love with her. And, in Fanny's hour of need, he too deserts her and tries to persuade her to marry Henry Crawford. It is only after much tribulation that he recognises Fanny as his true mate. But for her, *all* the inheritors would have gone astray.

The interlopers are in many ways the most interesting characters in the book, and in depicting them Jane Austen reveals her great insight. For in making them attractive and investing them with many engaging qualities she shows how subtle their threat is, how intimately it is bound up with characteristics which we all like and respond to. (More than one critic has suggested that Mary Crawford, with her quick wit, her vitality and resilience, is much more like Jane Austen herself than is the shrinking Fanny.) We must examine the Crawfords' qualities carefully and see where they shade off into faults. From the start 'the manners of both were lively and pleasant', and they soon become the indispensable centre of all the gay goings-on at Mansfield Park during Sir Thomas's absence. Perhaps the first thing to stress is that they are both associated with movement, the unhindered expenditure of energy. They have the wealth and the vitality to scorn limits and limitations. They dislike 'quiet' and the absence of distraction. Mary reveals much of her temperament when she takes to horse-riding, for she is soon going at an exhilarating canter. Indeed, the hint is there that her taste for movement is excessive: 'Miss Crawford's enjoyment of riding was such, that she did not know how to leave off.' As she herself confesses, she only feels 'alive' when she is doing something. Similarly, Henry is a keen hunter, and, more generally, 'to any thing like a permanence of abode, or limitation of society, Henry Crawford had, unluckily, a great dislike'. In addition they both have 'lively' minds, and are accomplished, witty, amusing talkers. Neither mentally nor physically do they like to be still. They are both 'active and fearless' in a way which, initially, is decidedly attractive. Where then are the faults?

In a general way we can say that their energy has become divorced from any moral guidance or control: they respond to the opportunities of the world but they are deaf to the claims of principle. Mary, for instance, regards marriage as 'a manœuvring business' and, a true Londoner, thinks that 'a large income is the best recipe for happiness I ever heard of'. More serious is her contempt for the profession of clergyman: she thinks it insignificant socially, and cannot believe that anyone could choose it out of a sincere sense of vocation. Since she is attracted to Edmund, she does all she can to tease, mock and seduce him from his high calling. When she finds he is still intent on ordination she is angry and sets out to harden herself against him. Worldly considerations distort her emotional instincts. She is indeed frankly selfish and ambitious: 'It is every body's duty to do as well for themselves as they can.' She can simulate affection and devotion but, as Fanny sees, she is 'careless as a woman and a friend'. This 'carelessness' finally reveals itself to Edmund after Henry has run away with Maria, since Mary blames them only for their 'folly' and cares nothing for the actual evil. Indeed, she even has suggestions as to how 'appearances' may be preserved. She has no feeling for the underlying realities. As Edmund says, 'This is what the world does.' When she makes one final effort to seduce Edmund with an inviting 'saucy playful smile', she is revealed as the purely worldly creature that she is. She is superb in the world of 'appearances', but as a moral essence she does not exist. She is not a conscious villain, more a product of her world. As Fanny can discern, Mary has a mind 'led astray and bewildered, and without any suspicion of being so; darkened, yet fancying itself light'.

Henry is comparably 'careless', 'thoughtless and selfish from prosperity and bad example'. He is not 'in the habit of examining his motives' and he regards other people only as they may provide 'an amusement to his sated mind'. He too is addicted to 'change and moving about'; he too has a 'corrupted mind' and mocks those who are concerned about genuine virtue. As Fanny says to herself, 'he can feel nothing as he ought'. What is most interesting is his attitude to Fanny. He starts by coolly deciding to make her love him and then break her heart – just for his own amusement. Then he finds he is seriously attracted to her, drawn perhaps by a quality and depth of sincerity he has never known. He presses her to marry him and does so in a manner which convinces the world of his sincerity. Yet Fanny is always aware of the element of selfishness in his apparently disinterested love. She sees, more subtly, that in fact he is really amusing himself by *playing* at being the honest devoted suitor. He is acting, albeit unconsciously. There is no genuine depth and staying power in his love, as is revealed by his sudden reversion to an old flirtation with Maria out of idle 'curiosity'. His relapse into adultery is a reversion to his true self. I shall return to the importance of 'acting' in this novel. Here let us just realise what would have happened to the world of Mansfield Park if Fanny and Edmund had succumbed to Henry and Mary Crawford – with their centreless energy, their taste for movement untrammelled by morals, their world-darkened minds, and their insincere hearts.

It is next to the ebullient Crawfords that we must try to appreciate Fanny's stillness, quietness, weakness and self-retraction. Her weakness, which is almost a sickness (she has to be lifted on to her horse, which, moreover, never canters when *she* is on it), we must attempt to understand by bearing in mind that, as Lionel Trilling has pointed out, the traditional Christian heroine is often depicted as sickly, enfeebled, even dying – as in *Clarissa* or *The Wings of the Dove*. It is a way of showing that she is not quite at home in the world, that she cannot compete with its rampant appetitive energies. In Fanny's case this weakness is also a token of the exhaustion and strain she incurs through her 'heroism of principle'. In her stillness she is not inactive: on the contrary, she is often holding on strenuously to standards and values which others all around her are thoughtlessly abandoning. Typically she welcomes the 'tranquillity' made possible by Mansfield Park at its best. She is content to remain apart, silent, unnoticed, out of the 'festivities'. Whereas Mary is a distinctly forward woman, always in her element in the arena of society, Fanny is marked by 'natural shyness'. Indeed, when all the others complain of the dullness which comes over the house after Sir Thomas returns, she defends it, saying, 'There must be a sort of shyness.' To appreciate the full implications of this we should bear in mind a late remark of Jane Austen's: 'What is become of all the shyness in the world?' By which she clearly means not a false modesty but a true unassertive reticence of soul. A selflessness; a quietness.

Fanny's position in Mansfield Park is at first ambiguous. Mary asks, 'Is she out, or is she not?' She means, has she officially come out into society, and in the widest sense the answer is that, although she is involved in it, she is never wholly a part of it. This is the significance of her little cold room at the far end of the house, to which she often retires and where she reads or meditates and communes with herself. It implies that she is not, at first, considered an integral part of the home. In a way there is a little of the artist about her: she speaks for the value of literature, of memory, of fancy; she alone reveals a true appreciation of nature. More important, she is in a way the supreme consciousness of the society she moves in. Like many Jamesian figures, she does not fully participate in the world but as a result she sees things more clearly and accurately than those who do. As Edmund says, 'Fanny is the only one who has judged rightly throughout, who has been consistent.' She prefers custom and habit to novelty and innovation, and her resolute immobility, frail and beset though it is, is a last gesture of resistance against the corrosions of unfettered impulse and change. She stands for the difficulty of delicate right thinking in a world of inadequate perception and subtly corrupted instincts. Her toils and her triumphs are all mental and moral. She suffers to be still in a world where pleasure seems to lie in release and movement. If she is vindicated it is only after much pain, for Jane Austen suggests that Fanny has to go through all 'the vicissitudes of the human mind'. But she remains firm . Her immobility, her refusal to be 'moved' are not symptoms of mule-like stubbornness or paralysed fear, but a measure of her integrity, her adherence to her own clear evaluation of how things stand. She speaks for the 'inner light' in a world of falling worldly standards. As she says to Henry Crawford (who instinctively comes to her for advice and approval), 'We have all a better guide in ourselves, if we would attend to it, than any other person can be.' We can see her as a lonely conscience – ignored, despised, bullied, at times besieged by the forces of worldly persuasion, yet finally recognised as the true preserver of the values represented by Mansfield Park. Her real significance is made apparent when Sir Thomas realises that 'Fanny was indeed the daughter that he wanted.' She is the true inheritor of Mansfield Park.

The characters, of course, reveal their inner qualities by their actions, and it is worth stressing the extraordinary skill with which Jane Austen describes the various incidents so that a meticulous surface accuracy carries at the same time a subtle symbolic power. She was indeed unusually meticulous and went to great pains to get her details correct. For instance, she checked that there were actually hedgerows of a certain kind in

Northamptonshire before deciding not to mention them in the book; she clearly used a calendar to get all the days and dates correct; she took the names of actual contemporary ships; and so on. Yet she can make the details of the comparatively uneventful country life she describes convey deep meanings and reveal crucial aspects of her characters. For example, the card game in chapter 25. The game is called 'Speculation' and during the game the real 'speculators' in that world reveal themselves. Fanny, significantly, 'had never played the game nor seen it played in her life'. Henry tries to involve her in the game 'to inspirit her play, sharpen her avarice, and harden her heart', but in the game, as in life, Fanny resists his urgings and compulsions. Henry is of course very good at the game and teaches it to other people, much as he so suavely meddles with other people's lives. Mary plays a daring, rash game which has many innuendos indicative of her particular outlook and temperament. After winning a round at 'an exorbitant rate' she says, 'There, I will stake my last like a woman of spirit. No cold prudence for me. I am not born to sit still and do nothing. If I lose the game, it shall not be from not striving for it.' As in all things she prefers action to prudence. 'The game was her's, and only did not pay her for what she had given to secure it.' That deceptively simple sentence goes to the heart of Mary Crawford. She is indeed one of those who wins the stakes and finds that the game was not worth the candle. One can think of her as winning the world at the too-high price of losing her soul. Ultimately all her energy is misspent. In such ways does Jane Austen make an ephemeral incident such as a card game reflect the hidden dispositions and drives of the participants (compare Henry James's use of the card game at a crucial point in *The Golden Bowl*).

We could similarly explore the symbolic significance of the moment when Fanny finds 'a fire lighted and burning' in her room. Again, we can note how suggestively Jane Austen exploits the matter of Fanny's cross and chain for the ball. The amber cross is from her beloved brother William and she is determined to wear it, just as she wears him, close to her heart. (Typically, this amber cross had a real origin, for Jane Austen herself was fond of the 'gold chains and topaze crosses' which the young Charles Austen had sent to his sisters from the Mediterranean in 1801: her symbolism is firmly grounded in the actual.) The question is, which chain will Fanny wear to carry the cross? Henry slyly forces a fancy chain on her, while Edmund later gives her a tastefully simple one. She is persuaded to wear Henry's (just as they are trying to force her to accept him as a husband), but fortunately it will not go through the cross, so she can wear Edmund's with a good conscience. Thus the two tokens of the two people she loves most are linked together round her neck when she leads her first ball: and in that moment the final emotional situation at the end of the book is foreshadowed. But the two most significant episodes we should consider are the journey to Sotherton to discuss the 'improvement' of Mr Rushworth's country home, and the theatricals.

The practice of 'improving' estates according to 'picturesque' principles gained in popularity throughout the eighteenth century, and there are frequent references in Jane Austen's work to the growing cult of the 'picturesque' (for instance, in *Northanger Abbey* Henry Tilney offers Catherine 'a lecture on the picturesque': 'He talked of foregrounds, distances, and second distances; side-screens and perspectives; lights and shades', and so on). In general, the taste for formal gardens had given way to a preference for a sort of contrived irregularity, obscurity and wildness in landscape, as later in architecture (the new taste for 'Gothic', the habit of placing artificial ruins at telling points on one's estate, and the novel interest in mountainous country are all symptoms of a more recent phase in this shift in taste). Clearly this move towards landscapes which were calculated to look more 'natural' reflects the increasing predilection for cultivating 'romantic' sentiments and responses. It is indeed an aspect of that emerging sensibility which we loosely call the romantic movement. In her novels Jane Austen often directs her satire at the cultivation of excessive 'sensibility' at the expense of 'sense', although she herself seems to have had some sympathy for, and appreciation of, the 'picturesque' and the principles of 'natural' landscape gardening (we know that she was fond of Gilpin on the picturesque). However, in Mansfield Park it is less important to estimate Jane Austen's own opinion of the habit of 'improving' estates than to be aware of its significance in the world of the novel.

Henry Crawford is a great and enthusiastic 'improver' – and not only of gardens. He tempts Maria with some seductive hints as to how he might improve the uninviting prospects of her life as Mrs Rushworth. He is a man who, for his own amusement, likes to tamper – with other people's estates, with other people's wives. He cannot let things rest. (Similarly Mary is in favour of 'modernizing' Edmund's vicarage at Thornton; just as she wishes to 'modernize' Edmund himself, so that he will abandon his old-fashioned sense of duty and vocation.) Henry and Mary are all for change, for novelty, for uprooting the old and interfering with the established. In this book such instincts are shown to be potentially dangerous and destructive. Fanny, who in her own way is something of a romantic, is not however in favour of the 'improvements' when they involve any excessive depradations and disruptions of the old. She is, for instance, very much against the suggested destruction of the avenue of trees, and she says, 'I should like to see Sotherton before it is cut down, to see the place as it is now, *in its old state*' (emphasis added). In the world of the book she is the preserver, holding out *against* the improvers. Mary, on the other hand, on viewing Thornton Lacey – Edmund's prospective living – immediately insists, 'The farm-yard must be cleared away entirely, and planted up to shut out the blacksmith's shop.' She wants to erase or conceal any signs of the actual productive work which goes on in the country. That must be masked to allow the country to appear as spectacle. (The definitive work on the importance and significance of 'improvement' of estates – and one of the best books on Jane Austen – is Alistair Duckworth's *The Improvement of the Estate*.)

Henry Crawford is an avid 'improver' (as indeed he is always interfering with the *status quo*), and Mr Rushworth eagerly seeks his help. When they are all at Sotherton they find the house oppressive, and, as soon as they come to a door leading to the open, 'as by one impulse, one wish for air and liberty, all walked out.' To appreciate what happens subsequently it is important to keep the layout in mind. First there is a walled lawn – nature tamed, ordered and civilised. But beyond that is a 'wilderness' – here things are less refined, less restrained, darker. Providentially the door into it is unlocked and into the dark wood they all, variously, go. It is a version of the Renaissance *topos* of the wood of love – *la selva d'amore* – always understood as a dark maze in which one loses one's way. Here it is that Mary tries to undermine Edmund's intention to be a clergyman. (In the course of this conversation they leave 'the great path' and take 'a very serpentine course' – again outer action mimics the life within.) It is here that Fanny desires to sit down and be still, and she does so on a bench which confronts an iron gate which separates the wilderness from the unenclosed spaces of the park beyond. This is one of the most important gestures in the book. Mary, typically, has no taste for stillness. ' "I must move," said she, "resting fatigues me" ', and leaving Fanny immobile, she entices Edmund back into the wood. Then Henry Crawford and Maria and Mr Rushworth appear. Maria, always impatient of all restraints and enclosures, wishes to go beyond the gates and into the wider freedom of the park. The gate – perfect image for the rigid restrictions imposed by the conventions of civilised life – is locked. Mr Rushworth goes to fetch the key. Being engaged to Maria, he is in many ways the lawful person to 'open the gates' (there is perhaps a reference to virginity here, just as the locked garden represents virginity in medieval paintings). But in his absence, Henry engages in some very persuasive and suggestive *double entendre* with Maria. The improver of the estate is also the disturber of conventional life. The whole conversation should be looked at carefully; particularly when Maria complains that the iron gate 'gives me a feeling of restraint and hardship' and Henry answers, 'I think you might with little difficulty pass round the edge of the gate, here, with my assistance; I think it might be done, if you really wished to be more at large, and could allow yourself to think it not prohibited.' Their final adultery – also a bypassing of the 'iron' codes of society – is here prefigured. Fanny warns against the danger, but Maria manages to slip round the gate without any harm from the spikes. Subsequently the spikes of convention will damage her more deeply. Again, Fanny is 'left to her solitude'. And so it goes on. Mr Rushworth appears, upset to find he has been left behind; Julia turns up breathless and angry; Edmund and Mary continue their 'winding' walk in the woods. Only Fanny is still, silent, alone; not involved in the confused antics of all the others, who are variously pursuing their own desires and indulging their impulses. When they do all meet up again, one feels that some irreparable damage has been done. 'By their own accounts they had been all walking after each other, and the junction which had taken place at last seemed, to Fanny's observation, to have been as much too late for re-establishing harmony, as it confessedly had been for determining on any alteration.' Nothing constructive has been achieved, but the seeds of future disharmony have been sown, for the confused, often furtive, criss-cross moving around in the increasing liberty and concealment of garden, wood and park portends the more serious disorder that many of the characters will make of their subsequent lives. Fanny's staying-put is a small gesture of moral tenacity while the others dangerously roam.

The theatricals provide the core of the book; and, indeed, they are the occasion of one of the most subtle and searching pieces in English fiction. We know from the *Memoir* by Jane Austen's nephew, James Edward Austen-Leigh, that amateur home theatricals were popular in her family and by no means disapproved of as they are in the book. But in the novel she uses them as a vehicle to explore the profound implications of 'acting' and 'role-playing' for the individual and society. Her brilliant exploitation of the suggestiveness and relevance of 'theatricals' to modern life amply justifies Lionel Trilling's claim that 'it was Jane Austen who first represented the specifically modern personality and the culture in which it had its being'. The theatricals represent the culmination of the irresponsible licence indulged in during Sir Thomas's absence ('They were relieved by it from all restraint'). Of course the idea of home theatricals seems harmless if not positively charming to us. But in terms of the world of the book we must see the attempt to turn Mansfield Park into a theatre as a dangerous act of desecration: it is like transforming a temple of order into a school for scandal. Interestingly enough, all the characters sense that Sir Thomas would disapprove, but Tom overrules Edmund's objections by saying, 'His house shall not be hurt.' But in a deeper sense Mansfield Park is all but destroyed once 'the inclination to act was awakened'. For Mansfield Park is a place where you must be true to your best self: the theatre is a place where you can explore and experiment with other selves. A person cannot live in both.

It is perhaps helpful to bear in mind the old Platonic objection to acting: Plato thought a person could not be both a good citizen and an actor, because just to simulate a base character has a debasing and demoralising influence on the civilised self. There is a long history of comparable suspicion of the insidious dangers of acting. On the other hand, at least since the Romantic movement, there has been an increasing interest in role-playing, acting, masks, and so on – the feeling being that perhaps the self can only come to a full realisation of itself through experiments in different roles and by trying on different masks. One of the prevailing Romantic convictions is that we are very much more than the conscious mind tells us, that a man is a crowd of almost infinite potentialities (thus Whitman: 'I contain multitudes'). There has been a corresponding desire to try to extend life and consciousness by acting out many different roles. By 'losing yourself in a part', as we revealingly say, you may find another, buried part of yourself: the stage is a great place for discovering those hidden inner multitudes that Whitman mentions. Even reading offers important scope for vicarious role-playing. Clearly one danger in all this is that, although the self might enjoy an enhanced and enriched life by going from role to role, it may dissipate itself until the inner man loses himself in the actor and the face dissolves into the mask. Certainly, role-playing must make against stability and fixity: if the self is fluid, there is no limit to what it might do, no knowing how it might behave. Instead of life conceived as a rigid adherence to firm moral standards, it may turn into a series of improvisations suggested by the milieu of the moment, an endless metamorphosis.

The theatrical germ is brought to Mansfield Park by Mr Yates, a foolish visitor from the world of 'fashion and expense'; very soon all the younger people desire to act or, as Tom puts it, 'exercise our powers in something new'. Again it should be noted that it is in the absence of Sir Thomas that a whole range of hitherto restrained 'powers' and impulses start to press for expression and indulgence. Lady Bertram, of course, offers no obstructions; Mrs Norris positively likes the idea, because 'she foresaw in it all the comforts of hurry, bustle, and importance'. Only Edmund disapproves – and, of course, Fanny. They both refuse to 'act'. Fanny's words have a special emphasis. 'I could not act any thing if you were to give me the world. No indeed, I cannot act.' Henry Crawford is, revealingly, 'considerably the best actor of all' – even Fanny admits his great talents in this sphere. The point is, of course, that these talents stray out of the theatre and into real life: off stage he is 'at treacherous play' with the feelings of Julia and Maria – the latter being only too happy to indulge her illicit passion for Henry under the guise of 'acting'. Mary is also in her element in the theatre, and it is her teasing and tempting which finally undermine Edmund's resolution so that he allows himself to be persuaded to take a part. For when she provocatively asks, 'What gentleman among you am I to have the pleasure of making love to?' Edmund cannot resist the proffered role. This has important implications. Edmund has chosen to be a clergyman by profession: a profession is, in effect, the fixed role that we choose, as responsibly as possible, for life. Edmund at this moment symbolically abandons his profession, his role in life, to play at being a stage clergyman indulging in a love affair (for such is his part). It involves an abdication of his true self in order to indulge a passional impulse. And with his defection to the actors only Fanny is left among the 'players' as a centre of judgement and responsible clear-sightedness. The rest are no longer their true selves: 'and no man was his own' in Shakespearean terms.

Everything about the theatricals portends disharmony. First of all the 'players' squabble selfishly over which play to choose, because, of course, everyone is solely concerned with seeking a desirable role. Then the house itself is physically disrupted as it is altered to make it more like a real theatre. The actual play, *Lovers' Vows*, turns on unnatural or dangerous relations. This was a play by Mrs Inchbald, adapted from *Das Kind der Liebe* ('Child of Love') by Kotzebue, first performed in England in 1798. The plot is roughly as follows. Baron Wildenhaim has seduced and then abandoned a chambermaid, Agatha Friburg, in his youth. When the play opens Agatha is in a state of poverty, where she is found by her illegitimate son Frederick, now a soldier. When he learns the true story of his birth he goes out to beg in order to help his mother. He happens to meet his father and tries to rob him. When he is arrested he reveals the identity of himself, the Baron and his mother. With the aid of the pastor, Anhalt, he persuades the Baron to marry Agatha. The Baron also consents to the marriage of his daughter, Amelia, to Anhalt, instead of forcing her to marry Count Cassel, a rich but brainless fop he had in mind for her. As the play was to be put on at Mansfield Park, the cast was as follows:

| | |
|---|---|
| Agatha Friburg | Maria Bertram |
| Frederick | Henry Crawford |

| | |
|---|---|
| Baron Wildenhaim | Mr Yates |
| Amelia | Mary Crawford |
| Anhalt | Edmund Bertram |
| Count Cassel | Mr Rushworth |

The two aspects of the play which offend Fanny, and reflect on the irresponsible passional behaviour going on at Mansfield Park, are the presence of a bastard (the issue of unlawful, thoughtless eroticism), and the shameless manner in which the coquette Amelia courts and proposes to Anhalt (in the original German her lovemaking was 'indelicately blunt', wrote Mrs Inchbald in her preface). This clearly gives Mary the opportunity to indulge her real nature, under the disguise of playing a part, and pursue her plans with regard to Edmund. As may be inferred from the casting, some of the scenes could give rise to embarrassing situations and 'improper' confrontations.

In particular, Maria playing an abandoned mother and Henry playing her illegitimate son have the opportunity to develop an insidious intimacy. As the rehearsals continue, supressed and dubious desires start to emerge because of the release permitted by the playing of roles. Only Fanny stays apart. In fact she becomes strangely necessary, receiving their complaints, hearing their lines, acting as prompter, 'judge and critic'. She is, moreover, 'at peace' (except for the agonising moment when she has to listen to Mary and Edmund rehearse their love scene in her presence). More significantly, only Fanny is truly *aware*. Aware, for instance, of Julia's suffering, and of what Henry and Maria are really up to, and of how Edmund is deceived in Mary. This clarity of consciousness is of paramount importance because it is the only clear-mindedness still remaining at Mansfield Park. Even Edmund 'between his theatrical and his real part . . . was equally unobservant'. There is no one left except Fanny to uphold the claims and necessity of lucid moral consciousness. The others are lost in their roles; blind behind their masks. This may occasionally make Fanny appear as a prig; but we must respond to her symbolic value. This is why the last moments of chapter 18 are so dramatic. Because of the indisposition of Mrs Grant just before the first full rehearsal, there is a role left vacant. In despair the actors turn to Fanny and try to persuade and bully her into just reading the part. Even Edmund exerts his pressure on her to

.participate in the play. And, indeed, it seems finally that she too must succumb to the actors. Then Sir Thomas suddenly returns, the actors scatter, and the theatre is once more Mansfield Park. The return may seem melodramatic, but what we are to feel is that, if Sir Thomas had not come back, then Fanny would have been forced to 'act' and Mansfield Park would have been fully transformed into a theatre. Again, one has to respond to the subtle symbolism of this and see Fanny's consciousness as a single clear light in the darkening house; so that, when the actors crowd round her, forcing her to play a part, one must feel that the last light of reliable awareness is about to be snuffed out. It is not extinguished, because of the potent authority of Sir Thomas's sheer presence. And, because it isn't, because Fanny does hold out, she will be the one who truly saves Mansfield Park when, at the end of the book, the disorder suggested by the theatricals becomes a moral chaos in real life.

It is worth noting in detail the key moment of Sir Thomas's return and discovery of his 'theatricalised' home:

> Sir Thomas had been a good deal surprised to find candles burning in his room; and on casting his eye round it, to see other symptoms of recent habitation, and a general air of confusion in the furniture. The removal of the book-case from before the billiard room door struck him especially, but he had scarcely more than time to feel astonished at all this, before there were sounds from the billiard room to astonish him still further. . . . He stept to the door . . . and opening it, found himself on the stage of a theatre, and opposed to a ranting young man, who appeared likely to knock him down backwards.

This is Mr Yates playing the Baron. Tom watches the meeting:

> His father's looks of solemnity and amazement on this his first appearance on any stage and the gradual metamorphosis of the impassioned Baron Wildenhaim into the well-bred and easy Mr Yates, making his bow and apology to Sir Thomas Bertram, was such an exhibition, such a piece of true acting as he would not have lost upon any account. It would be the last – in all probability the last scene on that stage; but he was sure there

could not be a finer. The house would close with the greatest eclat.

The disordering and desecration of Sir Thomas's 'own dear room' – the very centre and sanctuary of the paternal authority of the house – 'enacts' a destructive disarrangement, of potentially far-reaching significance, to the essential centre of social order and authority (and note that the books are displaced to give entrance to the irresponsible frivolities of the billiard room: a serious gap and point of leakage – or invasion – is thus opened up; the sober authority of texts give way to the giddy recklessness of games). This wanton penetration and rampant usurpation of what should be the sacred and inviolable centre of legally constituted power and authority is a species of blasphemous vandalism. It is as if a mob had rampaged through it. But 'the origin of *our* acting', as Tom points out, was Mr Yates, who 'brought the infection from Ecclesford, and it spread as those things always spread you know'. Revolutions spread like disease, as Jane Austen's age knew only too well. But Yates is not a working-class agitator but a feckless dissipated aristocrat from a family Sir Thomas regards as particularly 'undesirable'. The fact that Mr Yates 'playing' a loutish, libertine Baron inadvertently 'rants' at Sir Thomas and nearly knocks him over makes, comically, a potentially serious political point. *Lovers' Vows* itself offered something of a political critique of the aristocracy, and Mr Yates as Baron nearly knocking over Sir Thomas dramatises a possible threat to Jane Austen's ideal landed gentry from the wanton and destructive games and histrionics of an irresponsible aristocracy – a threat in class terms not from below but from above and within. (It is hardly surprising that Sir Thomas 'burns' every copy of *Lovers' Vows* that he comes across. It is an inflammatory text in many undesirable ways. The proper conduct of the aristocracy was felt by the ruling class to be essential to social order.) Which is Yates's 'true' acting – when he is ranting at Sir Thomas as a braggart Baron, or when he is apologising to him as a 'well-bred' son of a lord? When he is nearly knocking him backwards, or when he is 'making his bow' to him? Where in fact does all the acting actually stop? When Mansfield is transformed into a theatre – right to the turning upside-down of Sir Thomas's study – and 'metamorphosis' seems to have spread with dangerous speed throughout the house, who can say what the original or 'true' form is of anything or anyone (except for the never-acting, non-metamorphosing Fanny; *her* metamorphosis takes place at the end of the book – a traditional one, whereby the ugly duckling turns out to be a swan). There is a political and social point of some seriousness here. If the 'play' had been sufficiently extended into 'real life' then indeed 'the house would close' – not just the theatre 'house', but the house of Mansfield Park itself. (If, indeed, they are so totally distinct. Where does Sir Thomas demonstrate his 'true acting', a beautiful Jane Austen irresolvable paradox? At Mansfield – or in the West Indies?) Such a closure, or terminal collapse, might be accomplished with 'great eclat', but it would be the end of the 'Play' – the larger, unnamed play of Mansfield's Vows – all the same. And, if there were a burst of applause, it might well come from a larger audience of the disaffected and uninvited part of society. That Mansfield Park had the capacity for self-destruction Jane Austen makes very clear. Given that – at its best – it is a microcosm of a particular society and how it could and should behave as a model of true propriety in all things, such a possible act or process of self-ruination was clearly regarded by Jane Austen very gravely indeed. It is that which makes this novel seem so much more serious and sombre than the light and bright and sparkling *Pride and Prejudice*. It is here that Jane Austen's world starts to darken – when, we may say, the 'theatricals' call all in doubt. (Note that Sir Thomas is most offended by the 'impropriety of the scheme' of the theatricals. And remember that it is the Portsmouth house as an abode of 'impropriety' that so shocked and stunned Fanny. It is almost as though the theatricals could turn Mansfield into another Portsmouth – a chaotic social levelling indeed. It will be seen that notions of 'propriety' and 'impropriety' are doing important political as well as social work by this stage in Jane Austen's writing.)

One final word about 'acting'. With Sir Thomas's return, all traces of the theatre are erased and the house returns to its former 'sameness and gloom', so that even Edmund finds it distinctly less 'lively' than before. It is a long time before he can see the theatricals as 'that period of general folly'. Mary, as we might expect, recalls them as her finest hour. 'If I had the power of recalling any one week of my existence, it should be that week, that acting week.' And Henry, actor supreme, also rejoices in the memory of 'that acting week'. 'We were all alive . . . I never was happier.' And that is the profound truth about the Crawfords, brought up on the great stage of London life: they only feel alive when they are acting a role. In themselves, in repose, they are nothing. They are master stylists, with an easy mastery of the whole range of responses: like other great actors they can mimic all feelings because deep down they can feel none. They are doomed to be insincere, because they lack the instinct for sincere feelings. In this, in their strange combination of energy and emptiness, they are a very modern pair. Henry's acting-ability is again stressed when he is courting Fanny. He picks up a copy of *Henry VIII* (surely Jane Austen's joke, for both Henries show a decided preference for a plurality of ladies) and by sheer instinct he is able to read *every* part perfectly.

> The King, the Queen, Buckingham, Wolsey, Cromwell, all were given in turn . . . he could always light, at will, on the best scene, the best speeches of each; and whether it were dignity or pride, or tenderness or remorse, or whatever were to be expressed, he could do it with equal beauty. – It was truly dramatic.

Thus Henry Crawford, with his 'great turn for acting', reveals what is, in effect, his curse. For, if you can play every part equally well, how can you know who you really are? And, if you can simulate all moods and affections, how can you know what you really feel? Henry Crawford is a man of whom we say, 'he puts his heart into his acting': unfortunately he has also put his acting into his heart. In his courtship of Fanny, Crawford is perhaps trying to play the most difficult role of all – the role of sincerity. But, despite genuine efforts, he cannot keep it up, and Fanny, the most determined non-actor, is vindicated. We must feel that it is only because of her resistance and resoluteness that the actors – in every sense – are kept out of Mansfield Park.

In a letter Jane Austen said the subject of this book was 'ordination'; and certainly Edmund's choice of the profession of clergyman is a serious issue – Mary despising it and trying to entice him into the world, Fanny admiring it and giving Edmund all the support she can. It has seemed to some people a somewhat odd way of describing the main concern of the book, but Jane Austen was totally scrupulous in her choice of words and we should not regard her statement as an author's deliberate perversity. 'Ordination', besides its specific meaning, carries connotations of authority and 'order' (from Latin *ordo*). Given Jane Austen's concern with the problem of how a true social order could be maintained, particularly in that troubled period, she clearly considered the role of the clergyman as being of special importance – less for the saving of souls (though there is no reason to doubt of her genuine orthodox belief) and more for the saving of society. Here are some words of Edmund's as he tries to convince Mary Crawford of the important role played by a proper clergyman (to her 'A clergyman is nothing'):

I cannot call that situation nothing which has charge of all that is of the first importance to mankind, individually or collectively considered, temporally and eternally – which has the guardianship of religion and morals, and consequently of the manners which result from their influence . . . with regard to their influencing public manners, Miss Crawford must not misunderstand me, or suppose I mean to call them the arbiters of good breeding, the regulators of refinement and courtesy, the masters of the ceremonies of life. The *manners* I speak of, might rather be called *conduct*, perhaps, the result of good principles . . . it will, I believe, be every where found that as the clergy are, or are not what they ought to be, so are the rest of the nation.

We should note here that crucial distinction between what, in the Introduction, I referred to as 'manners' according to Chesterfield and 'manners' according to Locke – manners as decoration and 'ceremony' and manners as expressive signs of morality and civility. It was the latter alone, we should recall, that people such as Burke thought could save England from revolution. Edmund's 'ordination', seen as involving the 'guardianship' of true 'manners', has the 'national' importance he claims for it – not least as involving him in maintaining the social fabric. 'Ordination' implicitly refers to everything that the 'theatricals' would – and do – disrupt. Of course we can see that there are also other very important issues in this book. Some of these can be indicated by juxtaposing certain abstract words, for Jane Austen uses abstractions with the power and certainty and fine discrimination of an eighteenth-century writer. There is a contrast between appearance and reality, the Crawford's plausible stylishness offset by Fanny's reticent genuineness. We are also made aware of the conflict between the joys of personality and the rigours of principle. We are shown the need to distinguish between what is 'sweet' and what is 'sound', between what is 'pleasant' and what is 'prudent'. 'Duty' of course is deeply important, but superadded to it there must be 'delicacy'. Manifestations of 'propriety' and 'impropriety' lead us to appreciate the profound importance of the former. And, a harder lesson perhaps, we are shown that the delightfulness of 'wit' (and who enjoyed that more than Jane Austen?) is trivial compared with the soberness of wisdom. As she wrote in a letter, 'Wisdom is better than Wit, & in the long run will certainly have the laugh on her side.' In a more general way the book does seem, as some critics have noted, to speak for repression and negation, fixity and enclosure, the timidity of caution and routine opposed to the exhilaration of risk and change. But if we are sympathetic to the symbolic implications of the world of the book we can see that, at its most profound, it is a book about the difficulty of preserving true moral consciousness amid the selfish manoeuvring and jostling of society. Fanny is constantly subjected to persuasion, victimisation, coercion and opposition. At the end of Volume I she barely escapes being pressured into acting. At the end of Volume II we leave her isolated and uncomforted with everyone trying to force her into a much more false situation – marriage with Henry Crawford. As Lionel Trilling has noted, in our age we tend to believe that 'right action can be performed with no pain to the self', but Jane Austen knew that virtue was a hard affair and morality might involve renunciation, sacrifice, and solitary anguish. Again, we tend to admire energy; but, to return to Trilling's point, Jane Austen had a firm grasp of the paradox 'that the self may destroy the self by the very energies that define its being, that the self may be preserved by the negation of its own energies'. In the debilitated but undeviating figure of Fanny Price we should perceive the pain and labour involved in maintaining true values in a corrosive world of dangerous energies and selfish power-play. She suffers in her stillness. For Righteousness' sake.

Fanny of course gets her due reward – in the shape of marriage to Edmund and, effectively, Mansfield Park itself. She is the true 'inheritor'. We may just notice here how summary Jane Austen is in her account of the 'passional' resolution of the book:

> I purposely abstain from dates on this occasion, that every one may be at liberty to fix their own, aware that the *cure* of *unconquerable* passions, and the *transfer* of *unchanging* attachments, must vary much as to time in different people. – I only intreat every body to believe that exactly at the time when it was quite natural that it should be so, and not a week earlier, Edmund did cease to care about Miss Crawford and became as anxious to marry Fanny, as Fanny herself could desire.
>
> (Emphasis added)

The irony of the italicised words is obvious, and must necessarily spread to the 'transferability' of passionate attachments in general. Not that she implies that the 'object choices' of love and desire are interchangeable and arbitrary, but she would seem to be sceptical about the 'eternalisation' of any feelings, suggesting that they can, whatever their immediate intensity, be disengaged and reattached, not exactly opportunistically but appropriately, following the dictates of the rational needs of the characters – and of the novel (we are, after all, given to believe that Fanny – the immutable and constant Fanny – might have accepted Henry Crawford if he had persisted in his reformed life). What other novelists might spend a whole book in attempting to pursue and portray – the strange shifts in passional manoeuvres and adhesions, the unfathomable processes of falling in and out of love – Jane Austen effectively dismisses in a paragraph which tells us that, in this matter, she will tell us nothing. *That* area of experience is quite explicitly 'transferred' from the obligation of the author to the discretion (or fantasy) of the reader. We may fill in the blank or gap – write *this* part of the novel – as we please. Jane Austen 'purposely abstains'. Irony? Ignorance? Propriety? Tactful reticence? We'd better write the answer to that as we please as well. But we can say without any prejudicial implications that, among other things, Jane Austen is announcing her purposeful – deliberate – intention to 'abstain' from the whole realm of sexual feelings. Not that she is unaware of it, or too prudish to recognise it. She simply won't write about it. And, given the codes and 'conditions of representability' she respects in her writing, it is a perfectly 'proper' decision. But in the case of this novel at least it would be fair to add that she has effectively removed the relationship between Fanny and Edmund as far from the realm of the sexual as is compatible with their getting married. They are after all cousins, and prior to their marriage their relationship is more like that of brother and sister than that of potential lovers. It is perhaps the most nearly asexual marriage among the marriages achieved by Jane Austen's heroines. But a marriage it is, and a celebratory one, symbolising or suggesting more far-reaching reconciliations and restorations; a paradigmatic marriage for society in a larger sense, which transcends personal gratifications.

But, if Jane Austen could see that a world of frantic change was about to supplant the world of peaceful fixity she knew, why then does she allow the spirit of Mansfield, in the figure of Fanny, to triumph over the forces of change, as exemplified by the Crawfords? I think one could put it this way: to a world abandoning itself to the dangers of thoughtless restlessness, Jane Austen is holding up an image of the values of thoughtful rest. Aware that the trend was for more and more people to explore the excitements of personality, she wanted to show how much there was to be said for the 'heroism of principle'. *Mansfield Park* is a stoic book in that it speaks for stillness rather than movement, firmness rather than fluidity, arrest rather than change, endurance rather than adventure. In the figure of Fanny it elevates the mind that 'struggles against itself', as opposed to the ego which indulges its promiscuous potentialities. Fanny is a true heroine because in a turbulent world it is harder to refrain from action than to let energy and impulse run riot. This is a point of Sir Thomas's final insight when he comes to 'acknowledge the advantages of early hardship and discipline and the consciousness of being born to struggle and endure'. Fanny has that consciousness. Mansfield Park as a place has many faults and is inhabited by some silly and nasty people. Fanny's life there has many pains. But a place may be more valuable than the people living in it; and, moreover, as Anne Elliot says in

*Persuasion*, 'one does not love a place the less for having suffered in it'. As a place it symbolically upholds the stoic values of control, stability, endurance. And Jane Austen offers it in this book as an image of quiet resistance at the start of what was to be the most convulsive century of change in the whole of English history.

Finally, to suggest the sort of place *Mansfield Park* occupies in English fiction, I want to suggest a brief comparison with another work which was written about England at a moment of climactic transition, almost exactly one hundred years later. I am referring to Ford Madox Ford's *Parade's End*. If Jane Austen's novel can be said to be about eighteenth-century England giving way to the nineteenth century, so Ford's tetralogy is clearly about nineteenth-century England giving way to the twentieth century at the time of the First World War. Like Jane Austen, Ford portrays a world of traditional values being infiltrated and undermined by modern types – unscrupulous, ambitious, cruel, selfish and false. And the central figure, Christopher Tietjens, comes to represent all the old stoic values of rural England. Like Fanny he is abused, vilified, despised. But, though he is wounded, exhausted and abandoned, like Fanny he endures. He too displays the 'heroism of principle' in a world of self-aggrandising opportunism: as he says, 'Principles are like a skeleton map of a country – you know whether you're going east or north.' In his figure Ford, like Jane Austen, vindicates passivity and abstention. And Tietjens, like Fanny, strengthens himself by holding on to an image of old English rural peace and stability – in his case, as exemplified by the figure of George Herbert, the seventeenth-century poet–priest. Here is one of his meditations in time of war, from *A Man Could Stand Up* (the third volume in the tetralogy):

> But what chance had quiet fields, Anglican sainthood, accuracy of thought, heavy-leaved, timbered hedge-rows, slowly creeping ploughlands moving up the slopes? . . . Still the land remains . . .
>
> The land remains . . . It remains! . . . At the same moment the dawn was wetly revealing; over there in George Herbert's parish . . . what was it called? . . . What the devil was its name? Oh, Hell! . . . Between Salisbury and Wilton . . . The tiny

church . . . But he refused to consider the ploughlands, the heavy groves, the slow highroad above the church that the dawn was at that moment wetly revealing – until he could remember that name. He refused to consider that, probably even today, the land ran to . . . produced the stock of . . . Anglican sainthood. The quiet thing!

Jane Austen is a greater writer. But she too was aware of an England that was passing away. She too knew about the passion which turns to lechery, the activity which becomes destructive, the energy which results in the collapse of a world. And, quite as deeply as Ford, she appreciated the value of 'the quiet thing', and knew, too, the incredible moral strength required to achieve and maintain it. And that, above all, is what Mansfield Park is about.

# 6

# The Match-Maker:
## *Emma*

---

Emma is a match-maker who meets her match – and, in a sense,
her 'maker': the conflated words have to be properly separated
(and morally monitored) so that Emma can become most
properly – well, Emma. But that begs all kinds of questions,
which perhaps we should do well by raising. Emma is, arguably,
one of *the* great English fictional heroines: she is, so the general
feeling runs, to be 'loved' in *spite* of (which merges into '*because
of*') her more or less amiable faults. Jane Austen purported to
think that Emma would not be much liked, but in the event she
has been really adored by generations of readers, for her
brilliance, wit, energy, independence, fallibility, for her capacity
to learn from and recognise her own errors, and finally, it seems,
for her willingness to capitulate to a (rational) passion. All these
aspects of her character as they emerge in the book have served to
gain her generation after generation of admirers (even some
rather besotted lover–critics!). Which is fine: Emma has certainly
become part of our national heritage and nothing could – or
perhaps should – dislodge her from that position. But it might be
worth looking at this indulged paragon again. And then think
again about why she has become one of the best-loved of English
heroines. For, if you look at it carefully, she has a rather
undistinguished, if not culpable, record. For a start, she gets
everything and everyone *wrong*. An arguable exception would be
her appraisal of Mrs Elton where her particular kind of contempt
for the social-climbing *arriviste* behaviour of Mrs Elton elicits
(provokes) some of her sharpest and most accurate and telling
'criticism'. But, with one or two exceptions, Emma *is* wrong, *does*
wrong, can *speak* wrong (Box Hill), *judge* wrong, and can use her
power (hers because of her permanently ailing, hypochondriac,
dozing father) in a way that can be destructive of other peoples'
lives and happiness. She is the apparent insider (all should defer
to her) who is in fact a kind of outsider (there is really no one in

Hartfield, or Highbury, who can truly engage in conversation with her): she is, for the most part, alone with her own 'wit', which does not, of course, exclude a wisdom – or at least a way of looking at things/people which transcends the constricted and repetitive discourse of those who are more sanguinely, and mindlessly, adjusted to the Hartfield–Highbury mode of perceiving, and living, life. But why, in a word, does the English reader seem so ready to fall in love with Emma?

I do not think this is a trivial question. It has something quite important to reveal about the way we read fictions, and the reasons for which we read them. Here is a passage which you might think would serve to alienate most readers; it is in the privileged voice of the narrator although at the same time it is intended as a summary of what Emma thinks about herself:

> With insufferable vanity had she believed herself in the secret of everybody's feelings; with unpardonable arrogance proposed to arrange everybody's destiny. She was proved to have been universally mistaken; and she had not quite done nothing – for she had done mischief.

How is it that this ebullient, enthusiastic but erroneous woman has not been relegated to the sidelines of English fiction? There have of course been many answers to this kind of question, but I should like to look at it all in a new way, if possible – and that will take us to Emma the match-maker. I want to insert here some remarks from a book which may seem a long way from Jane Austen, as indeed it is. Nevertheless I think that they can throw some suggestive, if refracted, light upon the figure of Emma. The book is *Sex and Character* by Otto Weininger (published in 1903, in which year the author killed himself). It is in many ways the culmination of a nineteenth-century trend in misogynistic works and in the extremity of its formulations it could hardly seem further from the balanced ironic sanity of Jane Austen. But Weininger makes, in extreme form, some points which can make us think again about Emma and her position.

Having asserted that 'however degraded a man may be, he is immeasurably above the most superior woman', he goes on to ask, 'But has woman no meaning at all? Has she no general purpose in the scheme of the world? Has she not a destiny; and, in spite of all her senselessness and emptiness, a significance in the universe?' His answer is firm and clear: 'It is from nothing less than the phenomenon of *match-making* from which we may be able to infer most correctly the real nature of women.' And again: 'so far, we have had to deny to women many characters which they would gladly claim, but which are exclusively masculine: in match-making, however, we have a characteristic which is really and exclusively feminine'. As Weininger sees it, this match-making instinct stems from a boundless desire to detect evidence of the actual or potential sexual union of a couple:

> the full extent to which match-making influences the point of view of all women is not yet fully grasped . . . it is women who turn in the streets to look at nearly every couple they meet and gaze after them. This espionage and turning round are none the less 'match-making', because they are sub-conscious acts. . . . Her wish for the activity of her own sexual life is her strongest impulse, but it is only a special case of her deep, her only vital interest, the interest that sexual unions shall take place; the wish that as much of it as possible shall occur, in all cases, places, and times.

He renews his emphasis: 'This match-making is the most common characteristic of the human female . . . match-making is essentially the phenomenon of all others which gives us the key to the nature of woman. . . .' Weininger then goes on to say a good deal about the 'impressionability', 'duplicity', dependency, and 'universal passivity' of woman's nature. He describes in some detail 'the way in which woman can be impregnated with the masculine point of view' and then goes on to say, 'complications first arise when these acquired valuations come into collision with the only inborn, genuine, and universally feminine valuation, the supreme value she sets on pairing'. So we arrive at a succinct formulation of his notion: 'femaleness is identical with pairing'; 'femaleness and match-making are identical'. His contention is that he has 'shown the connection between woman positive as match-maker, and woman negative as utterly lacking in the higher life'. I shall add a further quotation to illustrate the extreme nature of Weininger's theory:

Woman seeks her consummation as the object. She is the plaything of husband or child, and, however we may try to hide it, she is anxious to be nothing but such a chattel. . . . Woman does not wish to be treated as an active agent; she wants to remain always and throughout – this is just her womanhood – purely passive, to feel herself under another's will. She demands only to be desired physically, to be taken possession of, like a new property.

Most of this will seem a long way from being relevant to Emma – and indeed it is. But one crucial point, I think, does obtain.

Match-maker Emma certainly is, or would be if she could. Knightley reproaches her early on for her 'love of match-making' and the phrase occurs often with reference to Emma. In the very first chapter she takes credit for effectively bringing about the marriage of her (ungoverning) 'governess' Miss Taylor and Mr Weston. She confesses that it is a 'matter of joy' to her 'that I made the match myself'. Her (even more ungoverning) father, a 'valetudinarian . . . without activity of mind or body', feebly deprecates her initiative – as he does *any* 'activity' at all – and asks her to make no more matches. Emma merrily replies, 'I promise you to make none for myself, papa; but I must, indeed, for other people. It is the greatest amusement in the world! . . . you cannot think that I will leave off match-making.' Note that 'must'; it is an imperative of her self-pleasing, ungoverned wilfulness. The serious and judicious Knightley denies her any credit in causing this particular marriage – it was just a 'lucky guess' on Emma's part: really she did nothing. Part of her answer is especially significant: 'You have drawn two pretty pictures – but I think there may be a third – a something between the do-nothing and the do-all.' That third picture would be of a 'do-something' – which can include 'do something constructive' and 'do something thoughtlessly or mischievously', 'do something damaging or simply wrong', or just 'do anything at all – to indulge caprice, to pass the time'. This third picture is the complex picture of Emma – high-spirited, vivacious Emma, with £30,000 and an untrained, undirected, 'ungoverned' will. And no 'job'. Her father is against match-making because marriages are 'silly things, and break up one's family circle grievously'. As if he *had* a family circle; as if family circles could be perpetuated and reproduced without marriages. But this moribund patriarch is a comic–serious example of the type of male who would indeed bring his society – any society – to a stop. He is the weak emasculate voice of definitive negations and terminations. He is a (barely) living embodiment of his society's entropic tendencies. But he is too weak to matter except as warning and symptom. More seriously, the responsible active male Knightley calls Emma's self-amusing, self-gratifying match-making 'interference'. He is of course right. The question implicitly posed here is, how can the well-endowed but unmarried Emma actually participate actively in society? Can she intervene constructively without interfering harmfully? Emma thinks of match-making as a diversion: in fact it is her occupation. (I shall return to this central problem of female occupation. Here I just want to note the significance of the fact that Emma is rich – in money. It is not property, which for Jane Austen always carried distinct responsibilities and patterns of behaviour with it – or should do. Unlike money, property supplied a specific agenda of duties, actions and rewards. The danger of money, on the other hand, was that not only did it not provide any pedigree: it conferred no specific obligations. Always 'circulating', it was as uncertain in origin as it was indeterminate in application. It embodied no entelechy and was teleologically morally neutral – and indifferent. Anyone could be a 'do-anything' with it. Emma is unique among Jane Austen's heroines in that she is rich enough to think that she does not need a marriage with a proper man – with property – in order to exist properly in society. Marriage is a game she can play with other people. Her apparent freedom based on financial independence is thus not only deeply ambiguous but carries with it a latent double danger: she can delude herself and she can toy and tamper with other peoples' relationships. She of course does both.)

Emma's match-making eyes gaze and glimpse and stare all around her, but of course they are most concentrated on Harriet Smith. Harriet Smith: of no known origin – perhaps illegitimate and certainly without a 'class'; good-natured but not clever; impressionable, pliable and grateful; easily seduced (I use the word with a minimum of sexual connotation) into believing that it is on the one hand 'beneath' her to love Robert Martin, but on the other (with Emma's ill-considered encouragement) not 'above' her to think that Mr Elton may love her, and – here things get amusingly/soberingly out of Emma's control – that perhaps Mr Knightley is making courting advances to her. This is Emma's Harriet. We all know how Emma responds to *that* – when she realises that her playing with Harriet could bring about a reality situation which would be to her intolerable. As to the relationship between 'play' and 'reality', Emma has a great deal to learn. Without wishing to get involved with irrelevant and extraneous speculations about the relationship between Emma and Harriet, I think it can be justifiably (and not salaciously) suggested that Harriet *is* used by Emma in various ways as a fantasy sexual object. Is Emma's imagination lightly stirred at the coming of Mr Elton? She pushes and promotes Harriet in every way so that they should form a 'union'. And Frank Churchill? More difficult of course, since there is something in her slightly superficial volatility which draws her to Frank Churchill (and, yes, there is perhaps as much of a Frank Churchill in her – with all his playful, devious, deceptive, even dangerous dalliance – as there is a Mr Knightley, who is not given, we may say, to any of the above). But, although she joins in some arguably reprehensible 'games' with Frank, there is no question (certainly for Emma) that there will or can be any kind of intimate relationship with him. So Harriet again is really put forward – indeed, one might say, exhibited – as the sexual bait (I am deliberately crude about this because I think that, under the more or less polite discourses being conducted and engaged in at this time, there *is* an underlying crudity or physicality), and Harriet in her innocent, ignorant, discourseless condition does not, cannot, realise where she stands in all this euphemistic manoeuvring. To be plain: Emma has a wider range of discourse than anyone else in the novel. She can out-talk, over-talk, everyone, and that includes Mr Knightley, because she has a kind of energy of articulation, an instinct for just playing with the words – she is marked by excess, an over-plus. She is an over-speaker (not like Miss Bates, but not so unlike either – I shall come back to that). She claims a right of unrestricted liberty of speech: trying to explain her conversations with Mr Knightley to her father she says, 'it is all a joke. We always say what we like to one another.' But for Mr Knightley conversation is never 'a joke'. He only says exactly what is right and becoming; he is not cursed – or blessed – with that kind of intermittent overflow, that saying-too-much, that over-dancing of language which we enjoy in Emma. So Emma talks – yes – but with whom to listen to her? We shall come back to talking, and to problems of discourse in such a small, restricted area. I want to stay just for a while with the consideration of the strange relationship between Emma and Harriet.

Does Emma ever really *see* Harriet Smith ('the natural daughter of somebody') *as* Harriet, in her ductile plastic flexibility, her vagueness of talent, style, discourse and opinion – all as uncertain as her origin? (Class and origin are of crucial importance in this novel.) Emma is perfectly and satisfactorily defined in every way – money, class, position – and she has a wit and a discourse which are equal to anyone she might meet in her limited circle (Knightley excepted, though if he has superior judgement he does not have her dancing wit – but we shall return to this pair). So why her obsession with this pretty little nobody from who-knows-where? One reason must surely be that Harriet can be persuaded/forced into a surrogate figure, a substitute of Emma's making, who will engage in all the potentially dangerous male–female (i.e. sexual – we can say it even if Jane Austen does not think it necessary to spell it out) relationships which might amuse or distract Emma (*something* has to distract her) and which she can enjoy vicariously. Her match-making plans or fantasies serve to fill the gaps in her time. At one point we read that 'She was so busy . . . in talking and listening, and *forming all these schemes in the in-betweens*, the evening flew away at a very unusual rate' (emphasis added). For the basically unemployed Emma, life is full of 'in-betweens' – in a way it is one long 'in-between' – and she fills them with 'schemes'. She has to fill them with something.

That it all rebounds or boomerangs on her – Mr Elton thinks Emma is encouraging *him*; Harriet thinks that Mr Knightley might be encouraging *her*; and so on – is all part of what Emma has to learn as a would-be match-maker. But it is important that we see her as a privileged, well-endowed manipulator, much more willing to put others (Harriet) than herself at emotional risk. It is also clear that Harriet provides a distraction. Emma sees what an opportunity she offers very early on:

*She* would notice her; she would improve her; she would

detach her from her bad acquaintance and introduce her into good society; she would inform her opinions and her manners. It would be an interesting, and certainly a very kind undertaking: highly becoming her own situation in life, her leisure, and powers.

The words to take particular notice of are 'interesting', 'leisure' and 'powers'. The way she forcefully persuades Harriet to give up Robert Martin while claiming to refuse to offer any advice is a good example of her 'powers'. Just as she effectively writes the letter of rejection – 'though Emma continued to protest against any assistance being wanted, it was in fact given in the formation of every sentence' – she tries to 'write', or rather 'rewrite', Harriet's life. Or again, when Mr Elton offers his charade, Harriet is persuaded into reading it the way Emma wants it to be read (as with so many signs of other kinds – Emma abuses her intelligence in *mis*reading): what she herself tentatively and uncertainly ventures to say is replaced by Emma's confident voice. 'Emma spoke for her.' Harriet is not allowed to write or speak for herself; just as she is not allowed to express her real, if inchoate, feelings for Robert Martin – just as, indeed, she is not allowed to live her own life. Emma's motives in all this are of course multiple and not always by any means clear to herself. But we can see that, in addition to whatever real 'kindness' there may be in her attentions to Harriet, there is also the inclination to experiment on her. It is a dangerous and always potentially cruel game. And of course Harriet duly suffers from disappointments of expectations roused in her by Emma. 'Poor Harriet' is a phrase that rightly occurs to Emma more than once. She is indeed – Emma comes to see – 'the dupe of her [Emma's] misconceptions and flattery'. But at last comes the apparent *peripeteia*: Harriet seems to be about to 'get' Mr Knightley. It is only then that Emma – intelligent but out of touch with her own desires – realises that Mr Knightley must marry no one but herself. Emma is no Frankenstein and Harriet no monster(!); but, with her meddling and planning and scheming, Emma has created a false 'Harriet' who now threatens to act beyond the control of her 'maker'. So we arrive at that spontaneous outburst of Emma's when she thinks that Harriet has moved beyond her control and threatens to act autonomously: 'Oh God! that I had never seen her!' But she has to face up to the fact that Harriet – this incongruously aspiring Harriet – is her own creation. If all her plans have gone wrong it is 'her own doing':

> Who had been at pains to give Harriet notions of self-consequence but herself – Who but herself had taught her, that she was to elevate herself if possible, and that her claims were great to a high worldly establishment? – If Harriet, from being humble, were grown vain, it was her doing too.

It is incipient nemesis. If all of Emma's scheming, planning, match-making (the words recur continuously) have caused pain and threatened to disrupt society, 'it was her doing'.

(Harriet of course turns out to be quite wealthy and the 'daughter of a tradesman – quite respectable'. Emma's reaction is as follows:

> Such was the blood of gentility which Emma had formerly been ready to vouch for! – It was likely to be as untainted, perhaps, as the blood of many a gentleman: but what a connexion had she been preparing for Mr Knightley – or for the Churchills – or even for Mr Elton! – The stain of illegitimacy, unbleached by nobility or wealth, would have been a stain indeed.

This is a fine example of how subtly and unsettlingly Jane Austen could use free indirect speech, or 'experienced speech'. Who is more shocked at the idea of the 'stain of illegitimacy' being 'unbleached' by rank or money – Emma or the writer? And what about the 'blood of gentility' or the blood of 'many a gentleman'? Harriet's blood is 'perhaps' – a wonderfully revealing hesitation and qualification perfectly placed *after* the initial speculation which briefly suspends the socially imposed notions of what may or may not be 'untainted blood' – 'as untainted as the blood of many a gentleman'. But the implied horror at the idea of a stained or 'unbleached' 'connexion' reinstates the most crude social prejudices at once. Clearly the irony must be at Emma's expense: she is still capable of being a snob, mindlessly internalising or reiterating the crass inequalities of her society. The idea that it would have been somehow disgraceful to marry Harriet to Churchill, or Mr Elton, after what we – and Emma – have seen is hardly to be considered an idea. It is an unconsidered reflex which reveals society thinking *through* Emma, as it were. As if those men did not have taints and stains of their own which need a good deal of moral bleaching – if indeed the incorrigible Mr Elton is not simply 'unbleachable'. And what kind of society is it that regards rank and money as necessary and sufficient 'bleach' for an unlucky draw in the lottery of birth? The answer of course is, all too many societies; but we can see in such perfectly cadenced ironic passages as this how Jane Austen could be – indirectly but quite lethally – bitingly subversive of the *mores* of her class and society. Of course, reducing or equivalising – through metaphor – rank and money to a common household object such as bleach, and relating them to the mundane activity of washing, which has to be done continually, quite devastatingly compounds the irony. Which is not to ignore the obvious fact that it is Jane Austen who confers upon Harriet her money and minimal 'respectability'. Making Harriet just about respectable enough to be – just about – acceptable might seem to reveal a Jane Austen colluding with the very *mores* and requirements of her class and society which she elsewhere ironises or seriously undermines. But who can be sure where the ironies stop!)

Emma has 'leisure'. She also has 'powers'. But what powers? We gather that she has insufficient application and commitment when it comes to such activities as reading, painting, music (Jane Fairfax provides a contrast here), and, while she is a good hostess, her discharge of such charitable activities as might be thought consonant with her station is, as she well knows, irregular and imperfect. So her 'powers' cannot be discerned in particular accomplishments and activities. In fact, what she has is 'power' – the power of money and rank or position. But in themselves these will not fill up the great voids of 'leisure'. So we come to a central problem – that of female occupation. A sobering aspect of this problem is sharply and suddenly brought before us in an exchange between Jane Fairfax and Mrs Elton (who, rather like a parody of Emma's treatment of Harriet, wishes and presumes to arrange Jane's life for her). Jane is quietly but resolutely holding out against Mrs Elton's planning for her employment.

'When I am quite determined as to the time, I am not at all afraid of being long unemployed. There are places in town, offices, where inquiry would soon produce something – Offices for sale – not quite of human flesh – but of human intellect.'

'Oh! my dear, human flesh! You quite shock me; if you mean a fling at the slave-trade, I assure you Mr Suckling was always rather a friend to the abolition.'

'I did not mean, I was not thinking of the slave-trade,' replied Jane, 'governess-trade, I assure you, was all that I had in view; widely different certainly as to the guilt of those who carry it on; but as to the greater misery of the victims, I do not know where it lies.'

The exchange comes as quite a shock in a Jane Austen novel, but it does serve to remind us that, far from being the know-nothing sequestered spinster which some people make of her, she was fully alert to the social miseries and injustices of her age – including the acute miseries of the governess situation (compare Charlotte Brontë's work – *passim*), as well as the actual slave trade.

What is a girl with all the spirit, energy and wit – not to mention the privileges – of an Emma actually to do? Mr Knightley's sombre, juridical voice makes the point which poses the problem: 'She will never submit to any thing requiring industry and patience, and a subjection of the fancy to the understanding.' Emma is a clever but 'spoiled' girl and, having lacked external authority (both from her father and from her governess) when she was young, she has not internalised any authority which can direct and control her as she grows into a young woman. She says rightly – if 'playfully' – that she is a 'fanciful, troublesome creature'. She also regards herself as a very 'independent' person, though, as Mr Knightley says with uncharacteristic cryptic incompleteness but a very English use of aposiopesis, 'when it comes to the question of dependence or independence!' Emma will have both to complete that 'question' and answer it, but it will take her a long time. Marriage would seem to be the obvious answer to this problem of occupation, but for a long time she rejects that as a possibility. There is nobody suitable for her, as is pointed out by the one man whom *we* can see is the only possibility for her, but whom Emma misreads as she misreads practically everyone and everything else – particularly herself: 'there is nobody hereabouts to attach her; and she goes so seldom from home'. (Not only has she never seen the sea, she has not even seen the nearby Box Hill – we must realise that, with all her powers and privileges, Emma moves in a very constricted circle.) We are told that 'she had always wanted to do everything' – but in truth it must be recognised that by certain standards of achievement she can in fact do almost nothing. It is Harriet who, in all innocence and guileless directness, raises the problem when Emma has once again told her of her intention never to marry.

> 'Dear me! but what shall you do? how shall you employ yourself when you grow old?'
> 'If I know myself, Harriet, mine is an active, busy mind, with a great many independent resources; and I do not perceive why I should be more in want of employment at forty or fifty than one-and-twenty. Woman's usual occupations of eye and hand and mind will be as open to me then as they are now; or with no important variation. If I draw less, I shall read more; if I give up music, I shall take to carpet-work.'

We have a fairly clear idea by now just how much reading, or carpet-work, Emma will do – at any age – and Harriet's crucial question remains totally evaded, if covered with a litany of confident but empty protestations. How will she employ herself – not only when she grows old, but tomorrow and tomorrow and tomorrow? John Knightley asks the question of the novel when he says, 'I wonder what will become of her.'

If Emma's occupation is not with books and carpets – not to mention those people in the classes below her – what is it? In a word it is in her imagination, or, rather, her imagination *is* her occupation. ('Fancy' and 'imagination' are here used fairly interchangeably and I cannot see that any Coleridgean distinction is intended.) A comment made by Emma as she – as usual, quite wrongly – imagines what Mr Elton is doing with her (characteristically) distorted portrait of Harriet, passing it round his family and planning a future with Harriet (how such an idea is to annoy Mr Elton!), applies more pertinently to herself: 'How cheerful, how animated, how suspicious, how busy their imaginations all are!' The main, and one might say generating, animated, suspicious busy imagination in the book is Emma's. Emma often makes a resolve to herself to 'repress imagination', but, as with her resolutions to give up match-making, the resolve is usually no sooner made than it is broken. You do not make the imagination unemployed as easily as she might think. She has, for instance, only to hear the barest fragments of information concerning the relationships obtaining between Jane Fairfax, the Campbells and the Dixons to put together in her mind the outlines of some slightly, but significantly, erotic – indeed adulterous – plot: 'At this moment, an ingenious and animating suspicion entering Emma's brain. . . .' Similar statements occur throughout the novel, and in this case we may note that the important word is 'animating'. Because what on earth – or, rather, what in Hartfield and Highbury – *is* going to 'animate' Emma, with her constantly brimming high spirits, if not the scenarios, indeed the fantasies, of her own brain? We can see her tolerably egoistical imagination at work in her relationship with Frank Churchill; we are told of 'the distinguished honour which her imagination had given him: the honour, if not of being really in love with her, of being at least very near it, and saved only by her own indifference'. This, we say at least, is not the description of a young lady in love – in any kind of love, unless it is with herself and her imagination. If we take a short sentence such as the following from chapter 46 – 'Her fancy was very active' – we can realise just where, for Emma, the action *is*. And it is not in Hartfield. Her playing, plying, ploying with the nobody–nothing, Harriet Smith, is just exactly a projection of her active 'fancy', her busy 'imagination'. Her occupation is principally concerned with tending a father who is the negative of a proper father, and tending her fantasies, which, because she is so curiously lonely (Highbury and Hartfield 'afforded her no equals'), encounter more collusions than obstacles. There is very little either in her upbringing or in her environment (apart from the solemn sageness of Mr Knightley) to prepare Emma for an unavoidable and significant encounter with the reality principle – or, things as they *are*.

Emma is 'perfection', 'faultless in spite of her faults', and many more enchanting things besides. But she is also, underneath the rank and money, a curiously displaced person, a centre without a circle, a figure-force of perpetual restlessness. In fact, although Emma is the centre of the novel, neither Hartfield nor she are actually at the centre of Highbury: 'Highbury the large and populous village almost amounting to a town, to which Hartfield, in spite of its separate lawn and shrubberies and name, did really belong, afforded her no equal. The Woodhouses were first in consequence there.' As Hartfield is slightly off-centre and separate topographically (and nominally) – literally just detectably ec-centric – so Emma is both 'first in consequence' and oddly out of social 'sequence'. She knows what is fitting but she herself doesn't quite 'fit'. She is at once an outsider and insider when it comes to Highbury (which means 'society' in this novel). And in fact, whereas in previous novels the potential threat to the given social order tends to come from outside (though not beneath, in class terms), it is in fact Emma herself, the central ec-centric, who is the potentially most disruptive figure in the society of this novel. She is the danger from within – if, that is, society itself is not beginning to seem like the danger from without. Perhaps the centre cannot hold because it is no longer worth holding. Certainly, things as they are being so unstimulating, narrow, repetitious, insufferably boring (evenings with her father, mornings with Miss Bates), Emma is a very active fantasist. From this fact springs many of the problems and fluttering (or boorish) misunderstandings in the novel. But from this fact also springs the novel itself.

We might perhaps remind ourselves of the potentially abrasive or claustrophobic aspects of the community in and through which Emma must move and have her being. The general tendency of course has been nostalgically to idealise the rural peace and placid sameness (or blessed routine) of the way of life of a society such as hers. But – as always, we might say – it is peace at a cost. Just consider the position Emma, Mr Elton and Harriet find themselves in after Mr Elton has literally pushed his way into a carriage with Emma, both on going to the Westons' and coming back, just as he pushes his way between people during his party. Mr Elton is indeed a pusher, or social climber as we might say, and his pushing his way into Emma's carriage is a paradigmatic gesture of his approach to the whole community. He will get in, and get on. The established class cannot stop that kind of insentient vulgarity. So it comes about that Mr Elton presumes to 'make love' to the surprised (though not entirely blameless) Emma. She of course rejects his advances with the kind of cold and devastating 'politeness' of which we know she must be a true mistress. Mr Elton is mortified and angry but he is also easily repulsed. But it means the end of Emma's schemes– dreams for Harriet (a match with Mr Elton) and it means a perpetual embarrassment between her and Mr Elton. Better if one, or all, could go away. But this is a 'no exit' society. 'Their being so fixed, *so absolutely fixed*, in the same place, was bad for each, for all three. Not one of them had the power of removal, or of affecting any material change of society. They must encounter each other, and make the best of it' (emphasis added). *Absolutely fixed* – that is Emma's society; indeed we might say it is one aspect of Jane Austen's society.

This might seem to contradict what is said in this book about the dangers involved in roaming, wandering, restless movement, 'moving around', as shown in Jane Austen's work – particularly *Mansfield Park* and *Sanditon*. But she differentiates between directionless, unfocused, self-gratifying (often amoral or even vicious) 'moving around', which can have a disintegrating and corrosive effect on true social stability and moral values, and the kind of self-delighting energy which serves to enliven and vivify life within the constricted space and at times the restricting and too-constraining forms and ceremonies of her society. At its best it is a small world in which a Fanny Price and an Elizabeth Bennet could cohabit. At the same time she can also point the difference between the value and importance of stillness and 'the quiet thing', and the life-denying stagnancy of a small society which has become airless, claustrophobic, inert and even moribund. For Jane Austen life (and people) could become too fixed or too free – excess and forms of transgression (or omission) were possible at both ends of the spectrum. There was a right time for stillness and a proper place for movement. Needless to say, the definitions of these two phenomena (and their abuse) are not themselves 'absolutely fixed' but constantly, if at times implicitly, debated and tested and re-examined in her work. The tension and dialectic between them is ongoing.

In Emma's society there is no room for manoeuvre, no room for rearrangement, no room for any kind of escape. In short, there is no room. This is an aspect of Emma's small hierarchical society which Jane Austen keeps before us. It explains a lot about Emma's spirited imagination, which is constantly unfixing and refixing things in a most irresponsible way, crossing hierarchies in all sorts of ways and encouraging a Harriet Smith to look at a Mr Elton or a Frank Churchill (even a Mr Knightley) even if she does not exactly encourage a cat to look at a king. There is also a force of inertia at work in such a community, based as it is on observed repetitions and a general disapproval of all deviations (such as going to London to get your hair cut!). After one social evening we read that 'every thing was relapsing into its usual state. Former provocations reappeared. The aunt was as tiresome as ever. . . .' As ever, as ever . . . : as-ever-ness is the condition to which such a society aspires. It might seem to welcome novelty (most notably in this novel in the form of Frank Churchill) but at the same time it distrusts 'difference' (a distrust voiced, of course, by Mr Knightley, who speaks quite unashamedly for the superior – if not exclusive – virtues of continuity through sameness; he does not like Frank Churchill for many reasons, not all of them to be attributed to an unacknowledged jealousy). Emma, we should remember, does in fact 'despise' Highbury, and can find it 'dull and insipid'. She will find herself in something of a whirl between Frank Churchill (who likes change, mystification, puzzles, a kind of deracinated playfulness) and Mr Knightley (who, need it be said, by contrast stands for stasis, clarity, traditional routine and a kind of deeply rooted dutifulness). To put it at its most extreme, one can be the most irresponsible flirt and the other can be in danger of being a lugubrious incarnation of convention (even if that convention does represent the best of English tradition). In between them what shall Emma do? An Emma Churchill is perhaps unthinkable (though it is certainly thought about as a possibility) – among other things, as she acknowledges, she is rather too like him for them to make a pair. So, it will be Emma Knightley. Very proper and satisfactory – certainly. Though we may just wonder what will happen to Emma's dancing, teasing wit when it finds itself immersed in farming-journals and the rather humourless moralising of a gentleman farmer.

One important word in considering Emma's society is 'elegance'. As in all Jane Austen's novels, the contestations between different vocabularies – discourses, if you will – is crucial. We can discern a clear opposition (sometimes playful – on Emma's part) between a vocabulary which adheres to maxims of right conduct and rationality, and one which talks more in terms of 'spirit' and 'gaiety'. Where, in these discourse, does 'elegance' fit in? To ask that is exactly to ask, where does Jane Fairfax fit in in this community? Emma has plenty of mixed feelings about Jane, as we are told, but (it is a crucial aspect of our liking her 'in spite of her faults') despite the very limited range of her experience she can instantly recognise class and real quality, and she as instantly approves and admires it – almost as a thing in itself. Thus, despite her reservations about Jane, her apparent 'reserve', her seeming coolness, her clear intellectual and artistic superiority (Emma recognises this and makes no attempt to belittle it), Emma perceives with no signs of jealousy that 'Jane Fairfax was very elegant, remarkably elegant; and she had herself the highest value for elegance.' What exactly is this 'elegance', since it is clearly not a matter of fine shoes and fancy hats (as Mrs Elton would perhaps have supposed)? It is something impalpable, but something which by its very presence (measure and discern that how you will) makes clear where and among whom it is absent. And this Emma – to her credit, as we say – perceives. She is contemplating, objectively and without jealousy, Jane's beauty.

> It was a style of beauty, of which elegance was the reigning character, and as such, she must, in honour by all principles, admire it: – elegance, which whether of person or of mind, she saw so little in Highbury. There, not to be vulgar, was distinction, and merit.

It is part of the attraction of Emma that, while she is quite capable of perversely and deliberately undervaluing a character – as she holds on to her theory (or preconceived notion) that Robert Martin must be coarse, illiterate, a boor, socially unacceptable, and so on (though on reading his first letter she knows she is wrong, but she does not want to know that she knows it) – she can and will also respond to 'the real thing' when she is confronted with it. Jane Fairfax aggravates her in all sorts of ways, but Emma can see that she is truly 'elegant', just as Highbury, which is her society, is – truly – not. In this regard Emma's consciousness is finer than that of her community. That community encompasses the good-natured, the honest and honourable, the decent, as well as the silly, the boring, the (truly) vulgar, the malicious. But, however we choose to take the word – alluding as it does to an indefinable commingling of manners, morals, and style – we see, because Emma sees, that her society is not 'elegant'.

It would be misleading to overstress the pains and oppressions of this society. But Emma often has to have recourse to silence rather than utter her real feelings – her one slip in this matter, her joke at Miss Bates's expense, looms amazingly large and serves to indicate, among other things, what a degree of repression such a community, and its manners, depends upon. And it would be wrong to mentally gloss over the difficulties – the tediums, the longueurs, the 'inelegancies' – of that society. Perhaps the most important and notable thing to emerge from the Box Hill excursion is not simply Emma's unforgettable little flash of inconsiderateness (or cruel wit, if you prefer), but the relevation or realisation that, familiar as all the people are to each other, they do not really comprise a 'community'.

> There was a languor, a want of spirits, *a want of union*, which could not be got over. They separated too much into parties. . . . It seemed at first *an accidental division, but it never materially varied* . . . during the whole two hours that were spent on the hill, there seemed a *principle of separation*, between the other parties, too strong for any fine prospects, or any cold collation, or any cheerful Mr Weston, to remove.
>
> (Emphasis added)

This is not to say that there is no genuine communal experience in that society – there of course is: at dinner parties, at the ball, at the strawberry party. But it is to suggest that there are disparate, incompatible (if not hostile) elements in that society which really reveal themselves at the Box Hill party. There is a group, many members of which are related in one way or another; there is social contact and contiguity (enforced and suffered, or sought-for and welcomed); there is indeed a community – it would be perverse to withhold the term. But it is a community on the one hand bound together by acknowledged hierarchy, and on the other riddled with potential – if not actual – divisiveness. And

Emma, it must be said, is quite as much of a divisive agent as she is a binding presence. Which brings us, inevitably, as it must at some point, to that peculiarly English vexed matter of class.

Too much has perhaps been made of the notion that the English novel is obsessed with – and trapped within – an obsession with class. It is often argued that this has made it less than open to the various experimentalisms of this century. To speculate further along these lines would be inappropriate here. The fact is – if you can have 'facts' of 'fictions' – that Emma is so very class-conscious that it would be difficult to defend her from the accusation of being a snob. But it is not just Emma: the effects of class, and class-crossings (or transgressions), may be found throughout the book. Consider, for example, the authorial description and comment when the author(ess) sums up what happened to Miss Churchill when she decides to marry Mr Weston – for love. 'Miss Churchill, however, being of age, and with the full command of her fortune . . . was not to be dissuaded from the marriage, and it took place to the infinite mortification of Mr and Mrs Churchill, who threw her off with due decorum.' 'Due decorum'? – who is speaking here? What sanctions and dictations prescribe this 'decorum' which in another vocabulary might appear as a heartless rejection of a daughter who made the unforgivable mistake of marrying for love – not money or property. Is this really an example of 'decorum', or a rather unpleasant parody of it? We know that those who enjoy their status owing to inherited property and those who achieved their status through trade have a very uneasy relationship in Jane Austen. Consider, for example, Emma's reaction to the Coles, who 'were of low origin, in trade, and only moderately genteel': Emma wants to receive an invitation from them to go to their dinner, but only so that she can exhibit 'the power of refusal' and teach them a lesson – 'that it was not for them to arrange the terms on which the superior families would visit them'. This is not a very attractive trait in Emma's character, and the author, who clearly sees this, nearly punishes Emma by leaving her 'in solitary grandeur'. In the event, she does go of course, and the 'Coles expressed themselves so properly' – i.e. with all due deference – that Emma is reconciled to the idea of attending a function which she thinks is in some ways beneath her. One might question on what grounds Emma thinks herself so very superior – it is all a matter of class position. But one could see her reaction – in its ambivalence – to the Coles, as the sign of a class on the defensive, wanting to assert its superiority but no longer sure on what, exactly, that superiority was based. (If, that is, we see Emma as truly 'representing' a class – or is she, in some way, outside of any class, ec-centric; a class on her own? We should remember that this is the only novel Jane Austen entitled with a person's name – and a Christian name at that. 'Emma', as such, has no title, no place, and refers to an unsocialised individual.) Emma's most crude mistake, of course, emerges in her attempt to belittle and degrade Robert Martin and his class: 'The yeomanry are precisely the order of people with whom I feel I can have nothing to do.' Her defensive, and in many ways willed and fabricated, 'contempt' for the farmer class, the yeoman of England, is perhaps one of her most manifestly stupid and unjust attempts to use class position to denigrate and reduce the importance of a class different from hers. She insists on disparaging Martin for his 'want of gentility', lack of 'manners' and 'air'. She sees him – or pretends to – as 'clownish'. But here Emma is the 'clown' and the 'joke' is on her. As we see in the course of the novel, so-called 'gentility' and 'manners' are indeed so much 'air', if not even emptier – and worse. Martin is something more solid and valuable. He is a 'gentleman-farmer' (and indeed, like Mr Knightley, lives in an 'abbey' – Abbey-Mill Farm). Harriet is the real 'nobody', underneath Emma's reinvented version of her, and it is simply 'nonsense' for her to assert that Martin is 'her inferior as to rank in society'. In this discourse 'rank' and even 'society' simply don't mean anything any more. Emma affects to despise 'farming', 'business', 'the market', 'profit and loss', but, quite apart from supporting her and her like in unproductive idleness, this section of society she despises is of course supporting the whole nation. Farming and trade were contributing crucially to both the stability and the growth of England, while Emma, with her 'leisure' and her 'powers' – what is *she* doing which, by any criterion, is of any use whatever?

A related matter concerns what constitutes a real 'gentleman'. (The debate about what constituted a real 'gentleman' had a very long history by Jane Austen's time and was to continue long into the future. Perhaps no other descriptive and prescriptive term for the socially – and morally, at times – most desirable and 'best' kind of man has undergone more mutations and transformation than 'gentleman'. Trollope, to give only one example, said that the idea of a 'gentleman' was absolutely central to his whole system of social ethics but that he could never define what exactly a gentleman was. For a history of this fascinating topic see *The Idea of a Gentleman* by A. Smythe-Palmer.) Emma seems to think that Mr Elton and Frank Churchill are 'gentlemen', while Robert Martin is not. But the term is already becoming so vague that Emma's use of it is very unsurely grounded and open to abuse. The term is labile and imprecise and Emma's use of it turns out to be shallow and inaccurate. Emma can only see marriage to Robert Martin as 'degradation', but her sense of hierarchy is deeply questioned by the novel. Socially, things are changing more rapidly than Emma can fully perceive. She dislikes having contact with the good-natured but impoverished Mrs and Miss Bates – 'a waste of time – disagreeable women – and all the horror of being in danger of falling in with the second and third rate of Highbury'. But who are the 'first rate' – Mr Woodhouse? – and what makes them so? Mr Knightley – who is indeed the 'knight' of the book, with his exemplary abode Donwell Abbey – is really the only clear embodiment of the 'gentleman'. (Except perhaps for Martin in *his* Abbey.) And even Knightley is not without a disqualifying defect, signalled by the fact that he will not dance: 'There he was, among the standers-by, where he ought not to be; he ought to be dancing – not classing himself with the husbands, and fathers and whist players.' Initially, then, he is emotionally retarded (or prematurely old). (As David Monaghan has suggested, it is only when he ventures to dance with Emma that he begins to mature towards marriage – which is necessary to complete him as a true 'gentleman'.) Mr Elton, for all his superficial ingratiating graces, is, as Emma comes to realise after he has had the presumption to make love to her, 'nobody'. But again, the bases for this judgement are family, money and property. Thus Emma thinks to herself: 'he must know that in fortune and consequence she was greatly his superior. He must know that the Woodhouses had been settled for several generations at Hartfield, the younger branch of a very ancient family – and that the Eltons were nobody.' Whatever she might say or pretend in her games and schemes with Harriet, when it comes to the point Emma falls back on the criteria of her class. But in her reflections Emma can see both the arbitrariness and injustice in the social designations of a 'somebody' or a 'nobody'. She is musing on what seem to be the respective fates of Jane Fairfax and Mrs Churchill. 'The contrast between Mrs Churchill's importance in the world, and Jane Fairfax's, struck her; one was everything, the other nothing, and she sat musing on the difference of woman's destiny. . . .' The real key to this class system, behind considerations of family name, property, money, rank, and so on, is, really, marriage. It is this which socially creates 'somebodies' and 'nobodies'. The book, among other things, is itself a 'musing on the difference of woman's destiny', and, before the author decides to tidy up these destinies at the end, so that every woman more or less mates with the appropriate man, we see – with Harriet, with Jane, even with Emma herself – just how precarious those destinies can be.

So what of Emma in this society? She is not simply a snob (though she is snobbish); she is not simply a fool (though she can be foolish). She is 'playful' – which perhaps marks her off from the other members of that society, who are not given to 'play'. She is more given to 'laughter' than others; she finds it 'much pleasanter to let her imagination range and work at Harriet's future, than to be labouring to enlarge her comprehension or exercise it on sober facts'. She has a clear eye for true 'elegance'. And she is quick to detect 'vulgarity', but her conceptions interfere with her vision (as with Mr Elton at an early stage: 'Emma too eager and too busy in her own previous conceptions and views to hear him impartially or see him with clear vision . . .'). She is in fact 'blind and ignorant', though it takes her some time to realise this. She is more attracted to ideas (internally generated) than facts (externally perceived): for instance, 'there was something in the name, in the idea of Mr Frank Churchill, which always interested her'. She moves between 'perturbation' and 'quiet reflection'. She is an inveterate 'schemer' and she likes riddles, mysteries and surprises. With – really – nothing to do, she lives in a state of 'schemes and hopes, and connivance'. It could fairly be said that part of her lives in 'errors of imagination'. Miss Bates, who does indeed 'chatter on', quite inadvertently describes Emma's chief proclivity without having any sense that she is doing so: 'One never does form a just idea of any body beforehand. One takes up a notion, and runs away with it.' Which is exactly what Emma does, all the time. When Emma reproaches Mrs Weston with the following words, she is in effect describing herself: 'You take up an idea, Mrs Weston, and run away with it. . . .' But nobody runs away with more ideas than Emma herself. She is indeed an 'imaginist' always 'on fire with speculation and foresight'. Not only is she wrong about Harriet and all the men she plans for her: she is equally wrong when it comes to discerning what is really going on – as between Jane Fairfax and Frank Churchill. When Mr Knightley proposes the possibility that there is some kind of attachment between Jane and Frank, Emma dismisses the idea with all the confidence with which she has previously conceived of other attachments:

> Oh! you amuse me excessively. I am delighted to find that you can vouschafe to let your imagination wander – but it will not do – very sorry to check you in your first essay – but indeed it will not do. There is no admiration between them, I do assure you . . . they are as far from any attachment or admiration for one another, as any two beings in the world can be.

No wonder that Mr Knightley – always correct in his careful observations – is 'staggered' by Emma's confidence. But Emma cannot see the world as it is, only as she imagines it to be; in this, at least, she is as much a fantasist or 'imaginist' as Madame Emma Bovary.

The first words of the novel are, of course, 'Emma Woodhouse', and one of the dramas of the book is concerned with the question of whether that name will undergo a mutation into Mrs – well, who? It is part of the narrative skill of the book that we both sense that she will become 'Mrs Knightley' and also wonder how it will come about, since Emma – as Emma – seems at once to be so confident and feel so self-sufficient, and also seems so perversely ignorant about herself. Perverse – because she does know when she is wrong or has made a mistake or been guilty of a rudeness or a neglect, but she has all manners of strategies of self-deception, repression, even self-misrepresentation, so that she can even translate some of her faults into appropriate and self-approving actions. Some – but not all. She would not be Emma if there was not a level of her consciousness which did not know when she had done wrong – whether it is in one of her paintings, or in one of her endeavours at social rearrangement. She knows when she is pretending not to know. She is given to error but not, at all, to evil. She can and does create confusion in society but never contemplates transgressing its norms and restrictions and obligations. She knows many people and some she is able to judge quite accurately immediately (e.g. the Eltons). Her most difficult task will be to come to know the person she partially knows and partially mystifies and misrepresents to herself – namely, Emma. Her confidence is that of a blind person: seeing nothing, she is convinced she sees all. It is only much later that she can admit that 'I seem to have been doomed to blindness.' It is because of this capacity to learn and see her own mistakes and erroneous perceptions and preconceptions that we are attracted to the meddlesome match-maker, Emma. She knows that she lacks 'common sense'; and, despite her sense of self-importance, and her need for 'being *first*' (particularly with Mr Knightley, but also at a ball or a dinner – anywhere in Hartfield in fact), she can arrive at the realisation – rare in such a privileged and spoiled heroine – that 'I was a fool.'

We like Emma because of her desire to play – whether it be at word games, charades or match-making. Meddle/play – it is not always easy to discriminate between them; but Emma has an energy for rearrangement which, well, makes the novel possible. Among other things, we can see Emma as an aspiring but failed novelist who wishes to 'rewrite' the community around her. She likes, and helps to generate, 'good enigmas or conundrums', and, if she partially enigmatises herself and other people when she should not, and produces riddles where they don't exist, well that too is part of her 'novel', her waywardly 'creative' response to the de-enigmatised, unriddling – and basically boring – society around her. For (and in) all her errors, she is a force against inertia, repetition, what Pope would have called 'dullness'. She flirts – with Frank Churchill, with Harriet Smith's marriage prospects – and such flirtations can be seen as culpable. A 'flirt' can of course refer to a 'fickle, inconstant person' and a woman of 'giddy, flighty character', but it can also carry the meaning of a 'darting motion', 'a smart stroke of wit', and (of a person) 'one who mocks or finds fault.' (All these definitions are taken from the *Oxford English Dictionary*.) In seeing Emma as something of a flirt – correctly enough – we should perhaps do well to bear in mind all the connotations of the word. The novel is a 'flirtatious' genre. We cannot easily imagine a novel entitled (and centred on) 'Mr Knightley'. Which can lead us to a consideration of the relationship between 'speech' (as it is transcribed in the book) and narrative discourse. The range of speech habits displayed in the novel is quite wide. If we omit the honest decency of the Westons and the crass vulgarity of a Mrs Elton, we can still note the considerable difference between the discourses of Mr Woodhouse, Miss Bates and Mr Knightley – not to mention Emma's own way of talking (and keeping silent). When we consider all the different voices that are supposed to conjoin in a community of shared discourse, we can appreciate such a statement as 'her heroism reached only to silence'. Needless to say, it refers to Emma, who would, and can, have a witty retort for anyone. It is precisely because she ruptures that heroic silence on Box Hill with her witticism at Miss Bates's expense that we realise how fragile and vulnerable is the relationship between all the 'voices' in the book. The wonder is, not that it can be so boring, but that it isn't Babel.

Mr Woodhouse, described by the rather elusive authorial voice as a 'kind-hearted, polite old man' has for some time been reseen and redefined as a selfish old hypochondriac, a travesty of a father whose minimal energy is expended in speaking out against marriage (his passive power is made all too clear in Emma's unthinking resolve never to leave her father or her father's house; the Knight must leave his Abbey to come and live with Emma and her father if the marriage is to take place). Emma blesses his 'favouring blindness' and he himself speaks of himself as living 'out of the world', but of course the apparently 'blind' father apparently living 'out of the world' can be a very powerful figure indeed. And it is Mr Woodhouse who stands between Emma and marriage – not only the actual act but all thoughts of it. (It is not the first time in literature that a daughter has seemed almost to become like a mother to the child-father. Indeed, one could trace a line of such instances from King Lear and Cordelia to Maggie and Adam Verver in *The Golden Bowl*.) But here I just want to point to the bizarre fatuity of Mr Woodhouse's discourse. He can ramble on about pork, or muffins – and, of course, 'gruel'. He commends the 'remarkable' cleverness of his grandsons because they will come and stand by his chair and ask, 'Grandpa can you give me a bit of string?' The peak of his aphoristic wisdom is reached by such statements as 'An egg boiled soft is not unwholesome.' The point is not worth belabouring that such a discourse could not have written the novel, *Emma*. But we have to say the same of Mr Knightley's discourse. He never wastes or squanders a word; his comments are economical, just, correct, somewhat terse and occasionally just this side of pomposity. He is as little likely to 'play' with language as he is inclined to dance. He could, no doubt, produce an admirable set of moral maxims – but not a novel. We may indeed see him as the true, even somewhat mythical, figure of the English gentleman, and we can scarcely forget how much he dislikes, or disapproves of, Frank Churchill – from his handwriting to his haircut; his mystifications and his puzzles; his excessive gallantry coupled with his apparent neglect of duty to his parents. Knightley is perhaps prejudiced because of unconscious jealousy. Emma opts to be prejudiced the other way. In her 'serious spirit' – as opposed to her 'vain' one – she knows that Knightley is the true gentleman, very much Frank's superior. But she plays the game of defending Frank – as she plays games *with* him – because at least he adds some 'spirit' to the community: his advent means a novelty, a disruption, a mystery, an uncertainty – in a word, a novel. He is of course roundly judged by Mr Knightley (and here the background hostilities between France and England are of course relevant):

> No, Emma, your amiable young man can be amiable only in French, not in English. He may be very 'amiable', have very good manners, and be very agreeable; but he can have no English delicacy towards the feelings of other people; nothing really amiable about him.

Harsh, perhaps; but a judgement mainly endorsed by the book. But here exactly is the paradox: no Frank Churchill, no *Emma*. Mr Knightley would be against the novel in which he figures. The author and what seems like her ideal character are profoundly at odds, no matter how much superficial justice is meted out at the end. If Mr Woodhouse *couldn't* have written a novel, Mr Knightley *wouldn't* have.

The general talk of the community is full of 'nothing-meaning terms' – such provide much of the verbal currency of this, as many another, society. There are deviants of course: on the one hand Mrs Elton with her 'licentious' tongue, and on the other Mr Knightley and his brother, who speak only sense, and only speak sense. A potentially more interesting deviant is Miss Bates, who suffers from a kind of logorrhoea which no one, not even Emma, can withstand: 'her words, every body's words, were soon lost under the incessant flow of Miss Bates talking'. It is indeed an incessant flow, and, while it would be misleading to deem it a portrayal of a 'stream of consciousness', it is certainly a discontinuous but connected jumble of fragments of conscious and semi-conscious (and perhaps unconscious) thought. As she admits: 'I do sometimes pop out a thing before I am aware. I am a talker, you know; I am rather a talker. . . .' Yes, she is 'rather a talker' and things do 'pop out', not all of them nonsense by any means. James Joyce has been invoked in connection with the teeming monologues of Miss Bates, and not inappropriately. If we let Miss Bates 'talk' on, with a merely arbitrary point of termination, we could have a novel – of sorts. But it would not be anything like the kind of novel that Jane Austen wrote. Nevertheless, part of the shock of Emma's rude little mockery of Miss Bates during the Box Hill outing is not only that it is an offence to good and kind manners, but also that it is a check (albeit temporary) on that 'cheerful volubility'. But what kind of a society would it be in which all that kind of 'cheerful volubility' was silenced? In which one moved between the extremes of the stern silence of Mr Knightley and the feebly wailing dottiness of Mr Woodhouse? Miss Bates, in her way, is as important to that small society as she is to Jane Austen's novel. Mr Woodhouse, Mr Knightley, Miss Bates – these are perhaps extremes, and we have not considered, and need not consider, the vulgar Eltons, the 'amiable' over-gallant Frank Churchill, the good-natured if somewhat platitudinous Westons when it comes to thinking of the kind of speech which makes the novel possible. Of course, the novel contains all the modes of discourse in a larger discourse which can 'place' them all, though it is not so univocal a narrative discourse as one might at first think. The question of this narrative discourse will occupy us in a moment, but what we can assert is that, of all the 'voices ' in the book, it is Emma's which seems to come nearest to the narrative voice itself – not in knowledge, but in tone and style. In terms of 'knowledge' her voice is of course full of errors, and, as I have said, she 'tells' most things wrong. But that is part of what the book is all about. Emma is a bad 'novelist' who is the central subject of a great novel.

But then another problem arises. Given this wider variation of discourse within such a small society, with whom is Emma really to speak? We hear quite a lot about the 'evils' of this society – rather a strong word to use, given that the first time we encounter it is in the reference, on the first page, to 'the real evils of Emma's situation', which turn out to be 'the power of having rather too much her own way, and a disposition to think a little too well of herself'. Such 'evils' are obviously social and secular – no theological considerations are involved. The word is used more than half a dozen times, but we never react to it as we should, say, in *Macbeth*. The real 'evil' or terror in *Emma* is the prospect of having no one properly to talk to, no *real* community, in fact. Imagine those long evenings when Emma has only her father to converse with, which she has to get through with the aid of backgammon. For a person of her 'wonderful velocity of thought' they must be nearly intolerable. Hence Emma's dread, near the end, when she foresees the possibility of all the society she knows dispersing for one marital reason or another: 'Hartfield must be comparatively deserted; and she left to cheer her father with the spirits only of ruined happiness. . . . All that were good would be withdrawn . . . what would remain of cheerful or of rational society within their reach?' And that really is a dreadful threat. We have noted how various and potentially discordant are the discourses within this small society, so that it is a question of who really listens to, or is heard by, whom. But the image of Emma spending long hours with her father and no one else brings home to us the real threat to her and her position. Not that she might not find the appropriate husband, not that she might not find sexual satisfaction (that question is scarcely raised), but simply – and terribly – that she might be condemned for years to have no one to talk to wittily, playfully, rationally, or in any way at all that transcends pork, eggs, muffins and gruel. That would be a doom indeed.

The virtues and blessings of 'domestic happiness' are firmly supported in the novel just as vague gregarious socialising (here as elsewhere epitomised by Bath) is devalued or discredited. Thus Emma can appreciate the strong domestic tendency in John Knightley:

> there was something honourable and valuable in the strong domestic habits, the all-sufficiency of home to himself, whence resulted her brother's disposition to look down on the common rate of social intercourse, and those to whom it was important. It had a high claim to forebearance.

Fair enough, and we know that Jane Austen is no novelist of the *pícaro*, the unhoused and unhomed, the deracinated (a comparison with the male 'peregrinating' world of Smollett would be interesting on this point). But it would be a generous view indeed of 'domestic happiness' to see an image of it in Emma's evenings alone with her father, just as it would be perverse to see the empty frivolities of a Bath as the only alternative. What Jane Austen knows – and shows – is that, while 'domestic happiness' is an admirable ideal, it is not easy to come by. She also knows and shows (who better?) what domestic misery could be like. And how much more common it was than 'domestic happiness'. In the event Jane Austen ensures that Emma does marry Mr Knightley and we are to imagine that her playfulness will harmonise nicely with his sobriety. (One of the most memorable things he says to Emma is 'If I loved you less, I might be able to talk about it more.' Emma can be a sport of language while Mr Knightley is, if anything, an under-talker; but between them we can conceive how they might work out a converse – a conversation – which will be energising and vivifying for them both.)

Emma and Mr Knightley wed, and the little community regathers in closer intimacy. But that 'little community' is small indeed and notably contracted. Harriet was 'less and less at Hartfield' and is clearly dropping out of the social picture; 'Jane Fairfax had already quitted Highfield'; John Knightley is about to return to London. There is as much dispersal as regrouping. The social circle is not enlarged and renewed and regenerated. It has shrunk and turned inward. Effectively it is composed of Emma and Knightley together keeping watch over Mr Woodhouse – that negation of family and society. At the end we read that

'Hartfield was safe' (Mr Woodhouse's last appropriate flicker of emotion being a paranoia about *'housebreaking'*). Hartfield – not Highbury. Hartfield, we remember, was always in some way just separate from Highbury, and the ending could be seen as a symbolic retreat from society at large to a single, anxiously defended – and isolated – house. The last words of the book – 'the perfect happiness of the union' – apply of course to Emma and Knightley. If one read this optimistically one might be tempted to see it as a paradigm of a more general reassertion and re-establishment of a larger 'union': a community which undergoes so many various threats of *dis*union in the course of the novel. But the end is marked by so many dispersals and such a specific exclusive and excluding retreat that it has hard not to see the conclusion of the novel as being centrifugal as to society even while it is cetripetal as to individual pairings and families. (The resonances of 'the union' in this novel are very different from those which emanate from the words 'united them' which conclude *Pride and Prejudice* – different, and greatly reduced. If we look at the trend in the 'sentimental novel' we can see that there, too, there was an increasing tendency to depict a withdrawal from the 'world' or society at large, into the 'little society' of the family. Even Pemberley and Mansfield Park – figures of a larger social harmony and restoration – depend on a 'withdrawal' from the incorrigible and unassimilable parts of society. Thus Primrose, in Goldsmith's *The Vicar of Wakefield*, says, 'If we live harmoniously together, we may yet be contented, as there are enough of us to shut out the censuring world and keep each other in countenance.' In the 'sentimental novel' we often find such a retreat from the world – the tendency is reclusive. The wider social world of relationships is rejected. But this is an idealised, non-prescriptive mode of fiction. *Emma* is not in that tradition, nor is Jane Austen one of the 'sentimental' novelists. Nevertheless there is clearly discernible in her later work a somewhat similar reclusive tendency and at least a comparable inclination to exclude or reject society at large. But the reasons for this are infinitely more complex in her fiction than they are in the 'sentimental' novel, and in *Emma* it is far from unambiguously clear that the odd little family group – hardly a circle – will be enough to keep them all 'in countenance'. The family itself may have to be reconstituted before it can provide any kind of adequate alternative to the rejected society-as-it-is. That will be one of the matters explored in *Persuasion*.) There is no sign that Emma will become the restorer and renewer of Highbury in the way that Fanny does of Mansfield Park. Rather we sense that to a large extent individuals will go their separate ways. I find it hard not to feel that the felicitous personal 'union' here coincides with something approaching social dissolution rather than figuring its reharmonisation. It would seem that Jane Austen was growing distinctly more pessimistic about her society's ability to re-establish and renew its vital bondings and cohering power. Society has not collapsed. But in this novel it has started to scatter.

The novel: so simple a term for us, yet so ambivalent for such a writer as Jane Austen. To put it very crudely, if the novelist upholds the values the novel seems to endorse and celebrate, there would be no novel. Let me run a few quotations together to try and make clear my point. Mr Knightley: 'There is one thing Emma, which a man can always do if he chooses, and that is, his duty; not by manoeuvring and finessing, but by vigour and resolution.' And again from Mr Knightley: 'Mystery; Finesse – how they pervert the understanding! My Emma, does not every thing serve to prove more and more the beauty of truth and sincerity in all our dealings with each other.' Mystery and finesse – and surprise (e.g. the arrival of the pianoforte) – yes, they pervert, or confuse, the understanding. But they make the novel possible. 'Secrecy and concealment' cause pain to characters within the novel (not least Jane Fairfax), though they also of course cause the novel. But Mr Knightley has a very different way of describing Frank Churchill's behaviour:

> But I shall always think it is a very abominable sort of proceeding. What has it been but a system of hypocrisy and deceit – espionage and treachery? – To come among us with profession as of openness and simplicity; and such a league in secret to judge us all!

And again, later, having colluded with Frank Churchill – just for the fun (or distraction) of it – Emma says to Jane 'Oh! If you knew how much I love everything that is decided and open!' And, when Emma and Mr Knightley are finally engaged, the author tells us, 'It was all right, all open, all equal.' Later again, as Emma sees everything becoming clear; 'the disguise, equivocation, mystery, so hateful to her in practice, might soon be over'. The desire, the drive, to arrive at what is open, decided and simple is also the desire and drive of the novel. But, if everything had been 'decided', 'open' and 'simple' from the start, there would of course have been no novel. In one form or another, the novel depends on some form of disguise, equivocation and mystery. In an ideal world, such as wished for by Mr Knightley, there would only be 'openness and simplicity'. But it would be a world without any novels – there would be nothing to clarify, nothing to demystify, nothing closed to render open. No 'disguise', 'concealment', 'equivocation' – and no 'amusement' (which Emma feels about the whole goings-on while Mr Knightley feels only disapprobation) – would mean no novel. From one point of view one could say that this novel works towards establishing its own dispensability. When everything is 'open', the novel is – quite definitively – *shut*.

But the author has a little warning for us, unobtrusive as it may seem: 'Seldom, very seldom, does complete truth belong to any human disclosure; seldom can it happen that something is not a little disguised, or a little mistaken.' This should not be equated with the truism that 'the whole truth cannot be told'. It is more a matter of what we should take to be a warning from the narrative voice itself. There is no possibility of a complete 'human disclosure'. Apart from (or in addition to) the 'disguises' and 'mistakes' displayed in the novel itself among the characters, there are possible 'disguises' and 'mistakes' in the narrative itself. 'Closure' is not to be equated with full 'disclosure'. The narrative voice itself oscillates between apparently full knowledge and confessedly partial knowledge. The illusion of perfect and total clarity is as much of a fiction as 'the perfect happiness of the union' which concludes the book. Emma learns a lot about herself; but that does not mean that she arrives a total self-knowledge. Similarly, the novel *Emma* makes many discoveries about Emma and her community; but we are quietly warned to be alert to those little 'disguises' and 'mistakes' which are inseparable from any narrative – as they are from any 'human disclosure'.

# 7

# In Between: *Persuasion*

*Persuasion*. Not 'Persuasion and . . .' – Resistance, Refusal, Rebellion, for instance. Just *Persuasion*. In previous titles using abstract nouns Jane Austen had deployed pairs. This time the debate, the struggle, the contestation, the contrarieties and ambiguities are all in the one word. As they are all in, or concentrated on, the one girl. Anne Elliot is the loneliest of Jane Austen's heroines. Persuaded by others, she has to repersuade herself.

> Sir Walter Elliot, of Kellynch-hall, in Somersetshire, was a man who, for his own amusement, never took up any book but the Baronetage; there he found occupation for an idle hour, and consolation in a distressed one; there his faculties were roused into admiration and respect, by contemplating the limited remnant of earliest patents; there any unwelcome sensations, arising from domestic affairs, changed naturally into pity and contempt, as he turned over the almost endless creations of the last century – and there, if every other leaf were powerless, he could read his own history with an interest which never failed – this was the page at which the favourite volume was always opened:
>
> 'ELLIOT OF KELLYNCH-HALL'

Jane Austen opens her book with the description of a man looking at a book in which he reads the same words as her book opens with – 'Elliot, of Kellynch-hall'. This is the kind of teasing regression which we have become accustomed to in contemporary writers but which no one associates with the work of Jane Austen. It alerts us to at least two important considerations the dangers involved in seeking validation and self-justification in book as opposed to life, in record rather than in action, in name as opposed to function; and the absolutely negative 'vanity' (her key word for Sir Walter) in looking for and finding one's familial and social position, one's reality, in an inscription rather than in a pattern of behaviour, in a sign rather than the range of responsibilities which it implicitly signifies. We learn how fond Sir Walter is of mirrors and how hopelessly and hurtfully unaware of the real needs and feelings of his dependents he is. This opening situation poses someone fixed in an ultimate solipsism gazing with inexhaustible pleasure into the textual mirror which simply gives him back his name. The opening of Jane Austen's text – a title, a name, a domicile, a geographic location – implies a whole series of unwritten obligations and responsibilities related to rank, family, society and the very land itself, none of which Sir Walter, book-bound and self-mesmerised, either keeps or recognises. He is only interested in himself and what reflects him – mirrors or daughters. Thus he likes Elizabeth because she is 'very like himself' – this is parenthood as narcissism – and Mary has 'acquired a little artificial importance' because she has married into a tolerably respectable family; 'but Anne, with an elegance of mind and sweetness of character, which must have placed her high with any people of real understanding, was nobody with either father or sister: her word had no weight; her convenience was always to give way; – she was only Anne'. Only Anne – no rank, no effective surname, no house, no location; her words are weightless, and physically speaking she always has to 'give way' – that is, accept perpetual displacement. Anne we may call the girl on the threshold, existing in that limboid space between the house of the father which has to be left and the house of the husband which has yet to be found. No longer a child and not yet a wife, Anne is, precisely, in between, and she lives in in-betweenness. She is a speaker who is unheard; she is a body who is a 'nobody'. I emphasise this because the problems of the body who is, socially speaking, a nobody were to engage many of the great nineteenth-century writers. We might recall here that in one of the seminal eighteenth-century novels, *La Nouvelle Héloïse*, Julie's father refuses even to listen to the idea of her marrying Saint-Preux, because Saint-Preux is what he calls 'un quidam', which means an unnamed individual or, in dictionary terms, 'Person (name unknown)'. This is to say that, as far as the father is concerned, Saint-Preux exists in a state of 'quidamity'. As far as

her father is concerned, Anne also exists in that state of quidamity
– she was nobody, she was only Anne: 'He had never indulged
much hope, he had now none, of ever reading her name in any
other page of his favourite work.' Until she is, as it were, reborn
in terms of writing in the Baronetage, she does not exist – not to
be in the book is thus not to *be*. We may laugh at Sir Walter but
Jane Austen makes it very clear what kind of perversity is
involved in such a radical confusion or inversion of values
whereby script and name take absolute precedence over
offspring and dependents; or, to put it another way, when you
cannot see the body for the book.

Anne Elliot, then, is perpetually displaced, always 'giving way'
as opposed to having her *own* way – it is worth emphasising the
metaphor. The story of her life consists precisely in having had
her own way blocked, refused, negated. One might almost think
of the book as being about dissuasion, for she is urged or forced
not into doing something which she does not want to do, but into
*not* doing something which her whole emotional self tells her is
the right thing (that is, marry Captain Wentworth at a time when
he had no fortune). Her words carry no weight. The word
'persuasion' echoes throughout the novel of that title just as it is
constantly haunting Anne Elliot (it occurs at least fourteen times).
It is as if she cannot get away from what she has done in allowing
herself to be persuaded not to marry Frederick Wentworth – or
dissuaded from marrying him. Yet 'persuasion' implies some sort
and source of 'authority' – preferably moral authority; mere
power can work by simple imperatives or prohibitions backed up
by force. But what is striking about the world of *Persuasion* is the
absence of any real centre or principle of authority. Among the
possible traditional sources of authority we might include the
family, parents, the clergy, social rank and respected names,
familiar and revered places, codes of manners and propriety,
codes of duty and prudence, the care and concern of friendship,
or true love so certain of itself that it becomes self-authorising.
But in this novel all such potential sources of authority have gone
awry, gone away, gone wrong; they are absent, dispersed or
impotent; they have become ossified, stagnant or – worse –
totally unreliable and misleading. Everything is in a condition of
change in this novel, and as often as not it is change as
deterioration or diminution. In such a world it becomes a real

question, what can and should remain 'constant'? To retain an uncritical allegiance to certain decaying inert social hierarchies and practices means dehumanising the self for the sake of rigidifying deathly formulae; to abandon oneself to the new might be to opt for a giddy dissolution. Just about all the previous stabilities of Jane Austen's world are called into question in this novel – in which things really are 'changed utterly', with no terrible beauty being born. It is a novel of great poignancy and sadness, as well as one of real bitterness and astringency, for it is deeply shadowed by the passing of things, and the remembrance of things past.

It is hardly surprising, then, that time plays a larger part in this novel than in any other of Jane Austen's works. It is the only one of her novels which gives a specific date for the opening action – 'summer 1814' – as *Emma* is the only novel to use a single name as a title. The significance of that date (the end of the Napoleonic wars – apart from 'the hundred days' of Napoleon's abortive return, concluded by the battle of Waterloo in 1815), becomes increasingly obvious: it marks a big change in English history and society. But in the novel the crucial passage of time is that which has elapsed since Anne was 'persuaded' to give up Wentworth and he disappeared into the navy – 'more than seven years were gone since this little history of sorrowful interest had reached its close.' Indeed *Persuasion* is in effect a second novel. (Part of its rare autumnal magic – not unlike that of one of Shakespeare's last plays – is that it satisfies that dream of a 'second chance' which must appeal to anyone who has experienced the sense of an irreparably ruined life owing to an irrevocable, mistaken decision.) The 'first novel' is what might be called (warily) a typical Jane Austen novel and is told in telescopic brevity in a few lines in chapter 4:

He [Wentworth] was, at that time, a remarkably fine young man, with a great deal of intelligence, spirit and brilliancy; and Anne an extremely pretty girl, with gentleness, modest taste and feeling. – Half the sum of attraction, on either side, might have been enough, for he had nothing to do, and she had hardly any body to love; but the encounter of such lavish expectations could not fail. They were gradually acquainted, and when acquainted, rapidly and deeply in love. It would be difficult to say which had seen the highest perfection in the other, or which had been the happiest; she, in receiving his declarations and proposals, or he in having them accepted.

End of story. To get there could have taken the younger Jane Austen some hundreds of pages. But times and things have changed. That was a happy novel of yesteryear, here no more than a distant trace, a radiant but receding, summarisable memory in this second novel. 'More than seven years were gone since this little history of sorrowful interest had reached its close.' The first novel ended when the totally vain, egotistical anti-father (he is even described as womanly in his vanity) Sir Walter Elliot 'gave it all the negative of great astonishment, great coldness, great silence'. His 'negative' blocked the marriage and the novel alike. It is a 'negative' which is against generational and narrative continuity and renewal and it has far-reaching social implications.

Here it is enough to point out that it provides the starting-point for a new kind of novel for Jane Austen; a novel which arises precisely out of the thwarting and 'negating' of her first (earlier type of) novel. Hence the stress on time past. What has happened in between then and now? And what can happen next? It must be something quite different from the action and resolution of any previous Jane Austen novel, because something – history, society or whatever it is that is embodied in the sterile, life-denying figure of Sir Walter – has given that kind of novel 'all the negative'. What Jane Austen does say is this: 'She [Anne] had been forced into prudence in her youth, she learned romance as she grew older – the natural sequence of an unnatural beginning.' Most of Jane Austen's heroines have to learn some kind of prudence (not Fanny Price, who has suffered for her undeviating dedication to prudentiality). Anne, born into repression and non-recognition, has to learn romance – a deliberate oxymoron surely, for romance is associated with spontaneous feelings. But in Anne's case these had been blocked; her father gave them all the negative. To find her own positive she has, as it were, to diseducate herself from the authorities who, whether by silence or disapproval or forceful opposition, dominated that early part of her life when she was – in relation to Captain Wentworth – becoming somebody. Anne has to start on a long and arduous second life, which is based on loss, denial, deprivation. This is the 'unnatural beginning' to her life, and to Jane Austen's novel, which differs quite radically from her previous works in that there, as I said, her heroines tend to graduate from romance to prudence. And because of what she has lost and regretted losing (again an unusual condition for the Jane Austen heroine, who has usually not yet had any significant romance when the book opens) Anne undergoes a new kind of ordeal and tribulation, since any reference to Captain Wentworth offers 'a new sort of trial to Anne's nerves' so that she has to 'teach herself to be insensible on such points'. Among other things, Anne Elliot has to combine sense and *in*sensibility – again, a marked change from Jane Austen's earlier work.

The novel starts, then, with Sir Walter contemplating 'the limited remnants of the earliest patents' in a volume which records 'the history and rise of the ancient and respectable family'. 'Limited remnants' are indeed all that now remain, and *this* volume will complete the work by recording the 'fall' and self-destruction of this 'respectable family' – if not the traditional family in general. Around the unnaturally well-preserved appearance of Sir Walter he can only see the 'wreck of good looks of everybody else'. Did he but realise it, the 'wreckage' goes a good deal deeper than that. What is irremediably wrecked and what might yet remain to generate new life from among the 'remnants' becomes a key question of the book. Anne has to live with the regret for what she has lost, while her one friend and mother-substitute, Lady Russell, while feeling sorry for Anne, 'never wishes the past undone'. As a result 'they knew not each other's opinion, either its constancy or its change'. When Sir Walter decides to move with his daughters out of the family home, Kellynch Hall, Anne is aware of 'the general air of oblivion among them'. It is an air which partially pervades the book. When Anne does finally meet Wentworth again, her concern is very much with the possible effects of time:

> How absurd to be resuming the agitation which such an interval had banished into distance and indistinctness! What might not eight years do? Events of every description – changes, alienations, removals, – all, all must be compromised in it; and oblivion of the past – how natural, how certain too!

In the event Anne finds that 'to retentive feelings eight years may be little more than nothing'. Time can obviously mean one thing to a couple in love – and something quite different to the society around them. Anne is a lonely figure of emotional constancy living in a society of 'changes, alienations, removals'. She hears that Wentworth finds her 'altered beyond his knowledge', but his enlightened knowledge will find her essentially unaltered. There is of course much emphasis on the past and the pastness of the past: '*That* was in the year six'; 'There had been a time'; 'those rooms had witnessed former meetings'; and so on. The pluperfect tense is poignantly present. Even painful memories are precious; indeed even precious because painful.

> Scenes had passed at Uppercross, which made it precious. It stood the record of many sensations of pain, once severe but now softened; and of some instances of relenting feeling, some breathings of friendship and reconciliation, which could never be looked for again, and which could never cease to be dear. She left it all behind her; all but the recollection that such things had been.

The dominant mood before the end is autumnal, nostalgic, a sense of the most significant period of experience being in the past, recollectable but irretrievable and unrepeatable. 'One does not love a place the less for having suffered in it.' There are moments when Wentworth speaks to Anne 'which seemed almost restoring the past'. 'Restoration' on this personal level does prove to be joyfully – miraculously – possible. But on the social and familial level no such restoration is possible. This is made clear when the heir to Kellynch, Mr Elliot, enters the novel and is not only keen to marry Anne but *seems* a correct and suitable figure to assist at such restoration after the gross and ruinous derelictions of Sir Walter. Lady Russell, characteristically, would like to forward this marriage and see Anne 'occupying your dear mother's place, succeeding to all her rights . . . presiding and blessing in the same spot'. To Anne herself the idea of 'being restored to Kellynch, calling it her home again, her home forever, was a charm which she could not immediately resist'. But love is stronger than even the most precious property. Anne really has 'left it all behind her'. Whatever else it might be, this is not a 'restoration' age.

The question of 'what lasts' obviously figures most largely in this novel in connection with human feelings – even leading to a recurring debate as to whether man or woman is capable of the greater constancy, of loving longer. Captain Benwick is slightly reproached by Wentworth for having put aside his devotion to the dead Fanny Harville (whom he apparently worshipped) to marry Louisa Musgrove. 'A man does not recover from such a devotion of the heart to such a woman! – He ought not – he does not.' Wentworth obviously has his own motives for such an assertion: he is both indirectly signalling his own unbroken devotion to Anne, and questioning hers. And indeed such pointed exchanges proliferate towards the end of the book: 'You did not like to use cards; but time makes many changes.' Wenworth's statement is of course also a question. To which Anne replies, 'I am not yet so much changed' – 'and stopped, fearing she hardly knew what misconstruction'. In the crucial 'recognition' scene – in the revised chapter 23 – the central debate is between Captain Harville and Anne while Wentworth apparently writes a letter. Harville argues that men love longer, that women have a legendary reputation for inconstancy. Anne maintains that 'We certainly do not forget you, so soon as you forget us', and 'All the privilege I claim for my own sex . . . is that of loving longest, when existence or hope is gone.' This is all said for the benefit of the apparently preoccupied but all-attentive Wentworth. I shall return to the indirect mode of communication in this crucial scene. Here the point to note is that, as Lady Russell says, 'Time will explain' – certainly in this novel, in which time is so central, and 'explanations' (making intelligible, laying things out clearly) are both crucial and difficult to come by. And the novel itself is an inquiry into – an ex-planation of – the effects of time. As I have said, this is the 'second' novel, made necessary by the rude 'negation' of the first one, which remains as an aborted embryo in chapter 4.

I shall return to the relationship between Anne and Wentworth. First we should consider the general state of society as it is represented in this book. The normal sources of stability and order in Jane Austen's world would include social position, property, place, family, manners and propriety, as generating a web of duties and responsibilities which together should serve to maintain the moral fabric and coherence of society. In this novel all these institutions and codes and related values have undergone a radical transformation or devaluation. There *are* values, but many of them are new; and they are relocated or resited. Instead of a heedful regard for position and property and family, we have a new obsession with 'rank', 'connexions', money and private relationships. Lady Russell esteems Sir Walter not as a man or father (he is a wretched example of both) but as a baronet: 'she had prejudices on the side of ancestry; she had a value for rank and consequence'. There are discussions of 'rank, people of rank, jealousy of rank'. Mary, the most insufferable snob (she is not comic – she is unbearable), looks not at Mr Elliot but at 'the horses . . . the arms . . . the livery'; she regards only the insignia of rank, empty signifiers of another empty series of signifiers. For 'rank' in this book does not betoken a responsible authoritative position in society: it signifies only itself. It is rigidifying self-reifying system – signifying nothing. It is symptomatic of a 'state of stagnation' existing in the class which should be exemplary and active if it is to serve as, and deserve to be, a ruling class. Mr Elliot at one time of his life despises 'the honour of the family' and declared that 'if baronetcies were saleable, anybody should have his for fifty pounds, arms and motto, name and livery included'. 'Rank' is degraded into a mere commodity. On the other hand, when it seems that it would be more profitable for him to become the serious heir to baronetcy, he speaks seriously in favour of 'the value of rank and connexion'. This is a mark not of his conversion but of his ruthlessly selfish opportunism and hypocrisy. The discourse and ideology of 'rank' happen to be available to disguise or 'embellish' his crudely egotistical aspirations. The new realm where rank *does* have a genuine significance and is related to a hierarchy of real functions and obligations is the navy – but I shall come back to the navy. The emphasis on the 'value' of 'connexions', which Lady Russell upholds in an apparently rational way, as the unspeakably foolish Mary does in the crudest possible way ('It is very unpleasant having such connexions', she declares of the respectable Hayters), is a relatively new one in Jane Austen. It emphasises a merely titular or 'nominal' and fortuitous relationship rather than any true bonding or sense of reciprocal human relatedness. An extreme example of the meaninglessness and folly of this stress on 'rank' and 'connexions' is offered by Sir Walter's and Elizabeth's frantic anxiety and eagerness to cultivate the acquaintance of their titled cousins, Lady Dalrymple and her daughter. As people they are not even 'agreeable'; 'they were nothing'. Mr Elliot asserts that 'rank is rank'. The book confirms this as a meaningless tautology and counterasserts that rank is 'nothing'.

More than one person is said to be 'nothing' or 'nobody'. Anne 'was nobody' because unmarried; Mr Wentworth (Frederick's brother) 'was nobody . . . quite unconnected', because he was a curate and not 'a man of property'; Charles Hayter is 'nothing but a country curate'; Captain Wentworth, when he reappears as rich 'and as high in his profession as merit and activity could place him' was 'no longer nobody'. These are mainly the verdicts of Sir Walter, a 'foolish spendthrift baronet' who has neither money nor profession nor merit nor activity. He is also no longer married and has rented his property. If anybody is now 'nobody', it is he. It is indirectly Jane Austen's verdict – through Anne's silent assessment – that the Dalrymples 'were nothing'. But who then is somebody and something – and by what social criteria? It would seem that there are no longer any agreed-on standards, no authoritative modes of assessment, to discriminate the somebodies from the nobodies, to tell a something from a nothing. This in itself is a symptom of a crisis of values – a chaos if not a total absence and loss of 'common' (i.e. communal) standards of modes of identification and evaluation. There seems to be no correlation or connection between social title and social role, between rank and merit.

The honorific term 'gentleman' – always somewhat vague – now means different things to different people (Sir Walter is 'misled' when his agent Mr Shepherd refers to Mr Wentworth as a 'gentleman'), or it is meaningless (as applied to Captain Wallis) or worse it conceals heartless and ruthless anti-social egotism (Mr Elliott passes as 'completely a gentleman'). The true 'gentlemen' are now to be found in the navy, but they are neither recognised nor addressed as such. A whole social system of categorisation and terminology is slipping into meaningless or perverse misapplication, dangerously so when the label 'gentleman' is confidently affixed to a man who is the complete opposite (or inversion) of everything a true gentleman should be. Society's very taxonomy seems to have collapsed, being at best misleading and at worst totally corrupt. Names themselves seem to have lost any social significance – at least from the perverse and anachronistic point of view of Sir Walter, who laments thus: 'One wonders how the names of many of our nobility became so common.' One explanation may involve the dilution of aristocratic families with the wealthier members of other classes; another could simply point to the behaviour of Sir Walter himself, who effectively does just about everything he could to bring his family name into disrepute. It is he who, on hearing that Anne is going to visit her crippled and impoverished friend Mrs Smith, says disdainfully, 'Mrs Smith, such a name!' 'Smith' is indeed the archetypal anonymous English name, a name which is in effect no 'name' at all. But, here again, this novel forces us to question all kinds of social assumptions. What really *is* in a name? In the case of Sir Walter Elliot, an impoverished and fatuous vanity; in the case of Mrs Smith, a wealth of misfortune and misery; in the case of Lady Dalrymple, 'nothing'. Like 'rank' and 'connexions', names also no longer serve to facilitate any kind of social orientation. They now manifest themselves as truly arbitrary signifiers – designations unrelated to any coherent social design or structure.

Let us now consider property and places, houses and homes and families. We can note immediately that the action of the novel is dispersed among an unusually large number of different places (unusual for Jane Austen). Fanny Price visits her 'home' in Portsmouth; Emma goes to Box Hill. But Anne is variously 'removed' or 'transplanted' from Kellynch Hall to Uppercross cottage; to the Great House (of the Musgroves) to Bath; with a glimpse of Winthrop and a crucial visit to Lyme. This topographical diffusion and 'transplanting' is itself both a symptom and a part of a more far-reaching social fragmentation and mobility. One important scene takes place in an hotel in Bath. 'A morning of thorough confusion was to be expected. A large party in an hotel ensured a quick-changing, unsettled scene.' An hotel is the appropriate edifice for a transient, increasingly uprooted or unrooted society, and that 'quick-changing, unsettled scene' is – in little – the scene of the whole book. The 'thorough confusion' experienced in the hotel pervades society at large. This topographical dispersal and social scattering also have their effect on the style and vocabulary of the novel. Of the incident on the Cobb we are told parenthetically that '(it was all done in rapid moments)'. In a way that is true of the book as a whole, which is more episodic, more fragmentary, and more marked by quick and sudden changes and abrupt transitions and jerks of the plot than any of the previous novels. Related to that is a perceptibly new note of emotional volatility and irruptiveness, even excess. After the incident on the Cobb there is, not a cool discussion, but an 'interchange of perplexity and terror' – a significant dissolution of coherent speech in feeling. The word 'burst' appears a number of times in relation to sudden mental and emotional eruptions – 'extraordinary burst of mind', 'bursts of feeling'; phrases such as 'a thousand feelings rushed on Anne', 'overpowering happiness' contribute to the increased presence of sudden unanticipated and unpredictable inward intensities. And such 'bursts', 'rushes of feeling', emotional 'overpowerings' are not always the signs of a potentially dangerous and disorderly (or 'improper') lack of control, as they often are in Jane Austen's earlier work. On the contrary, they can now be the desirable manifestations of a capacity for authentic and spontaneous feeling. This means that there is a much more ruffled 'choppy' surface to the narrative. 'Tranquillity' is often 'interrupted'; 'restraint' gives way to 'disturbance'. 'Every moment rather brought fresh agitation.' This refers to Anne near the end, but in a way it is true of the novel as a whole.

There are further lessons to be learned from Anne's constant 'transplantation'. The following is crucial:

> Anne had not wanted this visit to Uppercross, to learn that a removal from one set of people to another, though at a distance of only three miles, will often include a total change of conversation, opinion, and idea . . . she acknowledged it to be very fitting, that every little social commonwealth should dictate its own matters of discourse; and hoped, ere long, to become a not unworthy member of the one she was now transplanted to . . . she believed she must now submit to feel that another lesson, in the art of knowing our own nothingness beyond our own circle, was becoming necessary for her.

This awareness that within the one common language – English – there can be innumerable discourses according to group, place, and so on, is a very crucial one. It is not the same thing as a dialect but what Roland Barthes calls a 'sociolect' – 'the language of a linguistic community, that is of a group of persons who all interpret in the same way all linguistic statements.' It is of course simply a general truth, and one well known to Jane Austen, that people speaking the same language can very often not 'hear' each other because they are operating within different discourses or sociolects. It is characteristic of many of Jane Austen's heroines that they are aware when people are operating within different discourses – an awareness which is an aspect of their sense and linguistic 'conscience' and very often a consequence of their detachment and isolation. And Anne learns another lesson; just as one language is in fact made up of many discourses, so society is made up of many 'circles' and in many of these circles one may be a 'nothing' just as in some discourses one is inaudible. Anne's 'word' initially 'had no weight' precisely because she was regarded as a 'no-body' within the first circle of her family – 'negatived' from the beginning. Her speech can only take on its full value when she is truly regarded as a 'some-body' – a person in her own right, not according to rank or status, and taken permanently into a new circle – the navy. In between she is, well, in between. But notice two things. Anne does not fight this state of affairs or lament the plurality of discourses. On the contrary, she is willing to try and adapt herself (within the limits of her unchanging sense of propriety). Yet her speech – like her love – is 'constant' in a society apparently given over to change. Having to negotiate a plurality of partial discourses, Anne comes to embody what we might call the conscience of language. She, and she alone, always speaks truly, and truly speaks. Indeed, Jane Austen may well be intending to depict Anne as in some ways old-fashioned – or, rather, out of fashion (which is by nature ephemeral and fickle). Not all change is regarded as unmitigatedly bad in this book – indeed, given the 'stagnation' and moral paralysis (if not something worse) which seems to prevail among the upper ruling clases, then some change may be not only unavoidable but positively necessary and welcome. But Anne's 'lessons' do point to the fact (glimpsed at the end of *Emma*) that society is breaking up into smaller and smaller 'circles' and units. This implies – indeed involves – the loss of any sense of a true, authoritative 'centre', and the possible disappearance of any 'common' language (and with that, a shared sense of 'common' values). Add to this the fact that even within the small separate 'sociolects' there are people who tend towards speaking an 'idiolect' (i.e. a language which is really private to themselves and not properly heard or understood by anyone else). This could portend a society which is no longer truly a society in any meaningful sense but rather an aggregate of contiguous but non-communicating groups or just families (or even just individuals), with no *real* connections, no overall coherence, no single structure binding them together. Separate 'commonwealths' with neither 'wealth' not anything much else held in 'common': 'Dictate-orships' perhaps (Jane Austen's words carry a weight of possible irony) of one kind or another. To a large extent this is our 'society' today. It is not 'society' as Jane Austen had thought it should or could be. But she saw that the change was coming and was inevitable. To a large extent she could see why. It is all there in this unique novel.

In this prevailing atmosphere of change it is not surprising that 'property' no longer plays the assured and essential role it did in earlier novels. Mary, for instance, 'had merely connected herself with an old country family and respectability and large fortune'. That 'merely' is Sir Walter's thought, Jane Austen's irony. The advantage for people 'living on their own property', according to the insinuating Mrs Clay, is that they 'are not obliged to follow any . . . profession' but can just 'follow their own pursuits'. Just what Sir Walter likes to hear, of course, but not at all what Jane Austen believed, since for her the owning of 'property' necessarily involved the recognition of obigations and duties to the community. If it is merely an arena for self-indulgence and hedonism, it is less than useless as a part of the maintained and maintaining order of society. It is still desirable to have property of course; but as a symbol of certain social values it is undervalued as Mary undervalues Charles Hayter's 'good, freehold property' because it confers no rank (adding, in her incomparably selfish way, 'it would be shocking to have Henrietta marry Charles Hayter; a very bad thing for *her*, and a still worse for *me*'), or as Sir Walter feels 'no degradation in his changes', seeing 'nothing to regret in the duties and dignity of the resident land-holder' and finding 'much to be vain of in the littleness of a town'. His is the quintessential abdication and dereliction of the ruling-class landowner. When he rents Kellynch Hall he causes a 'break-up of the family', and leaves behind 'deserted grounds' and 'so altered a village'. (There is quite possibly here a barely ironic allusion to Goldsmith's *The Deserted Village*.) He is an agent of 'desolation', helping both to precipitate and to accelerate the destruction of the old order of society. (Anne will be the first Jane Austen heroine who will not found her marriage on the once-necessary basis of 'property'.) Society in the form of Sir Walter Elliot has become all empty self-regarding form and display: he has no sense of responsibility to his position, to the land, and it is significant that he rents his house to go and participate in the meaningless frivolities in Bath.

This matter of renting his house is worth pausing over for a moment. The notion 'quit Kellynch-hall' is initially horrendous to Sir Walter. But he would, as he says, 'sooner quit Kellynch-hall' than undertake any economies or constraints on his unrestricted pursuit of pleasure. His relation to his house is not a responsible one: he does not see his house as part of a larger context, an interrelated rural society, an ecology, if you will; it is more like a pleasure-dome or a three-dimensional mirror which flatters his vanity. So he agrees to quit if he cannot have those pleasures. But note that 'Sir Walter could not have borne the degradation of being known to design letting his house – Mr Shepherd had once mentioned the word "advertise" – but never dared approach it again.' I shall come back to 'advertising' in the last chapter, but here again we note that Sir Walter wants the profits of 'renting' while still pretending to belong to an aristocracy which did not contaminate itself with contact with any kind of 'trade' or commerce. This is the self-deception of a figure no longer sensible of the significance of his social rank. When he does consider renting it he thinks of it in terms of 'a prize' for the fortunate tenants – 'a prize'; he has no appreciation of the real value of his inherited house. And I shall just note the areas to which he does not really want the new tenant to have access: 'The park would be open to him of course . . . , but what restrictions I might impose on the use of the pleasure-grounds, is another thing. I am not fond of the idea of my shrubberies being always approachable.' Funny of course – but again there is no sense of the importance and significance of the house of his fathers, the house in which he so signally fails in *his* paternal duties. To abandon it in exchange for money, for mere pleasure, rather than 'economise' is a very notable dereliction of his duties. This is an alteration which is most definitely not 'perhaps an improvement' but indisputably a degradation.

Even before Sir Walter decided to 'quit Kellynch-hall' we are told of 'the prosperity and the nothingness' of the life there, with nothing to fill 'the vacancies' – 'no habits of utility abroad, no talents or accomplishments for home.' Lady Elliot, the true upholder of domesticity, is dead. Anne would carry on her work – but of course is not allowed to. Rather than practise the slightest economy or curtail any of his indulgences, Sir Walter prefers to rent his landed house, which is indeed nothing of a home and merely parasitic on the community it should help to maintain and preserve. (We might note in passing that we are told that, if Sir Walter follows Anne's sensible suggestions, Lady Russell estimates that 'in seven years he will be clear'. Of course he cannot deprive himself of any of his private gratifications for any length of time at all. It is Anne, who can wait and economise scrupulously on her emotional expenditure, who after 'seven years' – when Wentworth returns – will finally 'be clear'. 'Clear', one might say, of the whole rotten pack of her family; as well as 'clear' of the obstacles, negatives and disuasions which had blocked the growth and consummation of her true love seven years previously.) Seeing the Crofts in Kellynch Hall after they have rented it, Anne feels that 'they were gone who deserved not to stay, and that Kellynch-hall had passed into better hands than its owners.' Unlike the 'improvements' suggested in *Mansfield Park*, the 'few alterations' the Crofts make to Kellynch Hall are 'all very much for the better'. It is almost as if Jane Austen was passing a verdict on the defection of a whole class in whom she had once invested so much hope. Initially Anne is sad at the thought of 'a beloved home made over to others' – but that home was no longer home. Her loyalties shift and are displaced or realigned elsewhere. For instance: 'how much more interesting to her was the home and the friendship of the Harvilles and Captain Benwick, than her own father's house in Camden Place'. The Harvilles and Benwick are naval officers of course, and, just as there is a shift of significant, active 'rank' from society to the navy, so it is the navy who – apparently paradoxically – reconstitute a meaningful domesticity, re-create the idea of home, ultimately redefine the notion of society itself. It is Mrs Croft who asserts that 'Woman may be as comfortable on board, as in the best house in England', and clearly her ship was more of a 'home' than Kellynch Hall. But even the house of the Harvilles and Captain Benwick – rather like a ship on shore – in all its apparent oddity and somewhat cramped idiosyncrasy offers to Anne 'the picture of repose and domestic happiness'. Note that the rooms are extremely small and the very limited space is crowded. This was one of the major deficiencies of Fanny's home in Portsmouth which contributed to its 'impropriety'. Nothing of that now. The small space is turned into 'the best possible account' and instead of the chaos of excessive proximity and discord there is the snugness of hospitable ease and intimacy. The 'hospitality' of the navy is emphasised – and usual 'forms' of etiquette are at the same time devalued. There was such a 'bewitching charm in a degree of hospitality so uncommon, so unlike the usual style of give-and-take invitations and dinners of formality and display'. A whole system of socially prescribed 'formal' reciprocities is here effectively displaced by an informal spontaneity. It is not prompted by custom but by 'the heart' – the rooms are so small as none but those who 'invite from the heart' would think of asking people to share their living-space. The shift of emphasis from socially prescribed 'invitations' to those which come from 'the heart' is part of a larger change from a socially based to an emotionally justified code of behaviour. It has quite radical implications. As already intimated, I shall have more to say about the navy, but I want to return to land matters.

There is an example of a relatively happy home unrelated to the navy: the home of the Musgroves, the Great House. But it is 'happy' in a new way. For a start, it is characterised by an 'air of confusion' owing to the accumulating objects belonging to the lively children. The originals of the ancestral portraits would have been 'astonished' at the general 'overthrow of all order and neatness'. So surmises Anne. But, again, though these were characteristics of Fanny's Portsmouth home, the Great House is in no way another version of that horrific non-home. The tone of the description is worth noting with some care:

The Musgroves, like their house, were in a state of alteration, perhaps of improvement. The father and mother were in the old English style and the young people in the new. Mr and Mrs Musgrove were a very good sort of people; friendly and hospitable, not much educated, and not at all elegant. Their children had more modern minds and manners . . . and were now, like thousands of other young ladies, living to be fashionable, happy, and merry. Their dress had every advantage, their faces were rather pretty, their spirits extremely good, their manners unembarrassed and pleasant; they were of consequence at home, and favourites abroad.

Alteration, *perhaps of improvement*: the qualification is not barbed. There is no biting irony, no malice in the text. Jane Austen is genuinely open and uncommitted. The gay hedonism of the children is not seen as dangerous or disruptive. The older generation lack education and elegance. Once that would have been a serious defect in Jane Austen's eyes. Now it doesn't matter. Because other values, such as friendship and hospitality, are coming to seem more important. 'There is so little real friendship in the world!' laments poor Mrs Smith later in the book, and it is now becoming for Jane Austen a cardinal virtue. The children's 'modern minds and manners' are not mocked. They may be somewhat giddy, perhaps a little shallow or frivolous. They are lively and good-spirited (*they* are not 'stagnant') and their 'manners' are at least 'unembarrassed and pleasant' – quite unlike the ludicrous snobbery, chilly hauteur, unpleasant seeming-politeness, and mean-spirited psuedo-etiquette of the upper classes. Jane Austen cannot whole-heartedly identify with these 'modern minds and manners', just as Anne 'would not have given up her own more elegant and cultivated mind for all their enjoyments'. But both Anne and her author can recognise their genuine happiness and applaud their 'good-humoured mutual affection'. Society – England itself – is altering, perhaps improving. Jane Austen does not take sides; she neither mocks the old style nor reprobates the new. Her stance is Anne's. But she is clearly undertaking a radical reassessment and revision of her system of values. She can be gently ironic about the domestic arrangements of the Great House, as when, later, she describes a tolerably confused and noisy scene there with everyone doing something different and contributing to a general disharmony, and comments, 'It was a fine family-piece.' But it is not Portsmouth. A new tolerance and relativism has entered Jane Austen's tone. What for Anne is a rather nerve-racking 'domestic hurricane' is for Mrs Musgrove 'a little quiet cheerfulness at home'. Jane Austen is amused but not censorious: 'Everybody has their tastes in noises as well as in other matters; and sounds are quite innoxious, or most distressing, by their sort rather than their quantity.' (Lady Russell would hear the street noises of Bath as signalling her 'winter pleasures' and would, says Jane Austen, have probably regarded them as part of 'a little quiet cheerfulness' after the deprivations of the country.) I do not believe that Jane Austen could have written that sentence at the time of *Mansfield Park*.

Having mentioned 'manners' I want to point to another major reversal or change in Jane Austen's habitual mode of assessment. We have seen how important manners were to her – as to Burke – and how crucial she made it seem to distinguish (if possible) between Lockean good manners and Chesterfield's type of good manners (alternatively, between English and 'French' manners). Again, this careful distinction – indeed the whole signifying role of manners – has become useless if not treacherously misleading. On Mr Elliot's first appearance he 'proves' by his 'propriety' that 'he was a man of exceedingly good manners'. By contrast, Admiral Croft's 'manners were not quite of the tone to suit Lady Russell'. Mr Elliot indeed serves single-handedly to undermine utterly any code of values attached to manners. 'His manners were so exactly what they ought to be, so polished, so easy, so particularly agreeable' that – as manners – Anne herself finds them as good as Wentworth's! His conversation leaves 'no doubt of his being a sensible man'. And it is not merely the cultivated appearance of manners. Lady Russell finds 'the solid . . . so fully supporting the superficial' that she perceives him as an embodiment of all the virtues. 'Everything united in him.' He even seems to have 'a value for all the felicities of domestic life'. True, Anne begins to have her suspicions and reservations, and Lady Russell is capable of erroneous judgements. But *nothing* in Mr Elliot's manners could have prepared anyone for the revelation of the 'true' man.

Mr Elliot is a man without heart or conscience; a designing, wary, cold-blooded being, who thinks only of himself; who, for his own interest or ease, would be guilty of any cruelty, or any treachery, that could be perpetrated without risk of his general character. He has no feeling for others. Those whom he has been the chief cause of leading into ruin, he can neglect and desert without the smallest compunction. He is totally beyond the reach of any sentiment of justice or compassion. Oh! he is black at heart, hollow and black!

Mrs Smith's description of the true Mr Elliot is never challenged or controverted. It is the most unqualified summary of unmitigated evil in all Jane Austen's work. Yet his manners are so perfect that even Anne can scarely differentiate them from her true, beloved, Wentworth's. Anne's own manners are 'as consciously right as they were invariably gentle', but as usual, in her constancy and genuine 'invariability', she is an exception. With the vivid example of the absolue non-correlation between 'manners' and character presented by Mr Elliot we have to accept that 'good manners' in the socially accepted and prescribed sense are simply no longer of any use in estimating or infering the inner qualities of anyone. Perhaps a new code of manners altogether is necessary – manners which, however 'incorrect' or even crude according to established social notions of decorum and propriety, do nevertheless reveal the true qualities of the inner man, or woman. Anne, and Jane Austen, find them in the rougher but sincere manners of the navy.

As I have tried to indicate, the usual sources, strongholds and tokens of social values have, in *Persuasion*, dried up, collapsed, or been eroded or travestied into meaninglessness. Even the family – which did seem to offer the possibility of a last stronghold in *Emma* – is at best a good-humoured confusion barely containing generational differences and at worst a hollow mockery or a claustrophobic prison of cohabiting egotists or a dreary vacancy. It may indeed have already 'broken up' – specifically in Anne's case, but that might be taken as a paradigm for a more general dissolution of the institution of the family. Mrs Smith seems to recognise this when she gives her opinion that 'even the smooth surface of family-union seems worth preserving, though there may be nothing durable beneath'. It would be idle to speculate whether or not this was Jane Austen's own opinion. It does indicate a felt apprehension that the 'family' was in danger of becoming an empty form, a mere name – or collective noun – when it should be the cornerstone and microcosm of society. The fate and future of 'the family' is an ongoing debate and problem in our own times. Jane Austen could already see that it was at a crisis point. We have very little to add to her diagnosis. What Jane Austen does offer as a potential source of new values, new bondings is the navy. About which now a few comments.

The specific dating of this novel – 1814 and after – and its obvious significance has been mentioned. Britain has won the wars against Napoleon and primarily through her navy. Many specific references to the war – including Trafalgar – are made in the book, and indeed the whole novel is not properly comprehensible without appreciating the importance of this background. As Warren Roberts rightly states, '*Persuasion* could only have been written by someone whose life was deeply affected by the Revolutionary and Napoleonic wars' (see *Jane Austen and the French Revolution* for detailed evidence of the relationship between the novel and the wars). The 'peace' brings Captain Wentworth back to England; more generally, 'This peace will be turning all our rich Navy Officers ashore.' That many of them *were* rich – through capturing enemy ships and the like – is important, since, for example, it enables the Crofts to rent Kellynch Hall and makes Wentworth completely independent of any snobbish social disapproval (such as had separated him from Anne). Indeed, it makes him a 'somebody', since money was becoming a more powerful means of gaining social acceptance and esteem than land or even rank. But what is more important is that they bring back with them a wholly different scheme of values, and a potentially new model of an alternative society or community, alive and functioning where the traditional land society seemed to be moribund and largely 'stagnant'; a new community which, among other things, accepted wives as equals. Thus Anne delights in seeing the Crofts walk about Bath, meeting and warmly greeting their friends, and observing 'their eagerness of conversation when occasionally forming into a little knot of the navy, Mrs Croft looking as intelligent and keen as any of the officers around her'. That admiration and respect for 'a little knot of the navy' brings Jane Austen curiously close to

Conrad and his sense of the hypocrisies of society on land and the values of fidelity within the ranks in the navy. (As it happens he also uses the work 'knot': 'the dark knot of seamen drifted in sunshine' – *The Nigger of the 'Narcissus'*.) This, if you like, is Jane Austen's ultimate displacement or shift of values in the novel: to redefine and relocate her vision of a 'possible' society in relation to that most potentially precarious of occupations engaged with the most unstable element – an unlanded and unrooted community of people committed to the sea. Hardly a stable and fixed community, since that 'knot' could be disassembled and reassembled, depleted and augmented, indeed 'tied' or 'untied', at any time and in any place. In truth, the extreme of a dispersed community, a floating, drifting, changing, population which would have seemed the antithesis of the kind of society Jane Austen was writing to secure or maintain. But by 1815 much had changed. For one thing it was the navy which – to Jane Austen's eyes – had saved England, while the ruling aristocratic class had done almost nothing. Seen in this light, the fact that at Uppercross 'there was a very general ignorance of all naval matters' is deplorable, while Sir Walter Elliot's unbelievably patronising and condescending attitude to naval officers is beneath contempt. Without the navy there quite possibly would no longer have been any society left in England. (Jane Austen must have been aware of the invasion panics.) Her transfer of allegiance and emotional investment from the English ruling classes (about whom she had clearly been growing more and more pessimistic) to the navy (which not only appealed to her patriotism but also embodied new and welcome alternative values) is doubly understandable at this point in English history. Among other things, *Persuasion* is notable for some uncharacteristically lyrical passages about the sea, which also help to give the novel its markedly different atmosphere. (Emma, we may recall, had never seen the sea, and one of her father's more significant fatuities is, 'I have been long perfectly convinced . . . that the sea is very rarely of use to any body.' By this time the sea was 'of use' – of inestimable use – simply to the whole of England!) In the first description of the coast and sea at Lyme, so enchanting and beautiful in contrast to the 'melancholy looking rooms' and undistinguished buildings of the town, there is a curious sentence referring to the group 'lingering' on the seashore 'as all must linger and gaze on a first return to the sea, who ever deserve to look on it at all'. *Deserve* to look on the sea? Is this Jane Austen – or Melville? Here is a shift indeed. Not the awed and humble approach to Pemberley or Mansfield Park; but the privilege, for those who deserve it, of gazing at – the sea. Jane Austen seems to be turning her back on more than just the local inanities of a Sir Walter Elliot.

Of course the navy is on shore throughout the novel, and it is the effect they have there and the part they play in Jane Austen's redefinition and relocation of values that we must consider. At one point the enthusiastic Louisa

> burst forth into raptures of admiration and delight on the character of the navy – their friendliness, their brotherliness, their openness, their uprightness; protesting that she was convinced of sailors having more warmth than any other set of men in England; that they only knew how to live, and they only deserved to be respected and loved.

Allowing a little for her youthful hyperbole, this is in many ways – and with moderation – the verdict of the book. Anne finds Captain Harville 'a perfect gentleman, unaffected, warm and obliging' – it would seem that, by another shift, only sailors can be true 'gentlemen': Mrs Harville is 'a degree less polished' but has the 'same good feelings'. Above all, this naval group (or knot) are sincere, hospitable, open, warm and genuinely friendly. What they might lack in 'polish' they more than made up for in 'heart'. In any case, Jane Austen never set great store by *mere* 'polish' and by now she clearly distrusts it. The older values seem to have lost much of their force and degenerated into snobbish reflexes. Where the older civilities are somewhat peremptorily adhered to, it is often in 'an improper style'. Anne of course holds on to what was best in the older practices and codes. She believes in 'duties', in 'prudence' in 'propriety'. If she is somewhat shy and reserved, she appreciates the decent lack of these potentially inhibiting traits in others. Quiet herself, she responds to 'heartiness'. She suspects Mr Elliot precisely because he seems too controlled and good-mannered:

> Mr Elliot was rational, discreet, polished – but he was not open.

There was never any burst of feeling, and warmth of indignation or delight, at the evil or good of others. This, to Anne was a decided imperfection. Her early impressions were incurable. She prized the frank, the open-hearted, the eager character beyond all others. Warmth and enthusiasm did captivate her still. She felt she could so much more depend upon the sincerity of those who sometimes looked or said a careless or hasty thing, than of those whose presence of mind never varied, whose tongue never slipped.

The passage speaks for itself; we remember that Emma's most significant transgression occurs precisely because her tongue slips and she says 'a careless and hasty thing' to Miss Bates, and to get some idea of the kind of change in Jane Austen's values it represents just think how a Darcy or a Knightley would appear if tested by these criteria. These are primarily the manners of feeling, which may dispense with manners: spontaneity is always likely to annihilate etiquette. If we want to see a 'Romantic' side to Jane Austen, it would be in such passages. In a sense Jane Austen was fortunate to have the navy to turn to. Otherwise it is something of a question whether she would not have had to have gone further afield – perhaps into socially 'dangerous' areas – to find suitable embodiments of these preferred values and characteristics.

Anne is also always 'useful', and willingly so, in anybody's home. (When Mary leaves her sick child in the care of Anne so that she can go to a dinner party, her excuse is 'I am of no use at home – am I?' It is the literal truth. In fact she is 'no use' anywhere. In this, she is not alone in the book.) When Anne speaks up for the navy – 'The navy, I think, who have done so much for us, have at least an equal claim with any other set of men, for all the comforts and all the privileges which any home can give. Sailors work hard enough for their comforts, we must all allow' – Sir Walter speaks disparagingly of them as a class and merely allows that 'the profession has its utility'. But 'utility' is becoming a very positive word in this book. When someone is sick, Anne is glad to know herself 'to be of the first utility'. Whether or not there is some influence of Bentham here it is impossible to say. But it is clear that for Jane Austen 'utility' was becoming a word of approval. We must allow, for instance, that

Sir Walter and his ilk have no 'utility' whatsoever. 'Utility' is something which Anne has in common with the navy. All the more appropriate that she should find her true home here at last. Of course, there is already an example of a 'useful' woman happily integrated into the 'little knot of the navy' – Mrs Croft. From the start we gather that she is no 'lady' of idleness leaving the 'real' world to men. She is in fact better at business than her husband. 'A very well-spoken, genteel, shrewd lady, she seemed to be . . . [she] asked more questions about the house, the terms, and taxes than the admiral himself, and seemed more conversant with business.' Thus Mr Shepherd. When Anne meets Mrs Croft we are given the description of effectively a new kind of woman in Jane Austen's world. Quite outside any structure of dominance and deference, she seems to belong to no class at all. She is both inseparable from her husband – does all that may become a man – sharing all his travels; and also strongly independent – and still very much a woman. If she seems 'rougher' than many Jane Austen heroines, she is also in many not unadmirable ways tougher. Anne is not (yet!) like Mrs Croft. But she admires her.

> Mrs Croft, though neither tall nor fat, had a squareness, uprightness and vigour of form, which gave importance to her person. She had bright dark eyes, good teeth, and altogether an agreeable face; though her reddened and weather-beaten complexion, the consequence of her having been almost as much at sea as her husband, made her seem to have lived some years longer in the world than her eight and thirty. Her manners were open, easy, and decided, like one who had no distrust of herself, and no doubts of what to do; without any approach to coarseness, however, or any want of good humour.

Anne is 'pleased' with her, and so are we. So, obviously, was Jane Austen – and in that depiction of Mrs Croft she is offering a new model of a new kind of woman, scarcely imaginable in any of her previous novels. (One odd note: she is childless. But then Jane Austen never does actually *show* us a good mother. I think we must infer from this what we choose.)

A key area of the debate concerning old and new values

concerns resolution and wilfulness. A central problem here
hinges on Anne's early 'yielding' to the negative persuasion of
Lady Russell, which effectively involved her supressing the love
she felt for Wentworth and preventing a marriage both of them
desired. Was she wrong? Did she show insufficient resolution
and belief in her own instinct and desires? We shall leave a final
adjudication until later, but her behaviour in fact poses a problem
which reverberates through the book. For instance, in talking to
Louisa (who boasts that she is not so 'easily persuaded' and
derides 'nonsensical complaisance') Wentworth praises her for
her 'character of decision and firmness' and speaks with
understandable bitterness against the opposite: 'It is the worst
evil of too yielding and indecisive a character, that no influence
over it can be depended on. . . . Everybody may sway it; let those
who would be happy be firm.' And to emphasise his point he
picks up a hazel nut – one of the rare emblematic aids to discourse
in Jane Austen! – praising its exemplary enduring strength and
hardness, and asserting, rather foolishly, that its 'happiness' is a
function of its unpunctured 'firmness'. A 'nutty' happiness
indeed, but not perhaps a very helpful model for a young – and
virgin – woman! Is this fair to Anne? Was she too easily 'swayed' –
too indecisive and lacking in firmness? It is at least something of a
question. But Louisa's 'decision and firmness' reveal themselves
most graphically on the Cobb. We have been told that Louisa has
the habit of 'doing as she liked' and believed in 'the merit in
maintaining her own way' (against 'parental wishes or advice')
and is quick to advance 'heedless schemes'. On the Cobb she also
wants her own way: this times it involves jumping from the steps
into the arms of Wentworth. Enjoying the sensation, she
expresses a wish and an intention to do it again. Wentworth
'reasoned' against it, but 'in vain': she smiled and said, 'I am
determined I will.' And 'maintaining her own way' she jumps –
too precipitously ('heedlessly'?) – and as everyone knows she
falls and suffers a dangerous concussion. There lies the 'nut' of
'decision and firmness'! She indeed would not 'yield' to any
'persuasion', however 'rational' – and she will not be 'swayed'.
But how 'meritorious' or 'admirable' is that now? Is such a
character trait of determined wilfulness a virtue or a rashness? Is
it a real strength or an egotistical rashness (she not only causes
damage to herself but great anguish and a lot of trouble to other

people)? Is that jumping girl a finer character than the sedate and self-effacing – and apparently 'persuadable' – Anne? We might remember that another of the Musgrove children sustains a 'bad fall': young Charles falls and dislocates his collarbone in chapter 7. On that occasion 'Anne had every thing to do at once', since Mary retires into useless hysterics, and all the duties and responsibilities devolve on Anne. As, of course, they do after Louisa's accident on the Cobb. There even Wentworth reveals an uncharacteristic sense of helplessness: 'Is there no one to help me?' These are unusual words from a Jane Austen hero. He is not omni-competent and once again all eyes turn to Anne for advice and direction. She effectively has to help and advise them all. These modern youngsters are attractive and lively, and perhaps engagingly adventurous and independent in their wilful heedlessness of external constraints – or advice. The Musgrove girls are 'wild for dancing', 'wild to see Lyme' – 'wild' is one of their favourite words and, as a word, harmless enough as a youthful hyperbole (as for a more recent young generation everything was 'fabulous', 'fantastic', and so on). But are they perhaps in fact *too* wild? After all, Elizabeth Elliot is also accustomed to 'go her own way' and there is nothing at all attractive about her ice-cold selfishness. After the Cobb incident Anne might well wonder whether

> it ever occurred to him [Wentworth] now, to question the justness of his own previous opinion as to the universal felicity and advantage of firmness of character; and whether it might not strike him that, like all other qualities of the mind, it should have its proportions and limits. She thought it could scarcely escape him to feel, that a persuadable temper might sometimes be as much in favour of happiness, as a very resolute character.

Of course she is right. Louisa, in 'jumping' at will, shows herself to have a very 'yielding' character, but she yields to her own whims and caprices. At least Anne thought that she was 'rationally' persuaded to yield to Lady Russell. It comes back to the problem of authority in a period of change when all traditional sources of authority are in doubt, if not disqualified or defunct. Whose persuasion or advice should one – anyone – listen to? When Wentworth cries for help he is articulating a larger need. In the event, in this novel it is the apparently yielding but actually steadfast Anne who becomes the authority to whom others turn. Wentworth's 'nut' lies sufficiently crushed to make us (and him) realise that she would be in no way an appropriate wife for him. He says he wants 'A strong mind, with sweetness of manner' in any wife he chooses. There is of course only one candidate. Anne is not a 'nut' – that visual image for the ideal wife was curiously infelicitous. For nuts are either totally hard or totally smashed (I suppose they can also go rotten). Anne's strength of character is peculiarly human. Which means that it must combine flexibility and firmness, the concessionary and the adamant, the rights of self with the obligations of selflessness, in a complex, ever-demanding way. Wentworth is right in seeking for an alliance of strength and sweetness (the lion and the honeycomb). He is only wrong temporarily and perhaps understandably – in not seeing that that ideal admixture is only to be found in one woman (in this novel). Anne. Only Anne.

How Anne will discover Wentworth's true state of feelings, how she will be able to convey her still 'unyielding' love for him, raises a problem familiar in Jane Austen's work: namely, that of private communication in a predominantly public world in which various taboos on certain forms of direct address between the sexes are still operative. It is again a problem of hermeneutics. 'Now, how were his sentiments to be read?' After his return they are 'repeatedly in the same circle', but that offers as many chances for misreadings (on both sides) as it does opportunities for reliable interpretation. People talk too little or too much. (As when Anne finds herself the unwilling repository of the 'secrets of the complaints of each house'. Regarded as nothing herself, a permanently available pair of hands or ears, she is 'treated with too much confidence by all parties'. On the other hand, the one man she wants to hear most from says least. She cannot control these asymmetries and excesses or shortfallings of com- munication.) Mary, inevitably, provides a constant example of lack of all communicative tact – as when she asks Anne to tell their father they have seen Mr Elliot. To Anne 'it was just the circumstance which she considered as not merely unnecessary to be communicated, but as what ought to be supressed'. For Jane Austen the imperatives of verbal repression were as important as the obligations of communication: social harmony depends on getting the balance right. Needless to say, in the world of *Persuasion* most people have lost that tact. Anne often has to 'smother' her own feelings and preoccupations, realising that they are of little or no interest to her interlocutors. She knows what it is to have to 'converse' without 'communicating'. She also knows what it is like to talk without being heard. 'They could not listen to her description of him. They were describing him themselves.' But of course her main concern is somehow to communicate with Wentworth and this in fact provides the climax of the book. At the concert near the end she is sure of his feelings and desperate to communicate hers. But she cannot contrive the necessary propinquity. As other Jane Austen women do, she has recourse to the eye – trying to catch Wentworth's when she is prevented from speaking to him: 'she was so surrounded and shut in: but she would rather have caught his eye'. But she is trapped by the unwelcome attentions of Mr Elliot and the general 'nothing-saying amongst the party'. How to find or create a place or position which would make 'something-saying' possible is again a recurrent problem for Jane Austen's heroines. Interestingly, she manages to choose a seat on the bench with a 'vacant space' next to her. Wentworth nearly takes it, but Mr Elliot breaks in. Here is a small parabolic tableau of the problem for a woman. She can create a space for the man but cannot invite him to take it. Man has to initiate, and if there is any hesitation the wrong (and more assertive) male may take advantage of that space. Mr Elliot does this – and a jealous Wentworth takes his departure. Anne still has her problem: 'How was the truth to reach him? How, in all the peculiar disadvantages of their respective situations, would he ever learn her real sentiments?'

So crucial is this problem that Jane Austen revised her first – excessively simple – resolution of it into two longer chapters which dramatise in detail the strategies of indirection to which the lovers have recourse. This revision (chapters 22 and 23) is of great subtlety and importance and is worth some particular examination and comment. In the first version Admiral Croft crudely contrives to leave them alone in his house and very quickly everything is cleared up. There is 'a hand taken and pressed; and "Anne, my own dear Anne!" bursting forth in the fulness of exquisite feeling, – and all suspense and indecision were over. They were re-united.' This is summary to a degree and a very lame solution to a problem which has been growing in importance until it becomes *the* main problem in the book. The revised and substituted chapters do not merely prolong the suspense and defer narrative gratification through gratuitous complication of plot: they comprise an infinitely richer and more searching examination of the whole problem of communication between man and woman.

The revised chapters add much. We learn more of the 'odious insincerity' of Mr Elliot and his dubious connection with that other plotting 'hypocrite', Mrs Clay, whose name is suggestive enough of a weak vessel and whose 'freckles' not only indicate a flawed and 'spotted' moral interior but may indeed suggest the remnants or traces of syphilis. (In a very interesting letter to *The Times Literary Supplement* on 7 October 1983, Nora Crook points out that 'Gowland's Lotion', which Sir Walter recommends to Anne 'on the strength of its supposed benefits to Mrs Clay's freckles', contained 'corrosive sublimate of mercury', which 'had a particular connection with the old-fashioned treatment of syphilis'. Mrs Crook produces evidence from contemporary journals such as *Reece's Gazette of Health* and, while admirably tentative in drawing any conclusions, rightly points out that 'so few are references to actual trade-names in Austen that one feels that this one must have had some sort of function other than "realism" '. I agree completely and feel surer than she does – though on no more evidence – that a hint of syphilis must be intended. After all, Mrs Clay ends up in London as Mr Elliot's mistress and thus with a status little better than that of a prostitute. The fact that she was a welcome intimate of Sir Walter's and Elizabeth's, in preference to Anne, not only confirms the worst we feel about their utterly corrupted judgement: it also suggests the presence of the most ruinous sexual disease among the upper classes. She is a fitting 'partner' for the totally corrupt Mr Elliot – who is also the heir of Kellynch Hall. A fine end to be inscribed in that volume chronicling the 'history and rise of the ancient and respectable family'!) We learn that Louisa is 'recovered' but 'altered' (perhaps improved?). There is no 'running or jumping about, no laughing or dancing'. Her newly acquired 'stillness' is not the result of achieved moral poise and undistractability – the stillness which Jane Austen admired – but the timorous cowering of a nervous wreck.

But centrally there is the extended problem of how Anne can communicate with Wentworth. It is he now who is acting under an 'unfortunate persuasion': namely, that she loves Mr Elliot. In the crowded hotel scene 'he did not seem to want to be near enough for conversation' and the 'circumstances' only expose them to 'inadvertencies and misconstructions of the most mischievous kind'. Eyes and glances – surreptitious, anxious, inquiring – are again active. More venturesomely (or desperately) Anne speaks words to others which are meant obliquely for Wentworth – as when she loudly proclaims her complete lack of interest in a party being organised for the theatre which would include Mr Elliot. She trembles as she speaks, 'conscious that her words were listened to, and daring not even to try to observe their effect'. When they do have to exchange social conversation, Anne has recourse to another strategy. Referring to trivia – whether she still enjoys card games – Anne uses the occasion to transmit a second meta-message by emphasising that 'I am not yet so much changed', hoping that the generalising response will not be lost on Wentworth – though she still fears 'she hardly knew what misconstructions'. It is indeed a tricky and dangerous game when a lifetime's happiness depends on the outcome. We may wonder at the need for all these tormenting ploys of indirection. Why cannot Anne be open and direct – qualities she admires in other people? The contrast is indeed made in the next chapter when Mrs Musgrove is talking. Her talk is marked by 'open-hearted communication', but it is all concerned with personal 'minutiae' and Anne feels that 'she did not belong to the conversation'. The obstacle – effectively a double-bind – seems to be that you cannot speak 'openly' and 'directly' about such important matters as your feelings of love, *to* the person you love, until you have achieved a certain intimacy (tantamount to engagement) which *then* permits such open talk. But how do you ever manage to get intimate enough to be intimate, as it were? I don't think this is just a matter of tiresome, overdelicate etiquette or the repressive interdictions of propriety. It certainly has something to do with true modesty. More generally I think it dramatises the delicacy and difficulty of identifying and establishing the right sexual partner. That social conditions and codes made this particularly difficult in Jane Austen's period we can hardly doubt. But one feels that there is some deeper correlation between the delicacy of the approach and the value and quality of the ensuing union. We have gained much by our less inhibited and less formalised ways of achieving sexual and marital *rapprochements*. Arguably our loss has been no less great.

Be that as it may, we now approach the actual moment of full communication. How it is achieved – the context, the method – could hardly be more interesting. The general talk has become meaningless to Anne – 'only a buzz of words in her ear'. She must look for (and send) the right signal in the noise. Then Captain Harville approaches Anne with a 'small miniature painting'. It is a portrait of Captain Benwick which was commissioned for Captain Harville's dead sister, Fanny. Benwick now wants it reset to give to Louisa, whom he is to marry. Harville finds the commission too painful and Wentworth has gallantly agreed to take care of it. He is seated nearby – 'writing about it now', as Harville explains. Harville almost tearfully muses that 'Fanny . . . would not have forgotten him so soon' and there ensues that debate about the relative constancy of men and women in their love. Anne argues that women do not forget so soon. 'We cannot help ourselves. We live at home, quiet, confined, and our feelings prey upon us. You are forced upon exertion . . . continual occupation and change soon weaken impressions.' Then follows a famous exchange in which Harville has recourse to the evidence and authority of literature – writing:

> But let me observe that all histories are against you, all stories, prose and verse. If I had such a memory as Benwick, I could bring you fifty quotations in a moment on my side the argument, and I do not think I ever opened a book in my life which had not something to say upon women's inconstancy. . . . But perhaps you will say, these are all written by men.

Anne replies,

> 'Perhaps I shall. – Yes, yes, if you please, no reference to examples in books. Men have had every advantage of us in telling their own story. Education has been theirs in so much

higher a degree; the pen has been in their hands. I will not allow books to prove any thing.'

'But how shall we prove any thing?'

'We never shall.'

Painting, writing, speech. The portrait is a fixed representation or 'quotation' of the man which he can dispatch to different women. The man changes in his affections; the portrait remains 'constant'. In this it is precisely a misrepresentation – an ideal image of the man which leaves all his emotional changeableness out. However accurate as to physiognomy, it is untrue to life. It is a detached token which can be sent through intermediaries – Harville, Wentworth – to now this woman, now that. And potentially any other. It is in all respects the opposite of an unmediated confrontation of, and communication between, a living man and a living woman. In this the portrait comes dangerously close to being like a piece of money, a coin of fixed, arbitrary 'value' which can circulate through different hands and purchase any object to be obtained at the price on the coin. There need be no relationship between the purchaser and the object. Indeed, the whole mode of transaction is marked by separation and im-personality. The model for this kind of 'relationship' is ultimately the open market. This is not to impugn the feelings of reciprocity which may have gone into the 'relationship' of Benwick, but only to point out that it is *excessively* mediated. Benwick is a man who lives in and by books. He woos and wins Louisa by quotations and a portrait (as he did Fanny and, we feel, would have tried to do with Anne). They are signs which are precisely *not* his own, not himself. They are substitutions for an essential absence – emotional if not ontological. Anne has no access to totally unmediated communication, but she must avoid the kind of mediation briefly but tellingly here alluded to. And so must Wentworth. Benwick's books and Harville's allusion to his 'quotations' might remind us that at the start of *this* book Anne was effectively written *out* of meaningful life because she was not written *in* to Sir Walter's 'book of books'. She has suffered from male 'writing' since indeed 'the pen has been in their hands' – starting with the originating male authority, the father. Her argument has of course a general and very important validity, relevant to the condition of all women in her – and our – society.

But one crucial little incident gives it a vividly local and specific point.

As she is arguing with Harville – and of course her words have a double target and dual purpose, as she hopes that the nearby Wentworth, seated and writing, will hear them and detect the personal message contained in the general statements – a 'slight noise' draws their attention to Wentworth. 'It was nothing more than that his pen had fallen down.' Nothing more – in many ways it is the most quietly dramatic and loaded incident on the book. The pen may, generally speaking, be in 'their hands'; but at this crucial moment the pen – a specific one – had dropped from *his* – specific – hand. However unintentionally, however momentarily, he is disproving the generalisation which Anne is enunciating. He is, perhaps by a 'slip', excepting himself from – revealing himself as an exception to – the rule. We tend to read a lot of significance into 'slips' now, but, at no matter what level of conscious or unconscious intention, Wentworth's 'slip' in dropping the pen at that moment is perhaps the most important signal – or unvoiced communication – in his entire relationship with Anne. I am not concerned with possible phallic interpretations of 'the pen': literalness is quite powerful enough here. No single definitive reading of the incident is either possible or desirable. But we can say at least this: Wentworth at this critical moment has, however inadvertently, dropped (let go of, lost his grip on) that instrument which is at once a tool and a symbol of men's dominance over women; the means by which they rule women's destinies, literally *write* (through inscription, pre-scription, proscription) their lives. It is as if he is open to a more equal (unscripted) relationship in which the old patterns of dominance and deference are abandoned, deleted – dropped. Benwick quotes from already written books; Sir Walter wrote in his book according to an ancient and now non-functional scriptural tradition (his 'book of books' is only a bible for himself – a mere mirror instead of the authorising and authoritative sacred text). Wentworth was writing a commission for another person – he drops the pen and, after that crucial lacuna or interruption, when he picks it up again it is to 'speak' to Anne. Under the 'public' letter he writes for Harville and Benwick he now writes a 'private' letter – like a sub-text – to Anne, which he hides under scattered paper. He goes out – formally – with Harville, and returning under false pretences (left gloves), furtively delivers the hidden – but 'true' – letter to Anne. Significantly the writing is 'hardly legible': we may guess that the impersonal 'public' letter was in a perfect hand. The hidden letter was indeed not really written, but rather 'spoken'. As he writes in it, 'I must speak to you by such means as are within my reach.' It is the desperate calligraphy of the heart – written under pressure and social constraints. No wonder it is 'hardly legible'. For this speech-writing is not done according to prescribed formulae or convention: it is an 'exceptional' writing which seeks to find a way through all the restraining and silencing rules and codes to communicate directly to the chosen woman. It attempts the apparently impossible – mediated im-mediacy. Like love. There is no need here to reproduce the contents of that letter-under-the-letter. With its delivery and reading the 'union' is assured. But two final points about it. Anne realises that, 'while supposed to be writing only to Captain Benwick, he had been also addressing her'. No doubt some of this final drama (or game) can be traced to the specific difficulties of intersexual communication in Jane Austen's society. But the episode points up and dramatises a larger truth. All 'writing' or communication is potentially double (at least exoteric and esoteric, to go no further: there may always be another message in – under – the ostensible message); we can 'address' more than one person at the same time, and likewise be 'addressed' by messages not apparently meant for us. Indeed, one might say that the addresser and the addressee of the letter – all 'letters' – are potentially indeterminate and plural. There is ultimately no single, definitively correct 'address'. The problems and difficulties which Anne and Wentworth have to negotiate are not a function of early nineteenth-century English society. They are inherent in language and communication itself. How important is this rather singular little parlour 'game'? Well – 'On the contents of that letter depended all which this world could do for her!' Life, and all that it might offer, can indeed depend on 'the letter'. It is a final joke that informs us that, as Wentworth is now rich enough to be 'accepted' as a husband for Anne by her father, it 'enabled Sir Walter at last to prepare his pen with a very good grace for the insertion of the marriage in the volume of honour.' It is of course a dead volume by now and the paternal pen is as irrelevant as it is powerless. Anne and Wentworth will 'write' their own marriage elsewhere, in a new book, in their own hands. Of course they will never 'prove' anything by the book, any book. When it comes to matters of love we can never *prove* anything – by writing, or speaking, or painting. And we never shall. When Othello asks Iago for 'ocular proof' of Desdemona's infidelity, he is lost. Her honour is 'an essence that's not seen'. You may fake 'proof' of infidelity (nothing easier for an Iago) and misread signs (and books) as evidence of inconstancy. But you cannot *prove* love – any more than you can 'see' honour or constancy. You must finally trust beyond the available evidence. The proof of the loving can only be in the living.

Before leaving the matter of language and communication in this novel, I want to draw attention to a rather surprising notion which Jane Austen inserts into Anne's thoughts while she is listening to another social conversation which combines the vacuous and the hyperbolic. 'Allowances, large allowances, she knew, must be made for the ideas of those who spoke. She heard it all under embellishment. All that sounded extravagant or irrational in the progress of the reconciliation might have *no origin but in the language of the relators*' (emphasis added). Of course social conversation can lie and fabricate – nothing unusual in such an observation. But Anne's thought is potentially more radical. Allow that language 'embellishes'; but what if *all* that people talk about has 'no origin but in the language of the relators'? Put it another way: language may be the origin of all that people relate. It is perhaps not such a new idea for us, but, coming out of the context in which Jane Austen was writing, the hint (it is perhaps no more) that language itself might be the origin of what we talk about – i.e. that language is the origin of what we think of as reality – is here startling. Language thus becomes capable of creating its own referents *and* referends – an awesomely autonomous, generative, and 'originating' power. If in fact we live primarily in the world we speak, then we should be careful indeed about the words we use. Jane Austen herself exemplifies that indispensable vigilance and scrupulousness.

What follows the final achieving of clarification and communication between Anne and Wentworth is characteristically summary. They stroll along a 'retired gravel-walk' and there can indulge their 'private rapture' in 'public view'. As usual Jane Austen does not pursue them into their private passional discourse. Whether we ascribe this to ignorance, repression or delicacy hardly matters. Jane Austen has shown us all that is essential to her novel; now she maintains a tactful distance.

> There they exchanged again those feelings and those promises which had once before seemed to secure every thing, but which had been followed by so many, many years of division and estrangement. There they returned again into the past more exquisitely happy, perhaps, in their re-union, than when it had been first projected. . . .

And so on. There they are oblivious of the passing groups – 'sauntering politicians, bustling house-keepers, flirting girls, nursery-maids and children'. The 'world' is temporarily lost, and well lost. They have made 'a separate peace'. But we should add a few words about Anne and her marriage. In some respects she is like Fanny Price, with her 'still' virtues, her essential loneliness, her general desire 'not to be in the way of any body'; her pleasure is only to be 'unobserved', her plight to be generally overlooked. She is glad just to do her duty and to be 'useful', however unappreciated. In her apparent weakness she is the real source of strength. But there is a crucial difference, related to the larger difference between the two worlds of the novels. At one point in the confusion of Uppercross, we are told of an insuperable problem: 'How was Anne to set all these matters to rights?' Fanny Price does effectively 'set to rights' all the wrongs, neglects, and partial deteriorations of Mansfield Park – which becomes something of a microcosm of society as it should be and might be. Anne's healing efforts are necessarily more local and limited in the scattered and diffused world of *Persuasion*. She would have put her father's house 'to rights' but is not allowed to. She can nurse a sick child here, tend a wounded girl there, sympathise with a grieving bereft lover, provide concrete help when Wentworth cries out for it (a hint of a possible new equality there). But society is too far gone in disarray to be 'put to rights' by an exemplary heroine. Fanny Price's marriage to Edmund symbolises and seals the restoration and renewal of a whole social order and structure. Anne's marriage to Wentworth signifies nothing larger than their own refound and reconstituted happiness in love. Their 're-union' is not a sign of any larger re-established harmony. To borrow that enigmatic and resonant phrase of Jay Gatsby's, it is 'just personal'.

Their marriage is not grounded in property – as all the previous concluding marriages in Jane Austen are. Mary – of course – gloats that Anne 'had no Uppercross-hall before her, no landed estate, no headship of a family'. And indeed it is one of Anne's regrets that she has 'no relations to bestow' on Wentworth, 'no family to receive and estimate him properly'. In fact it is he who offers a family – the new 'family' of the navy. She brings to him only her 'undistracted heart', in Henry James's memorable phrase. The marriage itself does not portend an endless stability: there will always be 'the dread of a future war'. She has to 'pay' for her marital happiness in a way unknown to any previous Jane Austen heroine. Thus the conclusion: 'She gloried in being a sailor's wife, but she must pay the tax of quick alarm for belonging to that profession which is, if possible, more distinguished in its domestic virtues than in its national importance.' (Contrast the conclusion of *Mansfield Park* and Fanny's return to the 'paternal abode' of Mansfield, which formerly 'Fanny had been unable to approach but with some painful sensation of restraint and alarm' but which 'soon grew as dear to her heart, and as thoroughly perfect in her eyes as every thing else within the view and patronage of Mansfield Park, had long been'. Her 'alarm' was definite but is in the past, replaced by an extended future of assured happiness and 'perfection'. Anne's 'alarm' is indefinite and in the future – an integral part of her happy marriage, out of an old society and into a new one, far away from the abandoned 'paternal abode', with nothing assured except her joy in her reciprocated love.) The final words of *Persuasion* effectively point to that radical redefinition and relocation of values which marks the whole novel. Established society and domesticity are now, as we say, 'all at sea' – metaphorically (they are in a state of chronic confusion, chaotic flux) but also literally. For the new social and domestic virtues are now to be found, indeed, 'at sea' – for those 'who ever deserve to look on it at all'.

(To base a marriage almost exclusively on feelings, no matter how tested and proved those feelings may be, inevitably entails a *new* kind of 'risk'. It is more than apt that this new kind of model for a more personal society, in which actions come 'from the heart', is situated both metaphorically and actually on the sea – traditionally regarded as 'the unstable element'. Even though Anne and Wentworth are models of emotional stability and constancy, the emotions are by nature inherently potentially unstable, and, without the reinforcement of some forms – formalities – and conventions, any society based on feelings must be precarious and in danger of ensuring its own impermanence. In founding a possible new society on the sea, even metaphorically, Jane Austen was engaging deliberately in what is almost a contradiction of terms. It is some measure of her disenchantment with 'landed' society that she felt prepared, or compelled, to take that risk.)

Was Anne right to give in to the 'persuasion' of Lady Russell? There is rich ambiguity or hesitation here, and phrases such as 'the fair interference of friendship' in their poised ambivalence indicate that Jane Austen knew all about the multiple motivations which are at work in the impulse to exert some apparently beneficent control over a person in a weaker position. There is, perhaps, no point at which you can clearly distinguish persuasion from constraint or constraint from coercion. It is something of a blur, a confusion if you will – and it is out of just that confusion that Anne the nobody has somehow to come to clarification and remake her life. In discussing the point with Wentworth at the end of the book, when they are privately conversing while 'apparently occupied in admiring a fine display of green-house plants' (a somewhat more auspicious adjunct to a discussion of love than 'nuts'!), Anne defends her decision without wholly exculpating Lady Russell:

> I must believe that I was right, much as I suffered from it, that I was perfectly right in being guided by the friend whom you will love better than you do now. To me, she was in the place of a parent. Do not mistake me, however. I am not saying that she did not err in her advice. It was, perhaps, one of those cases in which advice is good or bad only as the event decided; and for myself, I certainly never should, in any circumstance of tolerable similarity, give such advice.

Lady Russell is by no means one of Jane Austen's malign

characters. On the contrary she is a 'benevolent, charitable, good woman, and capable of strong attachments'. She is genuinely fond of Anne and truly appreciates all her qualities and virtues. Anne loves her to the end. She is indeed regarded by all who know her as a person of 'the greatest influence with every body', and that 'influence' is often wisely employed and invariably with disinterested concern for what is right or best. If she has a fault, it is not a kind of masked will-to-power masquerading as good advice. But 'she had prejudices on the side of ancestry . . . a value for rank and consequence, which blinded her a little to the faults of those who possessed them'. In a word, she favours the old order of society and cannot always see its derelictions and delinquencies. She is not – as she insists – a 'match-maker', though we can see her as a 'match-marrer' when it comes to not appreciating the reality and value of Anne's and Wentworth's love for each other. But her real importance and significance is that, for Anne, 'she was in the place of a parent' – a surrogate mother. This brings me back to the central problem of the lack of any reliable properly constituted authority in the book. Effectively Lady Russell fills – and is allowed to fill – an authority vacuum. As far as my memory and my notes go, I think I am right in saying that that key word is only once applied to any character in the book, and that is Lady Russell. When Wentworth is explaining to Anne that he could only think of her as 'one who had yielded', who had been 'influenced by any one rather than by me', he is referring to his apprehensions about the persuasive power which Lady Russell might still be exerting over Anne: 'I had no reason to believe her of less *authority* now' (emphasis added). As Anne explains, she thought she was yielding to 'duty', and, while she now admits she was wrong, she makes the point that she was yielding to 'persuasion exerted on the side of safety, not of risk'. Perhaps she was too cautious, but she learnt her lesson and she is justified, in the event, when Wentworth comes to see where 'risk' can lead to – as in Louisa's foolish jump. (Emma, in her capricious wilfulness, often abuses her powers of 'persuasion': for example, in relation to Harriet's 'rejection' of the perfectly suitable Robert Martin – as Knightley angrily accuses her, 'You persuaded her to refuse him'; and in relation to herself, as when she excuses herself for her 'deficiency' in not visiting the Bateses by 'the persuasion of its being very disagreeable – a waste of time – tiresome women' – a perverse act of self-persuasion which, at 'heart', she herself knows to be a culpable rationalisation for a more selfishly and snobbishly motivated disinclination and neglect.)

Wentworth had to learn his own lesson, 'to distinguish between the steadiness of principle and the obstinacy of self-will, between the darings of heedlessness and the resolution of a collected mind'. The old order was wrong; but Louisa's reaction is not the right one – self-destructive rather than reconstructive. Lady Russell's 'authority' was capable of error, but with no other reliable authority available in this society-without-a-centre (as in Anne's family-without-parental-guidance), it seemed to Anne – as to others – the only reliable substitute. But it *was* a substitute. Lady Russell is *not* Anne's mother and she is not a true central authority in society. And it is the lesson that *she* has to learn that is as important as any in the book. It is a lesson which centres on her radically incorrect appraisals of the respective worth of Mr Elliot and Wentworth:

> She must learn to *feel* that she had been mistaken with regard to both; that she had been unfairly influenced by appearances in each; that because Captain Wentworth's *manners* had not suited her own ideas, she had been too quick in suspecting them to indicate a character of dangerous impetuosity; and that because Mr Elliot's manners had precisely pleased her in their *propriety* and *correctness*, their general *politeness* and suavity, she had been too quick in receiving them as the certain result of the most correct opinions and well regulated mind. There was nothing less for Lady Russell to do, than to admit that she had been pretty completely wrong and to take up a new set of opinions and of hopes.                              (Emphasis added)

There is no more important passage in the novel. We remember that Anne had been 'prudent' (an old and basic Jane Austen value) but had had to learn 'romance'. Similarly Lady Russell will have to learn to re-educate her 'feelings' when judging people and not rely on the once-reliable signs of 'propriety' and 'correctness', 'manners' and 'politeness'. In a changing society a more emotional, 'romantic' personal code is emerging as both desirable and necessary – with a proper appreciation of the difference between 'spontaneity' and 'impetuousness', between the mere rashness of 'risk' and the securely grounded independence of individual feelings, whether or not these seem to be approved and ratified by the old standards and codes of society. The lesson that Lady Russell has to learn is not in itself revolutionary or subversive, but it does represent a radical assessment – and turning away from – many of the old values. I have said that Anne was initially 'in between', an uncertain status both socially and ontologically. The novel shows that English society is similarly 'in between': in between an old social order in a state of decline and desuetude, and some new 'modern' society of as yet uncertain values, hierarchies and principles. It may precipitately 'jump' to its own destruction and wreckage (like Louisa). It may, though it is a slim hope, reconstitute itself and its values as Anne – and 'only Anne' – has learnt to do with Wentworth. Meanwhile the message within the message of the book, the not-so-hidden 'letter' under the text of the story, reads like this: 'There was nothing less for English society to do, than to admit that it had been pretty completely wrong, and to take up a new set of opinions and hopes.'

# 8

# The Disease of Activity:
## *Sanditon*

At one point in *Persuasion* when Anne is tired from walking, she is persuaded by the Crofts to let them give her a lift home in their carriage. In keeping with his energy and robust directness, there is a certain confident heedlessness, even recklessness, about the Admiral's way of driving. His wife even has to caution him. 'My dear Admiral, that post! – we shall certainly take that post.' And in fact it is Mrs Croft who helps to guide the carriage safely:

> But by coolly giving the reins a better direction herself, they happily passed the danger; and by once afterwards judiciously putting out her hand, they neither fell into a rut, nor ran foul of a dung-cart; and Anne, with some amusement at their style of driving which she imagined no bad representation of the general guidance of their affairs, found herself safely deposited by them at the cottage.

It offers indeed 'no bad representation' of their marriage, for, if anything, it is the calm, experienced, cool-headed, practical Mrs Croft who really 'drives' the carriage (as she looks after their business interests). The carriage of their marriage is driven in a rather unconventional manner, even risking collisions and crashes because of the Admiral's good-natured, bluff impetuousness. But with the sensible hand of Mrs Croft also on the reins they negotiate the various obstacles – post, rut, dung-cart – which lie in their road. Their rather unusual, even risky, progress along the road, typifies their rather different way of moving in society – unconventionally direct and forthright, even to the point of hazardousness. But working in tandem they manage to just steer clear of the unanticipated hindrances and faults in the 'road' which might overturn them or block their eager, zestful progress, and arrive safely at their goal. It fares quite otherwise with the couple who are driving along at the beginning of *Sanditon*, that marvellous fragment of a novel which Jane Austen was working on during her last and fatal illness. 'A gentleman and lady . . . being induced by business to quit the high road, and attempt a very rough lane, were overturned in toiling up its long ascent half rock, half sand. . . .' For Jane Austen to *start* a novel with an accident is, of course, a complete departure from all her previous openings and points of commencement. It is as though instability, errancy, inversion, break-up, a general 'overturning' of established, secure, stabilising modes and procedures was the generative point of this very different novel, which starts, we might say, with a cameo of society wilfully, mindlessly, leaving the prescribed and proper road – and crashing: an admonitory token of a society which is in the irresistible and determined process of quite literally overturning itself, or, as we may say with a little (but only a very little) anachronism, going off the rails. And with all possible speed.

There is a carriage crash in Jane Austen's work as early as *Love and Friendship*, though there it was for fairly crude burlesque purposes. Carriages of course figure largely and importantly in her work as they would in her world. In that small society of very limited movement, the carriage could be a microcosm of a microcosm and might be a little heaven or a little hell according to whether Captain Wentworth was handing you into it with all due solicitousness and decorum, or Mr Elton pushing his uninvited way into it with all insufferable effrontery and insolence. The carriage could be an epitome of that society at its most comfortable and balanced and harmonious, the right company in the correct conjunctions, combining a requisite stillness with a graceful locomotion; or it could be the very image of a society of unendurable claustrophobia, intolerable proximities, penetrable and invadable vulnerabilities. The posts and ruts and dung-carts could as well be inside as out. It would depend not just on the company you kept, but also the company that kept you. However, in *Sanditon* the occupants are not at odds, and there are no posts and ruts. The carriage (which characteristically does not belong to the occupants: in *Sanditon* nearly everything is 'rented' is one way or another – little is truly 'owned') has been obstinately and quite deliberately driven off the road. They have driven up a narrow lane where 'no wheels but cart wheels could safely proceed'. They have attempted to penetrate an essentially agricultural territory where they no longer belong. The result is that the wife is 'terrified' and the man hurts his foot and is 'unable to stand'. They are off their own ground, in a place, a world, where indeed they no longer have any 'standing'. The novel opens with complete displacement.

However, the people who live there are very much in place. The 'proprietor of the place' is Mr Heywood, who is indeed first seen working in the fields among his haymakers, with the women and children close by. They comprise and compose a family–community, closely bonded and intimately related to the land. Mr Heywood is obviously intended as a simplified, somewhat mythological figure, exemplifying an idea, commitment to his property, his 'family', his locale. He and his wife are the epitome of stability: they have always remained in their 'station' – stationary. They 'never left home' and 'their movements had long been limited to one small circle'. (He only goes to London to 'receive his dividends', about which more later.) They have an old family coach, which is handed down from generation to generation. But they never travel or visit fashionable places. They believe in the 'maintenance and education' of their children and squander no money except to equip them. This commits them to 'a very quiet, settled, careful course of life'. In a word, they are obliged to be 'stationary and healthy at Willingden'. They would seem to summarise all of Jane Austen's ideals and preferred values. Yet such perfection comes across almost as a fading cliché, certainly an anachronism; a memory becoming a timeless generalisation, a nostalgic dream of a might-have-been that perhaps never was. Everything, but *everything*, represented by, and embodied in, the small, self-sealing circle of the Heywoods will be shown to be degraded, debased, forgotten or transgressed – 'overturned' – in the course even of the fragment we have. They are inscribed in the book to serve as a measure of the loss and transformation, or deformation, which prevail in the new social world of the novel, a world in which not only are all the old values – mythic or historic – changed utterly, but also everything is changing continually. Changing and yet repeating. Going round in circles. But we shall come to that.

The 'gentleman' (and the men in this book are all gentlemen if they are not labourers or tradesmen or members of the serving class – it is the first of many 'empty' terms in the book) who breaks into this small extra-historical circle of the Heywoods, crashing his hired vehicle, is Mr Parker. Mr Parker is an 'enthusiast', not for religion but for the new seaside resort town of Sanditon. He is a developer, a promoter, a speculator. He lives only for the success of Sanditon. 'A very few years ago, it had been a quiet village of no pretensions' (the original manuscript added that it was 'inhabited by one family of consequence, his own'). Mr Parker was a principal landholder, and, with the other landowner, seeing the potentialities of Sanditon for becoming 'a profitable speculation, they had engaged in it, and planned and built, and praised and puffed, and raised it to a something of young renown'. It has become Mr Parker's obsession; he can think or speak of nothing else. He had handed over his humanity to his own invention. He belongs to Sanditon, body – and soul. His attachment to it replaces all natural and human attachments.

> Sanditon was a second wife and four children to him – hardly less dear – and certainly more engrossing. – He could talk of it for ever. – It had the highest claims; – not only those of birthplace, property, and home, it was his mine, his lottery, his speculation and his hobby horse; his occupation his hope and his futurity.

It is quite simply his 'everything', in time and place; it has displaced and replaced everything which should have some significance and attract some allegiance, piety and respect, outside of himself. It has engorged and conflated all difference and otherness. He has indeed been swallowed by Sanditon as Conrad's Gould is devoured by *his* mine in *Nostromo*. His world is all Sanditon, and only Sanditon. He can talk interminably about it, because he can talk of nothing else. We may note in particular that Sanditon has become a *second* family to him, one which manifestly engages his passion more than the first, original or 'real' one. It hardly needs stressing what a perversion of feelings and attachments this transference of affective commitment from the human unit to a speculative project half fantasised out of his own 'puffing', half wrenched out of an older humane order, involves. His Sanditon is a second Sanditon as well – and there are other doublings or pairs in the novel: two cottages, two Willingdens, two families of expected lodgers (not guests) for the plentiful houses-for-rent in Sanditon, two portraits of Lady Denham's two husbands. These doubles, or 'seconds', are usually not only substitutions and replacements; they are invariably replications in an inferior and inauthentic mode or material, marked by artificiality and recency; not so much repetitions as debased fabrications, not generational organic re-productions but degenerate commercial productions, not imitative forms but debased and debasing anamorphs; not a supplementary reality, but a secondary unreality. (This does not apply of course to the pair of expected families. They, precisely, turn out to be one, or by extension – and the unconstrained inflation of loquacious cupidity – any number at all. Transient customers have no original, prior, 'founding' model. They are not a falling-off from a previous 'real'. In essence they will always be one and the same.)

A simple example of this devalued and devaluing repetition concerns the cottage. There is a real old cottage in Mr Heywood's Willingden parish, in which live a shepherd and three old women: it is ecologically functional, embedded in the lane, inhabited by figures who worked the same terrain. Sir Edward Denham, an impoverished baronet with no land (titles also no longer signify anything in this society) is 'running up a tasteful little cottage *ornée*, on a strip of waste ground Lady Denham has granted him.' A middle-class fake 'picturesque' pseudo-cottage, built by a non-baronet, on useless land which he does not own. This is the world of *Sanditon*. We have come a long way from the ideal combination of rank, domicile and property adumbrated in the earlier novels as being constitutive of a genuine and viable social order. But, of course, the best example of this process of 'doubling' and substitution is the second Sanditon itself. The original Sanditon was 'a quiet village of no pretensions', but of long history and old traditions – ancient beyond annals. The new Sanditon, and the disruptive and deforming effects it has had on the old village, are described as Charlotte Heywood is driven through both when she is taken to Sanditon as the Parkers' guest. A long quotation is necessary:

They were now approaching the church and the *real* village of

Sanditon which stood at the foot of the hill [emphasis
added]. . . . The village contained little more than cottages, but
the spirit of the day had been caught . . . two or three of the
best of them were smartened up with a white curtain and
"Lodgings to let" –, and farther on, in the little green court of
an old farm house, two females in elegant white were actually
to be seen with their books and camp stools – and in turning the
corner of the baker's shop, the sound of a harp might be heard
through the upper casement.

Such sights and sounds were highly blissful to Mr Parker. –

Not that he had any personal concern in the success of the
village itself; for considering it as too remote from the beach, he
had done nothing there – but it was a most valuable proof of the
increasing fashion of the place altogether. If the *village* could
attract, the *hill* might be nearly full. – He anticipated an
amazing season. . . .

'Civilization, civilization indeed! –' cried Mr Parker,
delighted – 'Look my dear Mary – look at William Heeley's
windows. – Blue shoes, and nankin boots! – who would have
expected such a sight at a shoemaker's in old Sanditon! This is
new within the month. There was no blue shoe when we
passed this way a month ago – Glorious indeed! – Well I think I
have done something in my day. – Now for our hill, our
health-breathing hill. –'

The ironies here hardly need underlining: the incongruities (the
harp in the baker's shop, elegant females with books and camp
stools in the old farmhouse, the blue shoes and fashion boots in a
rural shoemaker's), the cognitive dissonance generated by the
infiltration, if not invasion and colonisation, of the signs of a new
consumer culture and fashion and leisure industry, into an older
rural economy, the absurd aesthetic contamination which
characterises the 'spirit of the day' – all of which presage
'Civilization' to Mr Parker; all this bespeaks a usurpation and
despoliation which are as legible to us as they must have been to
Jane Austen's putative readers. Higher up the hill where 'the
modern began' the evidence of what constitutes that 'modernity'
is equally recognisable. Houses with names which sufficiently
indicate their owners' idle purposes, or purposive idleness
('Prospect House', 'Bellevue Cottage'), empty houses with 'bills

at the window', 'light elegant buildings', a 'plantation' (not a garden), a smart row of new houses called the Terrace, fronting onto a broad walk 'aspiring to be the Mall of the place', where there are 'the best milliner's shop', the library, the hotel and billiard room, and then on the beach the 'bathing machines' – it is exactly a resort catering entirely for leisure and consumption, with no evidence of productive labour and no sign of any significant attachment and relationship to the land on which it is built. In fact, though it is materially built on a hill, it is really (economically) built on the beach, which is its sole *raison d'être*. *This* modern Sanditon is indeed a sandy-town, a town built on sand, and thus no town at all. It has no connections with anything except the appetite for distraction and amusement and idleness which fabricated it out of words, money – and sand. Here 'all was new'. It is indeed a neoteric pseudo-town, a non-place, an anywhere most significantly marked by the empty houses with bills (indicating 'To Let', or 'For Rent') and a 'miscellaneous foreground of unfinished buildings' and 'waving linen' (courtesy of the best milliner's no doubt). It is a place for vacations, marked by actual vacancies ('To Let'), composed of the miscellaneous and the unfinished, a place for a vacating and vacant society – in truth, a vacancy, a vacuity. Devoid of any real occupations, but – as we shall see – very busy. (We might remember here Tess of the D'Urbervilles – a more pitiably displaced and abused girl than any of Jane Austen's heroines – who near the end of her weary travels finds herself taken to Sandbourne, a place of 'detached mansions', the very reverse of a community. It is a 'pleasure city', 'a glittering novelty', a place of meretricious fashion and amusement. ' 'Tis all lodging-houses here', says the postman, and, while it is the perfect place for the modern, deracinated Alec, it is no place at all for Tess, the 'cottage girl'. Again there is a prescience in Jane Austen's late work of matters which were to become more sombre and momentous later in the century. It is not far from the artificiality of Sanditon to the *anomie* of Sandbourne.)

What has been displaced to make way for this 'modern' artificial 'new' town is made sufficiently obvious in Mr Parker's attitude to, and treatment of, his first, original, inherited house, 'my old house – the house of my forefathers', where all the families of his ancestors, and indeed his own, were born and bred. It is 'snug-looking', well and modestly situated in a 'sheltered dip', 'well fenced and planted, and rich in the garden, orchards and meadows which are best embellishments of such a dwelling'. Mr Parker indeed refers to it as 'an honest old house', but 'I have given it up.' He discarded it in favour simply of what he regards as a 'better situation': that is, high on the hill, a most unsuitable, unnatural place for his second (again) house (which is no longer a home) – exposed, self-important and self-advertising, pointlessly elevated. 'Our ancestors, you know, always built in a hole.' Such a remark combines vulgar disrespect, crass aesthetic blindness, and complete ecological insensitivity. He has quite blithely sacrificed both the functional and aesthetic values of the architecture and archaeology of the past for the single supposed advantage of a passive, specular facility – 'a view'. This effortless abdication (even Sir Walter Elliot had some vestigial scruples and hesitations about renting the house of his forefathers) amounts to an ominously easy forgetting, an offhand rejecting of everything in the past which can give meaning to the present. It is at once a denial, a cancellation, an erasure, of a whole heritage. All for 'a view'. Though that 'view' is ambiguous. It is specular but also speculative. 'Speculation' was a card game in *Mansfield Park*. In Mr Parker's Sanditon speculation permeates all the activities of society. Indeed, his Sanditon is effectively constructed and constituted by and through 'speculation' (the word occurs at least six times in the fragment). Society itself has become an extended and endlessly proliferating 'game' of speculation. Any number can play. Everybody's doing it. The 'view' then offers a fine prospect of the sea; it offers a finer or more attractive prospect of unlimited financial profit. (We should notice that the neglected and superseded Mrs Parker looks back with a faltering and impotent nostalgia at the house in which she was a real wife and mother: ' "It was always a very comfortable house –" said Mrs Parker – looking at it through the back window with something like the fondness of regret. – "And such a nice garden – such an excellent garden." ' Of course she accepts her husband's assertion of the advantages of their move. 'But you know' (still looking back) 'one loves to look at an old friend at a place where one has been happy.' Jane Austen's novels themselves include a

'back window' through which she, and we, can look back at a
vanishing past, not sentimentally or even complainingly, but at
least with 'something like the fondness of regret'.)

Many key value terms are devalued and voided of a previous
significance in the new world of Sanditon, and the new novel
*Sanditon*; 'property', 'propriety', 'manners', 'gentleman', 'rank',
'title', 'family' – such words and concepts have been vacated of
meaning, or simply gone on vacation, with nothing or anything
to do. They have indeed become purely floating signifiers,
wandering at large, available for any kind of exploitative
appropriation. But perhaps the most notable devaluation and
debased appropriation concerns the sea, and all it signified in
*Persuasion*. In that novel it not only offered Anne the possibility of
a new life and was seen as nourishing virtues and strengths
which seemed to be no longer available in the society on the land:
it had also been the means of England's protection and salvation
from France. In *Sanditon*, although the sea itself is of course still
the sea, uncorrupted because incorruptible (thus Charlotte is
happy to see 'the sea, dancing and sparkling in sunshine and
freshness'), for Mr Parker, and all those he represents, it has
become an exploitable resource, a commodity. He stresses and
sells its benefits for health and availability for pleasure. Nothing
so very wrong in that perhaps – we all like a holiday by the
seaside. But his attitude encompasses a rather more far-reaching
devaluation and 'forgetfulness'. As when he boasts about his
new, superior house, which he has named himself (as he has the
naming of everything in his version of Eden, Sanditon):

> You will not think it a bad exchange, when we reach Trafalgar
> House – which, by the bye, I almost wish I had not named
> Trafalgar – for Waterloo is more the thing now. However,
> Waterloo is in reserve – and if we have encouragement enough
> this year for a little crescent to be ventured on – (as I trust we
> shall) then, we shall be able to call it Waterloo Crescent – and
> the name joined to the form of the building, which always
> takes, will give us the command of the lodgers.

The names of Britain's great victories are appropriated to adorn
not a tale, but a property development. This is not
commemoration or patriotism but commercialisation – and

degradation. Harmless in itself, it yet indicates how the significance of history can be exploited, and at the same time absorbed, by the opportunism of commercial 'speculation'. The glorious past is submerged into a street name in a building-development. It is another case of the second version. There was the original and unique, unrepeatable battle of Trafalgar, and now we have the name deployed as an item of fashionable 'packaging' which of course renders the name increasingly meaningless and non-significant. Our irreplaceable and indispensable heritage is disappearing into advertising. This renders it at once ephemeral and disposable, and endlessly reproducible. One battle of Waterloo; a potentially infinite number of Waterloo Crescents. For many the street name will become the only 'reality', with all sense of the original 'real' lost. This is what I mean by a 'forgetting'. It is a telling example of a form of modern nominalism. In a sense, most people in England (to go no further afield) now live in a 'Waterloo Crescent', if not in a 'Trafalgar House'. But of course it's just an address. The names could easily be changed for other names. Any other names at all. And so much for 1805 and 1815.

In such ways does Jane Austen's novel begin to offer a prevision of the future of her own, or rather, no longer her own, society. But now I want to return to the opening of the novel and its own present, and the story Jane Austen started to tell. The opening accident takes place where it does because Mr Parker is on an errand which is foolish and basically misinformed: he has been misled by advertisements in the newspapers concerning a doctor seeking a new place and this has brought him along an inappropriate road in the wrong place. Thus a basic and recurring note is struck which will be heard again throughout the fragment. People make themselves excessively busy in misdirected ways and at the same time they get things wrong. The unconstrained multiplication and diffusion of 'information' both vaporises reality and generates purely verbal 'facts'. Living in a world constructed simply of the often non-referential information secreted by advertising and desire, Mr Parker lives in error, not really in the world-as-it-is at all. This is clear from his first exchange with Mr Heywood, who is trying to help him after he has sprained his ankle. Mr Parker's first thought is to seek a 'cure' for his ankle, and his first request to Mr Heywood is to send for

the 'surgeon'. When Mr Heywood assures him that there is no
surgeon in this parish, Mr Parker politely contradicts him and
produces as evidence newspaper cuttings he has brought from
London. I shall just quote his words as he offers this undeniable
'proof' to Mr Heywood:

> I think you will be convinced that I am not speaking at random.
> You will find it an advertisement sir, of the dissolution of a
> partnership in the medical line – in your own parish – extensive
> business – undeniable character – respectable references –
> wishing to form a separate establishment. . . .

He doesn't talk exactly at random, he simply talks like an
advertisement. This is so throughout (and Jane Austen lets him
talk a great deal). His speech is conspicuously marked by
asyndeton (i.e. omitting particles which usually begin
sentences). This is exactly right; for in his hurry he does 'omit'
(forget) 'beginnings' and connectives. He is no longer concerned
with the syntactic rules which govern the correct linkings and
relationships and positionings of society. Among other things,
Sanditon is built on – and by – careless and eroding grammar.
Indeed, one could say that Sanditon is Asyndeton built large. Mr
Parker's speech is of course comic, but it also reveals a man whose
discourse is a repetition and extension of advertising with the
result that he is not only impervious to things-as-they-are: he
quite confidently asserts the primary authority and veracity of
newspaper advertisments over Mr Heywood's actual, local
knowledge, and tries to insist on the reality of a world of
things-as-they-are-not. He is a 'speculator' and would-be
improver and developer in language as well as land – an
investor in Sanditons of the word. In this instance he is only
disabused when Mr Heywood explains that there are in fact 'two
Willingdens' and Mr Parker is in the wrong one – because he was
in too much of a hurry even to read the newspapers correctly ('the
advertisements did not catch my eye till the last half hour of our
being in town; – when everything was in the hurry and confusion
which always attend a short stay there – One is never able to
complete anything in the way of business you know till the
carriage is at the door . . .'). What all this hectic business actually
consists of, the novel will soon make clear, and right from the

start we can see the foolish errors and accidents it can occasion. But Mr Parker is unabashed and immediately, compulsively, starts to talk about – or rather 'advertise' – Sanditon to Mr Heywood: 'everybody has heard of Sanditon – the favourite – for a young and rising bathing-place', and so on and so forth. Mr Heywood simply dismisses these instant constructs of fashion as 'Bad things for a country – sure to rise the price of provisions and make the poor good for nothing', an economic consideration to which Jane Austen returns. But meanwhile Mr Parker will not hear his cherished project maligned. I must quote the last part of one such promotional outburst (we can't call it conversation), which is not terminated but interrupted, at a most appropriate place:

> the growth of the place, the buildings, the nursery grounds, the demand for everything, and the sure resort of the very best company, whose regular, steady, private families of thorough gentility and character who are a blessing everywhere, excite the industry of the poor and diffuse comfort and improvement among them of every sort. – No sir, I assure you, Sanditon is not a place . . .

– at which point Mr Heywood interrupts him to politely reassure him that his criticisms of these overnight resort towns was not directed at any one such place in particular. But the interruption effectively draws the truth out of Parker's potentially interminable panegyric. The more he prolongs his empty asseverations, the more the underlying, unarticulated discourse becomes audible, and what *that* discourse is saying is, precisely, 'Sanditon is not a place'.

In this context Mr Parker's appropriation of the sea is revealed as simply a function of his advertising-discourse. But it is important to note here an intimate interconnection between Mr Parker's commercial interest in Sanditon and his preoccupation with health and medicine – in a word, 'cures'. Health, or perhaps we should more accurately say sickness, real or imagined (but particularly the latter), have become commodities and are thus indissolubly linked to the economics of the whole project. To encourage people to come and spend time by the sea in Sanditon, it is necessary to redescribe the undoubted pleasures and benefits of a sea bathe as a medically desirable treatment ('saline air and immersion'), which leads to the dissemination of a completely empty rhetoric of imaginary symptoms and cures. To 'sell' sea-bathing it is not enough simply to convey the indisputable fact that it is both pleasant and good for you: it is necessary (as far as Mr Parker is concerned) to stress its therapeutic properties. This in turn leads to the generation of a whole new rhetoric of 'sickness' or ill health which, as we see, is all too contagious. To put it very simply, if you want to sell the seaside as a cure, you must also 'sell' the notional illnesses which need curing. The invention and promotion of Sanditon is inseparable from the invention and promotion of sickness. Imaginary cures need – and thus create – imaginary complaints to work on. Sanditon is thus inseparable from quack medicine and hypochondria. On a small, local scale, as in this novel, all this makes for humour and obvious satire. It is, among other things, hilariously funny. But on a larger scale this would not necessarily be so. If advertising has the need to foster sickness for economic reasons, then we are confronted with something more far-reachingly pernicious than the amiable and easy-going Mr Parker would seem to represent. In himself he is hardly malign. But he is himself a symptom of what could become a very real and very serious sickness within sickness-as-manufactured-commodity.

I shall attempt to indicate how Jane Austen intimates the relationships between advertising, financial profit, invalidism, and activity or business/busyness, but here I just want to note how the opening incident concludes. Mr Heywood is simply concerned to do something practical about Mr Parker's ankle. Mr Parker, verbalising as always, starts to quote a bit of poetry and 'applies' it to a rival seaside resort. Mr Heywood politely enough says, 'apply any verses you like to it – But I want to see something applied to your leg.' Parker applies words, Heywood applies things: it is a meeting or 'collision' of different worlds. At the end of the chapter 'Mr Parker was therefore carried into the house, and his carriage wheeled off to a vacant barn.' I am reading this novel, in part, as a little parable of change – supersession, supplanting, and substitution; seen in this light, that 'vacant barn' now occupied by Mr Parker's hired and damaged carriage has a particular resonance. For the sort of enterprise Mr Parker is engaged in will indeed empty the barns, rob them of their original function, and put them to a different, non-productive use. Or, to put it another way, his 'business' will effectively lead to a 'vacating' of the barn (a rurally based way of life), while he creates another kind of vacancy – Sanditon (the second) with all those empty houses 'To Let'.

As a gesture of gratitude to Mr Heywood for his help, Mr Parker invites one of Mr Heywood's daughters, Charlotte, to come to Sanditon for a holiday. It is a sign of Jane Austen's realistic notation of generational differences (also seen in *Persuasion*) that the home-loving Heywoods are nevertheless quite keen to encourage their children to enlarge their circle and venture further afield: 'they were glad to promote *their* getting out into the world, as much as possible. *They* stayed at home, that their children *might* get out.' The result is that, in Charlotte Heywood, Jane Austen presents us with an entirely new kind of heroine. She is indeed displaced from her original home, but only for a holiday. Her roots, security and values are still firmly located at home. She has no emotional investment in the society she enters for a vacation period; the imperatives of making a right marriage are still distant from her. She is simply an observer (not unlike Jane Austen herself), not a blinkered and committed speculator but a relatively disinterested and uninvolved spectator. She tends to look on 'with the calmness of amused curiosity', with none of the anxiety of Anne Elliot nor any of the anguish of Fanny Price. She certainly has her feelings and, as well as being amused, can be indignant, offended, disapproving, compassionate, and even a little attracted to eligible men. What Jane Austen may have had in store for her by way of growing emotional entanglements we can never know, and surmises are fruitless. As she is, and as we see her, she is poised and undisturbed, unaffected by the action of the novel and at the same time the most reliable witness and critical evaluator of what is taking place. She quickly discovers that Mr Parker is the least possible reliable guide and assessor of his own world of Sanditon and realises, 'I must judge for myself.' We quickly apprehend that she is indeed the most reliable judge to follow. We do not worry *about* her: she has no stake in the game. Instead we are amused, amazed – and at times angered – *with* her. It is very much as if we, the readers, had gone on holiday with Jane Austen herself to Sanditon. The resultant pleasures and instruction are, alike, considerable.

The main figures whom Charlotte meets on her holiday are Lady Denham and her niece Clara Brereton; the nephew and niece of her second husband (Sir Harry Denham), Sir Edward and his sister Esther Denham; and Mr Parker's sisters and brothers, Diana, Susan, Arthur and – later – Sidney. There are also the 'two families' of expected lodgers, who turn out to be one, and not a family but three girls from a young ladies' seminary, Miss Lambe and the two Miss Beauforts. How they are all involved with each other – as much by confusion as by any actual relationship – is the very story of *Sanditon*, a comedy of errors, and a not-so-comic confusion of exploitations, of which Charlotte is the one stable and reliable witness. I wish to consider the other main characters from the point of view of the various discourses which they employ – or which employ them: namely, the discourses of advertising, hypochondria and quack medicine, money, and literary criticism(!). Like their speakers, these discourses turn out to be strangely interrelated, or confusedly mingled. So that, while there is very little true communication in the book (as there is no real community), there is a lot of discourse-imbrication (as there is plenty of overlapping in the way people keep running into other people). We must listen to the variety of voices – the group glossolalia – and in no previous novel has Jane Austen given us so much opportunity to do so. (The change in style of this last novel I shall consider later.)

The 'great lady' of Sanditon is Lady Denham, 'born to wealth but not to education'. From her first husband (Mr Hollis) she received her property or 'estates'; from her second husband (Sir Harry Denham) she acquired her title. From neither did she receive any children. (The Parkers have children, of whom we hear absolutely nothing except one short sentence from little Mary. The family voice is entirely absent in Sanditon, book and place; dumb, silenced or occluded.) Totally 'uncultivated', she only has her estates, her title and her money. And money is her only real interest; she only knows 'the value of money'. She is Mr Parker's 'colleague in speculation', his 'coadjutor' (perfect word to mask 'accomplice' or partner, hinting as it does at a debased and secularised ecclesiastical function). She takes a malicious glee in her power over the needy family relations and legitimate heirs who are constantly trying to win something from her. It is the power of an unstinting parsimony. The one exception she has made is a niece, Clara Brereton, of all her relatives 'more helpless and more pitiable of course than any – a dependant on poverty'. It becomes clear that Lady Denham has taken her in not out of generosity, but because she enjoys her power over her. Charlotte imagines Clara to be 'ill-used', seeing her as a literary stereotype of the persecuted poor female relation, then has to admit that this 'reading' is not borne out by what she sees (Lady Denham is deceptively good-natured), only to discover for herself that Lady Denham *is* cruelly mean and Clara suffers under all the constraints of 'dependence'. As Charlotte finds out, 'Lady Denham's discourse' is exclusively preoccupied with 'her own concerns', and those concerns are almost exclusively financial. She is more 'anxious' than Mr Parker about the prosperity of Sanditon, more worried about the possible arrival of the 'two families'. Her response is right to the point: 'That will bring money.' She is indeed entirely suitable to be the 'great lady' of Sanditon; the barren 'mother' of Mr Parker's second 'family'.

A particularly interesting aspect of her exchanges with her 'coadjutor', Mr Parker, concerns the possibility of inflation. On hearing that one of the putative families is composed of West Indians, who, Mr Parker asserts, always spend freely, Lady Denham is briefly worried as to whether this free spending will 'raise the price of our necessaries of life'. In answer to which Mr Parker proves himself to be a quick-thinking economist (and Jane Austen herself a very perceptive one). Parker replies,

My dear madam, they can only raise the price of consumable articles, by such an extraordinary demand for them and such a diffusion of money among us, as must do us more good than harm. Our butchers and bakers and traders in general cannot get rich without bringing prosperity to *us*. If *they* do not gain, our rents must be insecure – and in proportion to their profit must be ours eventually in the increased value of our houses.

It is a fallacious argument and ignores or elides the ramifying effects of inflation, which cannot raise the price of 'consumables' without affecting the cost of the 'necessaries', thus in turn impoverishing if not bankrupting the very service (and of course labouring) classes on which Mr Parker's (and Lady Denham's) class parasitically depend for their own unearned income – whether in the form of rent or in that of property value. We do not have to make Jane Austen into any kind of a Marxist to note that she saw with impressive clarity the potential dangers of the economic structure of a society which depended on the possible but precarious profits to be made from creating an ever-increasing demand for consumer goods. Remember that one of Mr Parker's points in favour of Sanditon was that it promoted 'the demand for everything', a potentially infinite, insatiable desire for 'consumable articles' which in the long run can only ruin a society, and in the short run can cause great hardship to those sections of the society who do not share in the distribution of 'profits' and can thus no longer afford the price of 'the necessaries', nor the increased 'rents', and of course not one of those ever-more-expensive houses. Jane Austen knows more about basic economics than Mr Parker knows, or at least wants to admit.

In this connection it is worth taking note of an uncharacteristic hesitation of conscience on the part of Mr Parker – concerning 'gardenstuff'. Having abandoned their kitchen garden (and 'the constant eyesore of its formalities, the yearly nuisance of its decaying vegetation'!) for a 'plantation' (!!), the question of where they are to obtain their 'gardenstuff' arises for the Parkers. There are three possible sources. They can still get it from their old garden (thus exploiting the present occupants); they can easily buy it from the gardener at Lady Denham's Sanditon Hall (convenient if parasitic); or – this is where an element of troubled responsibility begins to emerge – they can buy it from old Stringer and his son. They have in fact the 'higher claim', and why? 'I encouraged him to set up – and am afraid he does not do very well. . . .' To effect a compromise between convenience and obligation, Mr Parker suggests that they buy a 'nominal supply' from Lady Denham's gardener (so he won't 'lose his daily job'), but 'the chief of our consumption of the Stringers'. The multiplied source of necessary produce, and Mr Parker's uneasy division of his custom, reveal one thing tolerably clearly: that in setting up Sanditon as a 'rapid-growth' resort, Mr Parker (and, in a parabolic reading, take him simply as a representative developer) effectively brought into being both a new risk for the labourer (Lady Denham's gardener could now lose his job) and for the shopkeeper (Stringer could now lose his whole trade). Both have become dependent on the chance purchases of their patron and an anonymous, transient, fashion-following population. In his haste (and eager greed) Mr Parker has started to create the supply before he can guarantee the need. Sanditon is precisely not a manufacturing town in any sense. But it can effectively produce – not only sickness, but also unemployment and bankruptcy. It may be objected that I am making far too much out of a little aside. But not a word is wasted in the extraordinary pages of this last fragment, and the hint I have taken the liberty of expanding is undoubtedly there.

Lady Denham's discourse is fairly unambiguously concerned simply with money and financial gain. But that discourse is, like Lady Denham herself, in league with Mr Parker's discourse of advertising, which only imperfectly masks its concern with profits under enthusiasm for 'civilised' development, and a dedication to matters of health. It is Mr Parker's sisters and one of his brothers (Arthur) who are most immersed in the discourse of hypochondria – the discourses of advertising and hypochondria are complicit with each other, so it is entirely suitable that they should be in the same family, as it were. Jane Austen could perceive that there was a kind of perversion common to both, for both can become obsessions and take over the speaker until he or she is in the deceptive and fabricating grip of the discourse and increasingly out of touch with reality. In turning to the discourse of hypochondria, let me acknowledge in passing that other people have noted that there are a very large number of references to illness in *Sanditon* and that this, it is suggested, is explicable largely in terms of the fact that Jane Austen was herself ill, in fact dying, when she wrote it. This may of course have some truth in it, but, being the artist she was, whatever misery or pain she may have been experiencing, in her writing the obsession with illness is depersonalised and transformed into a significant social phenomenon which we are invited to consider and find, 'very striking – and very amusing – or very melancholy, just as Satire or Morality might prevail' (and note the willingness to sustain an ambivalence, or oscillate across a spectrum of attitudes).

Part of Mr Parker's advertising-rhetoric about the virtues of Sanditon is that the sea air and bathing are 'a match for every Disorder, of the Stomach, the lungs or the blood; they were anti-spasmodic, anti-pulmonary, anti-sceptic, anti-bilious and anti-rheumatic'. Of course bathing and sea air are good for us, but here as elsewhere Jane Austen is noting an excess, the language getting out of control, and in effect taking over and losing itself – and the world – in its own unchecked proliferations. (The sheer loquacity of the main 'discoursers' in the book is notable, and potentially interminable. There seem to be no constraints on utterance, as if language itself was embarking on an indefinitely protracted holiday.) The possible effect of this kind of excess is made very clear in the quite fantastic accounts Mr Parker's sister Diana gives of the family ailments. I quote from one of her letters to Mr Parker:

> your letter . . . found me suffering under a more severe attack than usual of my old grievance, spasmodic bile and hardly able to crawl from my bed to the sofa. – But how were you treated? – Send me more particulars in your next. . . . I doubt whether Susan's nerves would be equal to the effort [i.e. of a visit to Sanditon]. She has been suffering much from the headache and six leeches a day for ten days together relieved her so little that we thought it right to change our measures – and being convinced on examination that much of the evil lay in her gum, I persuaded her to attack the disorder there. She has accordingly had three teeth drawn, and is decidedly better, but her nerves are a good deal deranged. She can only speak in a whisper – and fainted away twice this morning on poor Arthur's trying to suppress a cough.

Now, of course people get ill – who better to know it than Jane Austen at the time? – and, by the same token, there is an obvious need for a discourse of symptoms, prescriptions, remedies, and so on. But what Jane Austen is here depicting, unsentimentally and indeed hilariously, is the way in which that discourse can take over the individual so that what should be in a normal person a reasonable concern for health becomes an entirely unreasonable obsession with *unhealth*, which creates the sickness it purports to be concerned with curing. Note Diana's interest in her brother's accident – 'Send me more particulars' – which is more a sign of morbid fascination than sororal affection.

It would be wrong to give the impression that there is anything excessively gloomy or ponderous about Jane Austen's treatment of this particular family of *malades imaginaires*. Her touch is as light as it is firm – as in her depiction of the younger brother Arthur, who, somewhat feebly to be sure, masks a truly fabulous gluttony and idleness under the terms of a neurological disorder. Drinking, it turns out, is very good for his nervous condition: 'The more wine I drink (in moderation) the better I am' – an unforgettable proposition which would not be out of place in *Alice through the Looking Glass*. At the same time she could see that what she calls 'enjoyments in invalidism' could have very destructive effects – on self and others. She saw, as other great writers have done, the dangers and perversities which could be involved in hypochondria and quack medicine, and for comparison we could look back to Ben Jonson or more pertinently forward to Flaubert's Monsieur Homais, the quack chemist in *Madame Bovary*, whose interfering intrusions of pseudo-medical advice and help are ruinous. He indeed is a man who destroys what he purports to cure. Jane Austen knew about such people. Given the obsessive dedication to 'illness' and 'cures' shown by the Parkers, there is a good deal of mordant point in the reported joke of Mr Parker's brother Sidney that Mr Parker should 'make a hospital' of his old house. ('He pretends to advise me to make a hospital of it. He pretends to laugh at my improvements. Sidney says anything you know.' What he says is nevertheless much to the point.)

We should note that Jane Austen traces both Mr Parker's obsession with advertising his semi-imaginary Sanditon, and his sister's devotion to the terminology of illness, to 'want of employment'. As she puts it, 'while the elder brother found vent for his superfluity of sensation as a projector, the sisters were perhaps driven to dissipate theirs in the inventing of odd complaints'. This 'want of employment' is the distinguishing feature of the main exploiters of discourses in the book. Mr Parker has 'no Profession' (his poor wife is simply described as 'useless' – her role has been pre-empted by Lady Denham and Sanditon); Lady Denham wants to make money without doing anything; and the parasitic Sir Edward is wholly engaged in efforts of ingratiation or seduction. As a group, the 'sick' family is best represented by Arthur, who is supposedly 'so delicate that he can engage in no profession'. Even by Mr Parker's account, this is a bad show:

> it *is* bad that he should be fancying himself too sickly for any profession – and sit down at one and twenty, on the interest of his little fortune, without any idea of attempting to improve it, or of engaging in any occupation that may be of use to himself or others.

Mr Heywood collected 'dividends', presumably for work done and things produced; Arthur simply waits for unearned 'interest'. Jane Austen deleted the words 'idle and indolent' in Mrs Parker's account of him. They were simply redundant. In his all-too-manifest idleness Arthur is only the gross representative of a whole class which follows no vocation, has no profession, and engages in no kind of productive or constructive employment. Its members have no meaningful occupation. But some of them make and keep themselves very busy, and it is to that 'business' I wish to turn.

From the opening Mr Parker's way of life is marked by 'hurry and confusion' and a perpetually self-distracting 'way of business' which prevents him from ever 'completing anything'. When he returns to Sanditon he 'longed to be on the sands, the cliffs, at his own house, and everywhere out of his house at once'. He wants to fragment himself in a kind of manic yearning for ubiquity; this suggests an extreme form of identity diffusion indeed, a permanently centrifugal and scattering self. Of course it is the result of his having no real anchoring-function, no unseverable tie with reality. Even more extreme (and comic) are his sister Diana's frantic perpetual motion and meddling, the reverse side of her hypochondria and arguably her real 'illness'. This is true of both sisters: 'they must either be very busy for the good of others, or else extremely ill themselves'. They are, indeed, busy-bodies, and no doubt that busyness is compensating for any number of lacks and frustrations in their lives. And, of course, all this unfocused busyness in misdirected ways means that they are constantly getting things wrong. Hence the comedy of errors about the 'two' families of lodgers. They have seemingly been procured by an inordinate amount of fuss and manoeuvring on the part of Diana. 'I will not tell you how many people I have employed in the business – Wheel within Wheel.' The confusion about the 'two' families comes about through the absurd multiplication of 'busy' communications along a chain of people who are said to be 'extremely intimate' but do not know each other. Diana keeps referring boastfully to 'constant correspondence', 'links of connection', 'chains' of contacts, but, since the links in the chain, or the wheels within the wheels, do not have any direct knowledge of one another ('I know them only through others', admits Diana, who is the 'chief of the family; principal mover and actor'), what we have is a parody, indeed a negative, of true communal interrelatedness. In a small but significant way, the incident puts the whole matter of 'communication' into question: what genuine contacts, links, connections, do in fact exist any more?

It is worth noting that the one item which was missing in this circuitous and displaced transmission of information was the actual *names* of the supposed families. The one thing that would be known in any genuine circle of acquaintances, that would have precluded error, that would have made the information properly referential, is absent. The 'circuitous train of intelligence' which Diana 'keeps up' is thus capable of transmitting, proliferating and circulating purely anonymous signs; here is no constraint on the possible number of 'representations' which can be engendered and fabricated by all the 'reports', 'letters and extracts and messages' which make up the permanently flowing, permanently deficient circuit. They are indeed 'enough to make everything appear what it was not'; and, we might add, such a system of information is also enough to make anything-that-is-not appear. Jane Austen could hardly have been surprised at the fabrications and fictions produced and disseminated by our own media and information systems. In the circumstances it is hardly surprising that 'the family from Surrey and the family from Camberwell were one and the same' and that 'the rich West Indians' and 'the young ladies' seminary', apparently so utterly different, are identical. The illusory 'differences' have been produced by the medium, which, lacking knowledge of, and commitment to, real names, can produce and reproduce not just two, but potentially any number of representations. (That the name of the 'family' is finally discovered – 'Griffiths' – in no way invalidates this phenomenon, for they still insist there must be two 'families' with the same name. Only the appearance of the actual girls – not a family – forces them to accept the 'reports' as false.) It is not so much the case that the medium is the message as that the medium itself manufactures the messages. We know that now, but Jane Austen was surely prescient to see it so clearly then; and it reveals the economy of genius to have condensed so much into what is apparently a trivial, laughable lapse on the part of a string of idle women trying to secure some lodgers for a new seaside resort.

Not only is Diana always 'running around': like the other discourses, she talks 'incessantly'; there is nothing to curtail her speech as there is nothing to terminate her activity. Both originate from nothing and have no certain direction or destination. The relatively unmoving and silent Charlotte, confronted with all this, thinks 'Unaccountable officiousness! – Activity run mad!', though she is too polite to say it, and Jane Austen later refers to the Parkers' 'spirit of restless activity', owing partly to the need for 'amusement' and partly to 'vanity'. 'There was vanity in all they did' – in both senses: it emanates from vanity, and it is all 'in vain'. That 'spirit of restless activity' originally read 'the disease of activity' in the manuscript, and we may well prefer to avail ourselves of the 'first' writing. Of course Jane Austen did not approve of more inactivity, inertia or indolence: Arthur Parker (who feels 'the want of some motive for action') is as much a member of the family as Diana (who invents motives for it), but she obviously regarded a certain kind of precipitate, unreflecting, interfering or 'improving' activity as indeed a kind of 'disease'. It is a hyperactivity which at the same time is a deranged activity, or motion and activity without a stable, organising centre. Mr Heywood has his 'one small circle' and he is clearly meant to embody a functioning centre. But other kinds of 'circles' are proliferating in Sanditon.

There is a 'Circulation Library', which 'of course, afforded everything; all the useless things in the world that could not be done without', and where as usual Mr Parker tries to 'encourage expenditure' (remember that 'demand for everything' which is one of the proferred advantages of Sanditon), so that Charlotte has to 'check herself' and 'repress further solicitation': it is a place for furthering the circulation of money as well as of books. Sir Edward talks 'a good deal by rote' (I shall come to him), and rote learning is exactly based on repetition, coming back to and echoing without understanding, a basic text again and again, a kind of 'rotation' (*rota* – wheel) or circling, to generate an illusion of knowledge, another fake simulacrum. Rote learning is the right kind of learning for Sanditon. And there are of course social circles. We read that 'the Miss Beauforts were soon satisfied with "the Circle in which they moved in Sanditon" to use a proper phrase, for every body must now "move in a circle" – to the prevalence of which rotatory Motion, is perhaps to be attributed the Giddiness and false steps of many'. Even the words referring to moving in a social circle have become a quotation, a second-hand phrase, picked up and used by rote we may say, an empty label available for easy circulation, like the money in Sanditon. For that society, or provisional and transient aggregation, everything must, ideally, move in a circle – money, 'consumable articles', books, phrases, people. Not only the economy, but the very existence, of Sanditon depends on endless 'circulation'. All societies do, to some (controlled) extent, of course. But here we notice an essential missingness at the heart, a central lack or absence. The circuit of information lacks the names which would make it function; the circulation library encourages a manner of 'rote' reading which loses the meaning of the original text; the circulation money is largely fiduciary, not backed by substantial or real wealth, and inevitably decreasing in value as inflation increases; the 'social circle' has already become an empty phrase because there *is* no society in Sanditon, no organising and authorising centre which could bring stability, significance and coherence to the movements around it. (To the extent that Lady Denham is the centre, the centre has become a vortex of pure, pointless, financial greed. It is a vortex which can only lead to a moral and spiritual vacuum.) It is in every way a decentred non-society. And, to the extent that accelerating rotation can erode and wear substance away, the kind of vertiginous, unemployed, unproductive 'circling' shown in the book can be seen as helping actively to destroy the accumulations and foundations of civilisation – the sediment of significance deposited by the past – and usher in a reign of endless unfocused demands, and more and more useless consumer things. In an important sense, a realm of nothing. The vacation town portends the institution of a larger vacancy.

(The depiction of vertiginous and frenetic 'circling' movement and a sense of accelerating 'circulation' of all manner of objects, discourses, names, consumer goods, and so on, to suggest a society in a state of increasing disarray and giddy frenzied uncertainty, collapsing distinctions and category confusions can be found in other novelists in the early nineteenth century – for example, Balzac. His social landscape is as vast as Jane Austen's is small; yet what Lucien, in *Illusions perdues*, experiences in the rapidly 'turning' world of Paris – 'la rapidité du *tournoiement* Parisien' [emphasis added] – is not intrinsically so different from what Charlotte perceives in Sanditon. Quoting this line of Balzac's, Christopher Prendergast in *The Order of Mimesis* comments on 'that highly mobile, ceaselessly "turning" landscape – of Balzac's Paris – in which the perception of ranks and occupations, origins and identities can no longer orientate itself within a fixed, reliable structure of differentiation'. In an admittedly small way I think *Sanditon* does contain an adumbration of such a condition of emerging modern society.)

One more discourse must be mentioned here, and that one not the least important. It is the discourse of literary appreciation or criticism, and it comes from the mouth of Sir Edward Denham. He is the impoverished baronet who is financially dependent on Lady Denham's whim, but when he first meets Charlotte he addresses himself eagerly to her and, since he is handsome and seems aimiable and of 'very good address', she is quite happy to let him do so. (Like all the others we have considered, he 'talked much' and has 'a great deal of conversation'.) Even when his sister signals her intention to go, he remains talking to Charlotte and she reacts favourably to his 'persisting in his station and discourse'. That means his particular position at the moment, and his conversation. But Jane Austen is exploiting a double meaning in a subtle but important way. 'Station' also means his position in society, and he no longer has a meaningful one to persist in. 'Discourse' may be extended to cover his whole habitual mode of speaking, and that, as we and Charlotte soon find out, is anything but his own. Appropriately enough, given the prevailing obsession, he begins 'to talk of the sea and the sea shore', not to turn them into advertising-copy, like Mr Parker, but into 'sublimity' via literary references. Charlotte is initially impressed by what she takes as signs of his being a 'man of feeling' (a glance at the popular writer of novels of sentiment, Henry Mackenzie, whose most successful novel, published in 1771, was entitled just that). But soon 'he began to stagger her with the number of his quotations, and the bewilderment of some of his sentences'. Indeed, he speaks wholly in quotations (more repetition and appropriation), but mutilated and confused quotations, which disfigure and maim the original texts. It is extremely amusing, of course – certainly at first:

> Do you remember . . . Scott's beautiful lines on the sea? – Oh! what a description they convey! – They are never out of my thoughts when I walk here. – That man who can read them unmoved must have the nerves of an assassin! – Heaven defend me from meeting such a man un-armed.

Charlotte confesses that she cannot remember any descriptions of the sea in Scott's poems, and nor can I (there is the odd reference to the 'distant Tweed' and 'Sweet Teviot'). But, then, nor can Sir Edward: 'Do you not indeed? – Nor can I exactly recall the beginning at this moment – But – you cannot have forgotten his description of Woman . . . ', and off he goes, now eulogising Burns for being 'always on fire'.

Sir Edward's main obsession begins to reveal itself: 'The man who cannot do justice to the attributes of woman is my contempt.' Charlotte begs to question the *'sincerity'* of the affections expressed in Burns's writing: 'He felt and he wrote and he forgot.' But Sir Edward will have none of it: 'some aberrations' there may be, but you must not expect 'the grovellings of a common mind' from such a genius.

> The coruscations of talent, elicited by impassioned feeling in the breast of man, are perhaps incompatible with some of the prosaic decencies of life, – nor can you, loveliest Miss Heywood, . . . nor can any woman he fair judge of what a man may be propelled to say, write or do, by the sovereign impulses of illimitable ardour.

Jane Austen comments, shifting into indirect speech, which she can since she and Charlotte share the same discourse (of which more later), 'This was very fine; – but if Charlotte understood it at all, not very moral.' Without ceasing to be very funny, Sir Edward's use (or rather abuse) of reading and quotation (or rather misreading and misquotation) is beginning to raise a more serious issue. Moreover, as she begins to be displeased with his ludicrous and 'extraordinary style of compliment', Charlotte starts to find him 'downright silly'. She wonders not just why he is speaking nonsense, but why he is speaking so very *much* nonsense. It – and he – is literally 'un-intelligible'. 'He seemed very sentimental, very full of some feelings or other, and very much addicted to all the newest-fashioned hard words – had not a very clear brain she presumed, and talked a good deal by rote.' His speech is all quotation and rote-ation. It is entirely appropriate that at this point he disappears into the library, while Lady Denham starts to expound Sir Edward's problems in terms of his need for money, property, an heiress. This is the actual penury under the lavish quotations, and Charlotte is amused by the contrast in the two discourses, as well she might be. Yet here again there is a similarity, a tacit collusion. Both discourses are essentially aimed at exploitation: financial on Lady Denham's part; sexual on Sir Edward's. He attempts a scrambled mystification – not so very different from Mr Parker's advertising, and Diana's invalidism. The result, as Charlotte and we have heard, is high-order balderdash. But there *is* a moral matter involved here, and to trace it further we must listen again to Sir Edward after he emerges from the library, followed by a youth carrying five volumes for him.

He starts by protesting too much: 'I am no indiscriminate novel-reader. The mere trash of the common circulating library I hold in the highest contempt' (having five volumes of such 'trash' meanwhile packed in his gig). He then embarks on a long, semi-intelligible 'discourse' about the kind of novels he approves of. Among other qualifications, they are

> such as exhibit the progress of strong passion from the first germ of incipient susceptibility to the utmost energies of reason half-dethroned – where we see the strong spark of woman's captivations elicit such fire in the soul of man as leads him . . . to hazard all, dare all achieve all, to obtain her.

The enthroning and dethroning of reason was becoming a problematic and contentious issue in the literature and aesthetic discourses of the time. There were some eminently serious writers who were challenging the imperial, and imperious, rule of reason (Blake, for example). But Sir Edward is only abusing such novels and discourses both to mystify and to dignify (or, we may say, to novel-ise and to aestheticise) his rank intention to seduce Clara Brereton. Here again Jane Austen shows how clearly she understood the problematical relationship between books and life. Indeed, she now takes over the discourse of her own novel to explain exactly what is going on.

'The truth was' – a rare gesture of omniscience in a book in which the 'truth' has become very far to seek –

> that Sir Edward whom circumstances had confined very much to one spot had read more sentimental novels than agreed with him. His fancy had been early caught by all the impassioned, and most exceptionable parts of Richardson's; and such authors as have since appeared to tread in Richardson's steps, so far as man's determined pursuit of woman in defiance of every feeling and convenience is concerned, had since occupied the greater part of his literary hours and formed his character.

As a result, he sympathises totally with 'the villain of the story' (Lovelace, from *Clarissa*, is the most important example) despite 'all his absurdities and atrocities'. Jane Austen then goes on to make an extremely important point. Sir Edward's identification with the villain goes far beyond anything that '*could ever have been contemplated by the authors*' (emphasis added). Then this: 'He read all the essays, letters, tours and criticisms of the day – and with the same ill-luck which made him derive only false principles of morality, and *incentives to vice from the history of its overthrow*, he gathered only hard words and involved sentences from the style of our most approved writers' (emphasis added). The italicised words point to a real problem in the history of the novel, indeed in the history of culture and feeling in the latter part of the eighteenth century – and beyond. Briefly the problem was this: Richardson, above all (but also later imitators), wrote his works not as novels, but as vehicles for moral instruction. Above all, he wished to demonstrate and celebrate the importance and power of female virtue. His purpose was explicitly didactic. Clarissa was created not as a plausible imitation of a young virgin, but as an ideal of absolute female virtue. However, to demonstrate the strength and unyieldingness of that virtue in action, he had to show it tempted, threatened, cajoled, coerced, vulnerable and victimised, in every possible way. Hence the varying stratagems, importunities, undeflectable lust, and final desperate violence and rape, revealed and practised by Lovelace. To show the strength of virtue, he had to dramatise the power and persistence of what it had to withstand and overthrow. But from the beginning it proved impossible to control the way his work was read. In making Lovelace plausible and convincingly threatening, he could not avoid making him fascinating and indeed glamorous to some readers. A story written to illuminate virtue necessarily and inevitably carries its shadow with it. The sexual threat had to be potently dark to give substance to the luminosity of female resistance. But that meant that sexuality was necessarily written into the book, and unavoidably *there* to be read. Meant to be repulsive, it could not prevent readers from finding it ambiguously attractive (as arguably Clarissa herself, half-consciously, does). Thus, what was intended as the most moral and virtuous book could also come to be seen as a 'disreputable', even scandalous, book. Richardson continued to make endless revisions and additions to his work to make the virtuous intention utterly unambiguous. It was not only an interminable project, but also an impossible one. There is simply no way an author, whatever his intentions, can both dictate and circumscribe how his texts will be read. This was an inherent danger in the whole tradition of the sentimental novel: intending to be admonitory, it could not escape seeming latently lubricious. In glorifying Clarissa it could not avoid raising Lovelace to a 'dark eminence'. (The problem with Milton's Satan is exactly parallel.) Its manifest purity inevitably carried with it its latent pornography.

The possible results of this ineradicable ambiguity Jane Austen deftly summarises in the portrait of Sir Edward, who is as manifestly 'absurd' and latently as 'atrocious' as the villains inscribed in his impressionable and ill-educated imagination. 'He felt that he was formed to be a dangerous man – quite in the line of the Lovelaces.' He has been de-formed by his misreading. He is the enactment of a perverted text. Clara Brereton in her vulnerable condition suggests the appropriate fictional victim of the fictionally prescribed rape. 'Her seduction was quite determined on. Her situation in every way called for it.' We should do well to remember that Charlotte herself has seen Clara, through books, as the archetypal victim–heroine. When she first sees Clara it is also in the immediate vicinity of the library.

> Charlotte could see in her only the most perfect representation of whatever heroine might be most beautiful and bewitching, in all the numerous volumes they had left behind them on Mrs Whitby's shelves. – Perhaps it might be partly owing to her having just issued from a circulating library – but she could not separate the idea of a complete heroine from Clara Brereton.

We are not back in *Northanger Abbey*, though we might seem to be. The difference is that Charlotte is a disengaged spectator and shown to be the most sensible, clear-sighted person in the region of Sanditon. Yet even she is not immune to the influence of reading. The implication is that by now *everybody* is likely to live a para-fictional life to some extent. The texture of everyday life now *includes* the texture of the fictions it produces. No one can ever be sure that he or she is wholly outside of some novel or other. They have become modes of visual instruction, and thus distortion. They engender preconceptions and pervert perceptions. In *Sanditon* this condition is not epidemic, but it is another possible 'disease' which can easily spread in that 'health' resort. Charlotte, endowed with the strength and self-correcting intelligence of what is in effect another world, can soon correct her vision. Sir Edward neither can nor wishes to. Jane Austen is very amusing about his preformed 'literary' plan of campaign against Clara – to offset the utterly humourless, and thus dangerous, seriousness of the Richardson way of treating the would-be seducer. Sir Edward thinks that perhaps a good place for the rape would be Timbuctoo; 'but the expense alas! of measures in that masterly style was ill-suited to his purse, and prudence obliged him to prefer the quietest sort of ruin and disgrace for the object of his affections, to the more renowned'.

Richardson was one of Jane Austen's favourite writers (and his

*Sir Charles Grandison* her very favourite 'novel'), so she would hardly wantonly ridicule his work. Rather, she is writing against that inherent danger in his work which he desperately tried to eliminate with endless rewritings, by, as it were, 'ludicrous-ising' it. In its brisk humour this is not a piece of carefree burlesque so much as a clean piece of fictional surgery – excising the possible areas of corruption in a virtuous text. Clara Brereton has none of the prolonged anxieties and tremulous apprehensions of a Clarissa. 'Clara saw through him, and had not the least intention of being seduced.' And that's that. A sentence of Jane Austen's sense displaces a thousand pages of Richardson's partially prurient anguish. And yet that is not quite the end of the matter. Sir Edward is not put off by Clara's calm resolution. 'He knew his business.' With that simple sentence Jane Austen suddenly aligns Sir Edward's misplaced and perverted sexual activity with all the other business/busy-ness in the book. It is, all alike, visibly (or audibly) comic but potentially (readably) exploitative and destructive. Of course Sir Edward is funny because transparently absurd. So too are Mr Parker, Diana and (though more sombrely) Lady Denham. But ruined girls are ruined girls (or at least used to be) and in the absurd figure of Sir Edward there are the flickering outlines of a more dangerous one. This is true of the other figures I have named as well. They are all more or less apparently harmless, softly aimiable, vaguely good-natured (again Lady Denham in her actual and detected meanness is something of an exception), certainly not evil and hardly threatening. They are also all in the grip of perverted, disfigured or debased discourses to the extent that, as we now say, they do not really speak the discourses, but the discourses speak them – endlessly. Hence the comic atmosphere of prevailing loquacious mindlessness. But all the possible dangers I have associated with these figures are latently there, the ominous sub-textual shadow of this superficially light and bright and sparkling fragment which was also Jane Austen's last testament. It has indeed a rare and very special brightness, written as it was in the strikingly non-visible shadow of death.

Clara is of course centrally involved in what hint of incipient dramatic plot the fragment contains. When Charlotte goes to visit Lady Denham in the last chapter we have, she sees Clara and Sir Edward in what must be a secret meeting. It is interesting that

Charlotte does not immediately conclude that Sir Edward is about 'his business' of seduction; at least they are said to be engaged in 'gentle conversation' and the atmosphere is that of a 'secret lovers'. Who knows what Jane Austen had in mind for the outcome of this relationship? But I think we can detect a curious change of atmosphere in general in this last chapter. In a word, it starts to become mysterious, not least because it does indeed take place in 'mist'. This means that vision is obstructed, clear perception is rendered uncertain; a new note of dubiety, unsureness, and even cognitive instability is struck. Consider the description of the arrival of the Parker brother Sidney, himself something of a mystery figure, of whom we (and Charlotte) have only heard through Parker's references to his wry, detached ironies. His actual presence in Sanditon would obviously introduce a new and problematising attitude to all that is going on. Sidney is thus already somewhat enigmatic, a deferred presence of a family difference, and, indeed, although he does arrive in the story at the end of the fragment, he still does not actually 'speak', as it were. He remains a silent voice, obviously about to become an important new agent in the story.

But we have his arrival described. It is in a carriage, of course, for, from the opening incident, the motif of the arriving carriage has often recurred. These arrivals often occasion questions and uncertainties, as the opening accident does. But Sidney's arrival is, appropriately, something different again:

> It was a close, misty morning, and when they reached the brow of the hill, they would not for some time make out what sort of carriage it was, which they saw coming up. It appeared at different moments to be everything from the gig to the phaeton, – from one horse to four; and just as they were concluding in favour of a tandem, little Mary's young eyes distinguished the coachman and she called out, ' 'Tis Uncle Sidney Mama, it is indeed.'

Why should Jane Austen introduce this most unusual note (for her) of sheer perceptual uncertainty? It might well adumbrate a larger change in the prevailing atmosphere, so that perception and interpretation are to become increasingly problematic, hesitant, tentative. A more general cognitive mist might be about to fall on the narrative, so that in a rather Jamesian way it may have become more and more difficult to 'make out' what was approaching, or going on. Certainly we can say that Sidney arrives shrouded in ambiguity, and mystery, and it may well be that his character was to prove as difficult to 'make out', as teasingly (and perhaps worryingly) protean, as his carriage in the morning mist. The problem might well have come to be of great importance to Charlotte, drawing her into the 'action' from her hitherto secure and untroubled peripheral position. But of course we can never know. As abandoned readers, we too are left in an endless mist.

But that new kind of perceptual uncertainty is also present when Charlotte goes to Lady Denham's. Again, there is an odd kind of specification concerning the actual conditions of vision which contributes to the rather mysterious atmosphere. There is an outside fence 'with an angle *here*, and a curve *there*' and a 'row of old thorns following its line almost everywhere'. Fine – but then: '*Almost* must be stipulated – for there were vacant spaces – and through one of these, Charlotte as soon as they entered the enclosure caught a glimpse over the pales of something white and womanish on the other side. . . .' Identification is deferred, vision itself is becoming narrativised – there are 'fences' but there are occasional 'vacancies', gaps and fissures in the 'almost' complete concealing screen, which make glimpses and partial sight possible. Just simply seeing what is *there* – and what is what – is no longer axiomatically an easy matter, even for the keenest, least obstructed eye. 'Scenes' have to be constructed from incomplete and fleeting notations, not simply observed. The hint of a new kind of phenomenological complexity can be discerned. It is only a hint, but as such it is certainly there and important. Charlotte on this occasion realises that she cannot 'judge' the situation. Having encountered Clara and Sir Edward in a clear social light in which the virtues and beauties of the one, and the plausibility and the absurdity of the other, were alike quite transparent to her (she is usually ready to 'judge' for herself – she has to), Charlotte now sees, or half sees, them in a different light, or mist. They have withdrawn into the impenetrable opacity of 'privacy'. Charlotte can only 'step back again, and say not a word'. Tact, of course; but also a gesture which seems to acknowledge a rather new kind of perceptual limitation, even perhaps a new kind of epistemological difficulty. Charlotte has indeed 'seen' Clara and Sir Edward together. But now to 'see' them in these conditions is also to see that she also *cannot* truly 'see' them. Perceptibly there, they have also become perceptibly unknowable, unreadable: present to the eye, and absent to the understanding. Charlotte's 'glimpse' is also a glimpse of the ignorance which inheres in vision. If this seems excessive, I think we can at least recognise that, just as Charlotte has to perceive things through 'a great thickness of air', so Jane Austen is introducing new atmospheric conditions into her novel. And Sanditon is becoming mysterious.

The last paragraph of the fragment takes Charlotte and us into Lady Denham's house. Charlotte, typically, has 'leisure to look about' and sees over the mantelpiece a 'whole-length portrait of a stately gentleman', Sir Harry Denham, while in another part of the room she notes a 'miniature' of Mr Hollis: it enjoys no position of singular eminence but is merely 'one among many'. 'Poor Mr Hollis! – It was impossible not to feel him hardly used; to be obliged to stand back in his own house and see the best place by the fire constantly occupied by Sir Harry Denham.' Thus the manuscript ends. It is perhaps a fitting-enough note. Here again we have an instance of the relegation and devaluing, even forgetting, of the 'original', and the elevation and promotion of the second, the secondary, the substitional, the glamorously decorative, which is also the mark of an astute purchase. Mr Hollis may only appear in the narrative consciousness as a somewhat pathetic and remote – indeed, 'removed', because displaced and superseded – figure. He is not even a ghost, hardly the trace of a memory. His original stature has indeed been miniaturised: his image is now merely 'one among others'. Meanwhile, the image of Sir Harry Denham has been enlarged – and centralised. It has pre-empted the visual space. It is the dominant 'advertisement' in – and of – the house. But, as I have said, we should remember that it was 'poor Mr Hollis' who actually owned all the property, which we may say was for Jane Austen true wealth, the real thing. Sir Harry Denham was simply 'bought' as a second husband, for his empty title, the merely nominal thing. The submergence of Mr Hollis and the ostentatious foregrounding of Sir Harry, in the iconology inside Lady Denham's house, perfectly recapitulates all that is going on outside it. It exactly parallels what has happened to the old and new Sanditon. In little it reproduces the process which Jane Austen is tracing and displaying in the whole book.

And here we may say something about the whole style of the book. It is often maintained that Jane Austen has reverted to the easy burlesque mode of her earliest writing, or that this is a crude first draft which she would later have written up in a more sophisticated way. This seems to me exactly wrong. The style is perfectly appropriate and adapted to the new world she is describing. There is a most uncharacteristic use not so much of dialogue as of actual unrefracted monologue. She lets the endless talkers talk endlessly, without the interposition of her own monitoring, adjudicating voice. The plentiful use of free indirect speech when it comes to transcribing what is going on in Charlotte's head – what she is saying to herself – indicates that she and Jane Austen share the same discourse, speak with one voice, as it were. But for the most part that *only* happens with Charlotte. It is as if Jane Austen were indicating that she no longer has anything in common with the other voices. They are alien to her. In effect she abdicates. In general she seems to be demonstrating that she can no longer exercise any authorial control over what is going on, as though there is no longer any true authority at work – only the dispersed driving force of money. Lady Denham is exactly a power which is no longer an authority, wealth coupled with ignorance. Here, suggests Jane Austen, is a world where she can no longer control or occupy the centre, because it has no centre, no organising values. Nor can she, literally, circumscribe this world, for it has no 'write-able' circumference, no discernible boundaries or shape. So she lets this world have its head – and its tongue. The inhabitants, for the part, run on and run around at will. Endlessly. Meaninglessly. And Jane Austen, like Charlotte for the most part, can only 'step back' and 'say not a word'. Thus she inscribes in the book her own redundancy. This is not mere burlesque. She is writing herself out of the world she is writing about. If, as author, she is necessarily and unavoidably omniscient, she counterbalances that fact by demonstrating that as curator and admonisher of values she is now effectively impotent. The world she creates is at the same time emphatically not her own. She shows her own unique discourse being submerged in and by what Merleau-Ponty aptly called 'the prose of the world'.

As a fragment, *Sanditon* is of course unfinished, but, without wishing to make a virtue of necessity or turning the unavoidable into a formal felicity, it seems to me that the abrupt termination, which is the reverse of a conclusion, could hardly be more appropriate. Remember Charlotte's first view of Sanditon: 'looking over the miscellaneous foreground of unfinished buildings, waving linen, and tops of houses, to the sea dancing and sparkling in sunshine and freshness'. Sanditon is 'unfinished' and incomplete, so it is right that *Sanditon* is as well. Sanditon (and all it stands for and embodies) is 'unfinished' because unfinishable, potentially interminable, containing a principle, or lack of principle, of uncontrolled expansion and extension, unco-ordinated proliferation, malignant hypertrophy. Just as it has no true centre, it knows no limit or boundary, it contains no criterion of sufficient size, it recognises no valid constraints. Unfinished and unfinishable then, it still is now. It is, as its creator boasts, in that aptly incomplete formulation, exactly 'not *a place*'. Mr Parker is somewhat dismayed that the list of names of subscribers to the circulating library is 'without distinction'. So, in every sense, is Sanditon itself. And so will always be. Never properly 'built', it is always a-building. It is potentially simply everywhere, and arguably is ever more rapidly becoming so. Starting, effectively, with an overturned carriage, it presages and foreshadows an overturned world. In all its comic fuss, it is nevertheless the very image of a sick society. For one cannot diagnose a 'disease of activity' without suggesting the activity of disease. Perhaps we should think again about the ironic suggestion, made by that clever Sidney, that Mr Parker, and all his 'coadjutors', should turn the house of his forefathers – the veritable house of old England – into 'a hospital'. Perhaps they already have.

# Bibliography

(i) *Works by Jane Austen*

*Emma*, ed. R. Blythe (Harmondsworth, Middx: Penguin, 1968).
*Lady Susan/The Watsons/Sanditon*, ed. M. Drabble (Harmondsworth, Middx: Penguin, 1974).
*Mansfield Park*, ed. Tony Tanner (Harmondsworth, Middx: Penguin, 1966).
*Northanger Abbey*, ed. E. Ehrenpreis (Harmondsworth, Middx: Penguin, 1972).
*Persuasion*, ed. D. W. Harding (Harmondsworth, Middx: Penguin, 1965).
*Pride and Prejudice*, ed. Tony Tanner (Harmondsworth, Middx: Penguin, 1972).
*Sense and Sensibility*, ed. Tony Tanner (Harmondsworth, Middx: Penguin, 1969).

*Jane Austen's Letters*, ed. R. W. Chapman, 2 vols (London: Oxford University Press, 1932).


(ii) *Works Cited in the Text*

Aers, David, Cook, Jonathan and Porter, David (eds), *Romanticism and Ideology: Studies in English Writing, 1765–1830* (London: Routledge & Kegan Paul, 1981).
Babbs, Howard S., *Jane Austen's Novels: The Fabric of Dialogue* (Columbus, Ohio: Ohio State University Press, 1962).
Brower, Reuben, 'Light and Bright and Sparkling', in *The Fields of Light* (London: Oxford University Press, 1951).
Deleuze, G. and Guattari, F., *Mille Plateaux* (Paris: Editions de Minuit, 1980).
Devlin, D., *Jane Austen and Education* (London: Macmillan, 1975).

Duckworth, Alistair, *The Improvement of the Estate* (Baltimore, Md: Johns Hopkins Press, 1971).

Foucault, M., *Madness and Civilisation* (London: Tavistock, 1967).

Hagstrum, Jean, *Sex and Sensibility* (Chicago University Press, 1980).

Heidegger, M., 'The Origin of the Work of Art', in *Poetry, Language, Thought* (New York: Harper & Row, 1971).

Horkheimer, M. and Adorno, T., *Dialectic of Enlightenment* (London: Allen Lane, 1973).

Jay, Douglas, *Sterling, Its Use and Misuse: A Plea for Moderation* (London: Sidgwick & Jackson, 1985).

Litz, A. Walton, *Jane Austen: A Study of her Artistic Development* (London: Chatto & Windus, 1965).

Monaghan, David (ed.), *Jane Austen in a Social Context* (London: Macmillan, 1981).

Mudrick, Marvin, *Jane Austen: Irony as Defense and Discovery* (Berkeley, Calif.: University of California Press, 1968).

Newton, Benjamin, *The Diary of Benjamin Newton, 1816–1818*, ed. C. Fendall and E. Crutchley (Cambridge University Press, 1933).

Porter, Roy, *English Society in the Eighteenth Century* (Harmondsworth, Middx: Penguin, 1982).

Said, Edward, *Beginnings* (Baltimore, Md: Johns Hopkins Press, 1978).

Smythe-Palmer, A., *The Idea of a Gentleman* (London, 1909).

Southam, B. C. (ed.), *Critical Essays on Jane Austen* (London: Routledge & Kegan Paul, 1968).

Thompson, E. P., *The Making of the English Working Class* (Harmondsworth, Middx: Penguin, 1968).

Tolstoy, Leo, *Anna Karenina*, trs. R. Edmonds (Harmondsworth, Middx: Penguin, 1977).

Trilling, Lionel, *The Opposing Self* (London: Secker & Warburg, 1955).

Weininger, Otto, *Sex and Character* (London, 1906).

Wellek, R. and Warren, A., *Theory of Literature* (Harmondsworth, Middx: Penguin, 1973).

Williams, Raymond, *The Country and the City* (London: Chatto & Windus, 1973).

Wingfield-Stratford, E., *The Squire and his Relations* (London: Cassell, 1956).

(iii) *Suggested Further Reading*

Barrell, John, *English Literature in History: 1730–80: An Equal, Wide Survey* (London: Hutchinson, 1983).

Butler, Marilyn, *Jane Austen and the War of Ideas* (Oxford University Press, 1975).

Cohen, Murray, *Sensible Words: Linguistic Practice in England, 1640–1785* (Baltimore, Md: Johns Hopkins Press, 1977).

Erdman, David, *Blake: Prophet against Empire* (Princeton University Press, 1969).

Hay, Douglas, Linebaugh, Peter and Thompson, E. P., *Albion's Fatal Tree* (Harmondsworth, Middx: Penguin, 1977).

Kelly, Gary, *The English Jacobin Novel, 1780–1805* (Oxford University Press, 1976).

Land, Stephen, *From Signs to Prepositions: The Concept of Form in Eighteenth-century Semantic Theory* (London: Longman, 1974).

MacIntyre, Alasdair, *After Virtue* (London: Duckworth, 1981).

Phillips, K. C., *Jane Austen's English* (London: Longman, 1970).

Poirier, Richard, *A World Elsewhere* (London: Galaxy, 1973).

Roberts, Warren, *Jane Austen and the French Revolution* (London: Macmillan, 1979).

Simon, Brian, *The Two Nations and the Educational Structure, 1780–1870*, Studies in the History of Education (1974).

Smith, Olivia, *Politics and Language, 1791–1819* (Oxford University Press, 1984).

Williams, Raymond, 'Society', in *Keywords* (London: Fontana, 1976).

# Index

Adorno, Theodor, *Dialectic of Enlightenment*, 50
Aers, David, *Romanticism and Ideology*, 5
Althusser, Louis, 5
Amis, Kingsley, 143
Arnold, Thomas, 145
Austen-Leigh, James Edward, *Memoir* 1, 162

Babb, Howard, *Jane Austen's Novels: The Fabric of Dialogue*, 37, 121
Bachelard, Gaston, *The Poetics of Space*, 49
Badiell, David, 19
Balzac, Honore, 5, 8; *Illusions perdues*, 274
Barthes, Roland, 54, 62, 220
Bellow, Saul, 142
Bentham, Jeremy, 231
Bernstein, Basil, 127
Blackstone, William, 16
Blake, William, 109, 140, 277; *Marriage of Heaven and Hell*, 140
Bonaparte, Napoleon: see Napoleon
Bowdler, John, 'Reform or Ruin', 18
Brontë, Charlotte, 3, 7, 35, 103, 120, 138, 186; *Shirley*, 3, 7
Brontë, Emily, *Wuthering Heights*, 101
Brower, Reuben, 121
Brown, Norman O., 131
Burke, Edmund, 2, 17, 26; *Reflections on the French Revolution*, 2; 'First Letter on a Regicide Peace', 27

Burney, Fanny, 19, 107; *Evelina*, 56; *Cecilia*, 107
Burns, Robert, 275
Butler, Marilyn, *Jane Austen and the War of Ideas*, 44
Byron, Lord, 140

Carroll, Lewis, *Alice through the Looking Glass*, 269
Chapman, R. W., 107
Chekhov, Anton, 48
Chesterfield, Lord, 26, 29, 170, 226; *Letters to His Son*, 26
Chopin, Kate, *The Awakening*, 49
Cobbett, William, 144
Cohen, F. S., 'Dialogue on Private Property', 19
Coleridge, Samuel, 95, 98, 140; 'Dejection: An Ode', 95
Congreve, William, 101
Conrad, Joseph, 70, 229; *Heart of Darkness*, 70; *The Nigger of the 'Narcissus'*, 229
Cowper, William, 82
Crook, Nora, 237

Defoe, Daniel, *Robinson Crusoe*, 50, 52
Deleuze, Gilles, *Mille Plateaux*, 52
Devlin, A., *Jane Austen and Education*, 25
Dickens, Charles, 21, 23, 54, 136; *Dombey and Son*, 21
Dostoevsky, Fyodor, 99
Duckworth, Alistair, *The Improvement of the Estate*, 160

Edgeworth, Maria, *Letters of Julia and Caroline*, 76, 77

Ehrenpreis, Henry, 44

Eliot, George, 8, 11, 23, 51, 76, 99, 100; *Middlemarch*, 21, 23; *Daniel Deronda*, 51

Ellison, Ralph, *The Invisible Man*, 136

Emerson, Ralph, 9, 10

Fielding, Henry, 52, 53; *Amelia*, 53; *Tom Jones*, 142

Fitzgerald, F. Scott, 113

Flaubert, Gustave, 11, 269; *Madame Bovary*, 269

Ford, Ford Madox, 48, 174; *The Good Soldier*, 48; *Parade's End*, 174; *A Man Could Stand Up*, 174

Forster, E. M., 99

Foucault, Michel, *Madness and Civilisation*, 82–4

Freud, Sigmund, 50, 77, 87, 99, 131; *Civilisation and Its Discontents*, 77, 99

Gilpin, William, 159

Gisborne, Thomas, *Enquiry into the Duties of the Female Sex*, 30–3

Goethe, Wolfgang von, *Elective Affinities*, 20

Goffman, Erving, 123

Goldsmith, Oliver, *The Vicar of Wakefield*, 205; *The Deserted Village*, 222

Hagstrom, Jean, *Sex and Sensibility*, 78

Harding, D. W., 125

Hardy, Thomas, *Jude the Obscure*, 142; *Tess of the D'Urbervilles*, 256

Hawthorne, Nathaniel, 8

Hay, Douglas, *Albion's Fatal Tree*, 16

Heidegger, Martin, 'The Origin of the Work of Art', 66–7

Herbert, George, 174

Hobbes, Thomas, *Leviathan*, 71, 73

Homer, *The Odyssey*, 50

Horkheimer, Max, *Dialectic of Enlightenment*, 50

Hume, David, 12, 71, 108, 109, 110, 139; *Treatise of Human Nature*, 72, 108; *An Enquiry Concerning Human Understanding*, 109; *Enquiry Concerning the Principles of Morals*, 109–10

Inchbald, Mrs, 76, 165; *Nature and Art*, 76; *Lovers Vows*, 164, 167

Jakobson, Roman, 64

James, Henry, 2, 8, 11, 36, 51, 98, 245; 'The New Novel', 11; *Washington Square*, 9; *The Portrait of a Lady*, 142, 147; *The Wings of the Dove*, 156; *The Golden Bowl*, 158, 200

Jay, Douglas, *Sterling: A Plea for Moderation*, 13

Johnson, Dr, 16, 19, 34, 36, 51

Jonson, Ben, 269

Joyce, James, 202

Keats, John, 99, 140

Kent, Christopher, *Jane Austen in a Social Context*, 104

Kotzebue, August von, *Das Kind der Liebe*, 164

Lawrence, D. H., *Sons and Lovers*, 142

Lewes, G. H., 103

Litz, Walton, 75, 76, 77, 121; *Jane Austen: A Study of her Artistic Development*, 75

Liverpool, Lord, 144

Locke, John, 16, 26, 29, 34, 76, 105, 106, 139, 140, 170, 226; *The Second Treatise of Government*, 16; *Some Thoughts Concerning Education*, 25; *Essay Concerning Human Understanding*, 106, 139

MacKenzie, Henry, 77, 275

Melville, Herman, 230

Merleau-Ponty, Maurice, 285
Mill, John Stuart, 98
Milton, John, 278
More, Hannah, *Strictures on the Modern System of Female Education*, 33–5
Mudrick, Marvin, 126
Mullan, John, 78

Napoleon, 2, 3, 4, 103, 138, 144, 228
Newton, Benjamin, *The Diary of Benjamin Newton*, 14–15
Nietzsche, Friedrich, *Beyond Good and Evil*, 63

Paine, Thomas, *Rights of Man*, 2
Pellew, George, 8
Pitt, William, 27, 70
Plato, 162
Pope Alexander, 76, 199
Porter, Roy, *England in the Eighteenth Century*, 18
Prendergast, Christopher, *The Order of Mimesis*, 274
Proust, Marcel, 36

Racine, Jean, *Phèdre*, 105
Radcliff, Mrs Ann, 48, 58, 71, 107; *The Mysteries of Udolpho*, 48–9, 58, 107
Reeve, Clara, *The Progress of Romance*, 57n
Reynolds, Sir Joshua, 117, 118; *Discourses*, 118
Richardson, Samuel, 2, 9, 52, 54, 77, 78, 118, 277–8, 279; *Pamela*, 53–5; *Clarissa*, 83, 156, 277; *Sir Charles Grandison*, 78
Roberts, Warren, *Jane Austen and the French Revolution*, 70, 228
Rousseau, Jean Jacques, *La Nouvelle Héloïse*, 209
Rowbotham, Sheila, *Hidden from History*, 44
Ruskin, John, 95–6
Ryle, Gilbert, 132

Said, Edward, 51
Sand, George, 8
Sartre, Jean Paul, 122
Scott, Sir Walter, 2, 138, 140, 275; *Old Morality*, 7
Shaftesbury, Third Earl of, 27, 132; *Characteristics*, 28
Shakespeare, William: *Hamlet*, 93; *King Lear*, 105, 112; *Macbeth*, 203; *Henry VIII*, 169
Shelley, Percy Bysshe, 140
Simpson, Richard, 13
Smith, Adam, 17
Smythe-Palmer, A., *The Idea of a Gentleman*, 196
Sophocles, *Oedipus Rex*, 105, 114
Southam, Brian, 106, 107, 121; *Jane Austen's Literary Manuscripts*, 106
Stendhal, 105; *Le Rouge et le Noir*, 142
Swift, Jonathan, 68

Thackeray, William, *Vanity Fair*, 142
Thompson, E. P., 2
Trilling, Lionel, 156, 162, 171
Trollope, Anthony, 196
Tolstoy, Leo, 11, 50, 131, 134; *Anna Karenina*, 131–2; *Resurrection*, 134

Warren, Austen, *Theory of Literature* (*with* Rene Wellek), 64
Weininger, Otto, *Sex and Character*, 177–9
Wellek, Rene, *see* Warren, Austen
Whitman, Walt, 10, 163
Williams, Raymond, *The Country and the City*, 15
Wingfield-Stratford, Esmé, *The Squire and his Relations*, 4
Woolf, Virginia, 35, 36, 85–6; *A Room of One's Own*, 35
Wordsworth, William, 95; *Lyrical Ballads*, 140